Citrus Growing in Florida

Citrus Growing in Florida

Third Edition

Larry Jackson

University of Florida Press
Gainesville

Library of Congress Cataloging in Publication Data

Jackson, Larry.
    Citrus growing in Florida / Larry Jackson—3rd ed.
       p.   cm.
    Previous editions by Louis W. Zeigler and Herbert S. Wolfe.
    Includes index.
    ISBN 0-8130-0964-2 (alk. paper)
    1. Citrus fruits—Florida. I. Zeigler, Louis W. Citrus growing
in Florida. II. Title.
    SB369.2.F6J33   1990
    634′.304′90759—dc20   89-20503
                                         CIP

    The University of Florida Press is a member of University Presses of Florida, the scholarly publishing agency of the State University System of Florida. Books are selected for publication by the faculty editorial committees of Florida's nine university presses: Florida A&M University Press (Tallahassee), Florida Atlantic University Press (Boca Raton), Florida International University Press (Miami), Florida State University Press (Tallahassee), University of Central Florida Press (Orlando), University of Florida Press (Gainesville), University of North Florida Press (Jacksonville), University of South Florida Press (Tampa), University of West Florida Press (Pensacola).
    Orders for books published by all member presses should be addressed to University Presses of Florida, 15 NW 15th Street, Gainesville, FL 32611.

Contents

Preface

Nearly fifteen years have passed since the previous revision of this book was published. The many changes that have occurred within the Florida citrus industry have dictated substantial changes in this text.

Florida no longer enjoys the number one position in the world citrus industry, having been supplanted by Brazil. A series of devastating freezes has further worsened the state's competitive position by reducing the acreage of citrus in Florida. In fact, a survey of acreage in 1986 indicated that nearly 30 percent of the acreage planted in citrus in 1982—over 200,000 acres—had been lost. Citrus blight (formerly called "young tree decline" or YTD) and tristeza continue to take a toll of our crop production, and outbreaks of a citrus canker-like disease have caused serious problems.

A great deal of new citrus-growing information has been developed, and much of it is summarized and incorporated in this new edition. Numerous changes in the citrus-production program are updated in this edition, and we expect to make similar updates in more frequent new editions in the future. The appendixes added to this edition are new. They should clarify the technical points of grove maintenance and financial management presented in more general language in the text proper.

Hopefully, the original style of the book has not been altogether lost in this revision. I have sought to make only revisions necessitated by historical and economic changes or the development of new technology. The publisher's editors have made minor changes in styling throughout to make the language more accessible to today's readers, and in sections that have needed extensive revision the style will not be that of the original authors. For the most part, however, the language of the earlier edition has been left intact so as not to compromise the thoughts and words of the original authors.

We mourn the loss of the senior author of this book, Dr. Louis W. Ziegler. He died in October 1976 and is greatly missed by all of those whose lives he touched during his great career.

Acknowledgments

Revising a book such as this seems a relatively simple task, and it certainly is much easier than starting from scratch. However, after nearly fifteen years, extensive changes were required. Many people have been involved in the process of getting the third edition of this book into production, and I am indebted to all of them. Significant contributions have been made by the persons noted below.

Much of the work begins with typing of a manuscript. This herculean task was undertaken in an exemplary manner by my secretary, Mrs. Beth Reus. Her tireless typing and careful editing set the stage for the text's production. Her contribution to this effort may have exceeded that of all the rest of us, and I am truly grateful for her part in this work.

The staff of the University of Florida Press has been particularly helpful throughout the production process. Their timely tips, numerous suggestions, and friendly persuasion have helped make this process a pleasant one.

The technical accuracy of any publication is ultimately the author's responsibility, which can be daunting unless assistance is available. A large group of reviewers provided tremendous help in this case by scrutinizing the text minutely for technical inaccuracies. As a group, they caught many errors and helped to clear up many inaccurate or misleading statements. Thanks to their hard work, we go to press comfortable with the accuracy of the text's technical information. I gratefully acknowledge the important contributions of all these reviewers, whose names and affiliations follow:

J. M. Bulger, Multi-County Citrus Extension Agent, IFAS, UF, Seffner

D. V. Calvert, Professor of Soil Science and Center Director, IFAS, UF, Ft. Pierce

W. S. Castle, Professor of Fruit Crops, IFAS, UF, Lake Alfred

T. E. Crocker, Professor of Fruit Crops, IFAS, UF, Gainesville

F. S. Davies, Professor of Fruit Crops, IFAS, UF, Gainesville

R. M. Davis, Multi-County Citrus Extension Agent, IFAS, UF, Lake Alfred

J. J. Ferguson, Associate Professor of Fruit Crops, IFAS, UF, Gainesville

C. J. Hearn, Adjunct Professor of Fruit Crops, USDA, Orlando

R. C. J. Koo, Professor of Fruit Crops, IFAS, UF, Lake Alfred

J. L. Knapp, Professor of Entomology, IFAS, UF, Lake Alfred

J. D. Martsolf, Professor of Fruit Crops, IFAS, UF, Gainesville

D. P. H. Tucker, Professor of Fruit Crops, IFAS, UF, Lake Alfred

W. F. Wardowski, Professor of Fruit Crops, IFAS, UF, Lake Alfred

Joe Wigham, Division of Fruit and Vegetable Inspection, Winter Haven

J. G. Williamson, Assistant Professor of Fruit Crops, IFAS, UF, Gainesville

W. J. Wiltbank, Emeritus Professor of Fruit Crops, IFAS, UF, Gainesville

1 /
Origin and History

Origins and Introduction in the Old World

The United States is the second largest citrus-producing country in the world. At one time in the late 1970s, the United States was number one, and Florida alone produced more citrus than any country outside the United States. Increased planting in Brazil and the loss of much Florida acreage due to a series of freezes has resulted in Brazil becoming the top producing nation. Florida continues to lead all other states in citrus production, and there is keen interest in both commercial and dooryard fruit production throughout much of the state.

The original home of nearly all citrus species was probably on the warm southern slopes of the Himalayas in northeastern India and adjacent Burma. Long before the dawn of history, primitive forms of the orange, shaddock, and some mandarins crossed over the Himalayan passes into western China—whether by the activity of primitive man or by other means, we will never know—and secondary centers of distribution developed in southern China and Indo-China. Lime, lemon, and citron remained south of the mountains, as did some of the mandarins, and spread southward into India and eastward into the Malay Archipelago. Only the trifoliate orange (*Poncirus*) and the kumquat (*Fortunella*) among citrus fruits seem to have come from China, originating in the eastern part of that country.

The sweet orange must have developed its present characters in southwestern China. Like the shaddock, it is not known anywhere in the truly wild state, and quite possibly it originated from other citrus species under cultivation and has always been a garden plant. It is impossible to say how long it has been cultivated in China because written records do not go back far enough in that country. The earliest mention of oranges occurs in a book compiled in the sixth century B.C., the *Shu-ching*, which purports to be taken from ancient records going back to before 2000 B.C. Chinese historians have long been aware, however, that any records dated earlier than 1000 B.C. (except inscriptions on bones used in divination) are highly

1

suspect, and that this particular reference cannot be credited to a period earlier than 600 B.C.

In the *Chou-li*, which deals with the Chou regime around 700 B.C. but was actually compiled some four hundred years later, a distinction is made between sweet and sour oranges, whereas the earlier *Shu-ching* speaks only of oranges. There are other reasons to think that the sour orange only reached the Yangtze Valley around 400 B.C., whereas sweet oranges may have been cultivated from much earlier times. Mandarins, as distinct from oranges, are first mentioned in Chinese literature about 200 B.C. The shaddock was included in the earliest mention of oranges, but citron was apparently not known until the fourth century A.D., and lemons not until the tenth century.

Fig. 1-1. A central Florida orange grove.

India seems to be the region where lemon, citron, and some species of mandarins have developed their present form. Sanskrit literature of the eighth century B.C. mentions both citron and lemon, but no Sanskrit name is known for the shaddock, and that of the orange dates only from the first century A.D.; however, we shall see that oranges had reached India long before this. This Sanskrit name for the orange, *nagarunga*, became *naranj* in Persian, *aurantium* in Latin, *naranja* in Spanish, and *orange* in English.

The citron and lemon (of some type) have greater written evidence of antiquity than the orange, although they are not necessarily older in cultivation. The evidence for reference to citron in Egypt in 1500 B.C. is very dubious. The lime is known truly wild only in the Malay peninsula, from whence it apparently spread westward into India and eastward into the Pacific islands.

The first citrus fruit known to Europe was undoubtedly the citron, prized for its fragrant rind. The naturalists who accompanied Alexander on his conquest of Persia and northern India brought back descriptions of the tree and its culture that were made widely known by Theophrastus around 300 B.C., but this was not the first acquaintance of the Greeks with the fruit. At least fifty years before this, citrons were being imported into Athens from Persia; and, since the Greeks called it first the "Median apple," it seems probable that they had known it when the Medes ruled Persia, before the sixth century B.C. Greek colonists apparently introduced its culture into Palestine about 200 B.C.

Eventually the citron replaced the cedar cone as the "fruit of the goodly tree" authorized for use in the Jewish Feast of Tabernacles. Tolkowsky advanced cogent arguments for this transition having been ordered by Simon the Maccabee in 136 B.C. The significance of this event for us lies in the probable explanation of the origin of the word *citrus*. The Greek word *kedros* originally meant the cedar, but apparently as the result of the substitution of citrons for cedar cones in this ceremony, the Palestinian Greeks began to say "cedar apple" (*kedromelon*) instead of Median or Persian apple. The Greek *kedros* became Latinized as *cedrus*, and this changed to *citrus*. By the time of Pliny (A.D. 70), *citrus* meant the citron tree. Of course, our word *citron* is derived from citrus, not the other way around; and *citreum*, *malum citreum*, or *malum medicum* were Pliny's names for the fruit. Cultivated in Asia Minor and Italy in the first century A.D., the citron was being grown in Greece a century later, and it seems to have been widely used in Moslem medicine in Egypt and Spain before A.D. 900, perhaps even long before.

The sweet orange in its present form must have reached India from China well before the beginning of the Christian era, for in the first century A.D. sweet oranges were known to the Romans as "Indian fruit." Certainly by the end of that century oranges were being imported into Rome, probably from Palestine and Egypt, where plantings had been established by seeds from India; for the time required for the journey from India to Italy was much too long for oranges to survive it. There is evidence that orange trees grew in southern Italy at that time, but apparently they could not mature fruit. By A.D. 300, oranges were being picked there, however; but in the Dark Ages following the sack of Rome by the Goths and Vandals, they may have been lost.

In Moorish gardens of southern Spain around A.D. 900, oranges were quite common, but it is not certain that some of these were sweet oranges, for accounts of citrus fruit rarely distinguished between sweet and sour forms. However, sweet oranges were certainly abundantly available in Baghdad and Cairo, and Spanish Moors imported a great variety of exotic plants from Iraq and Egypt for the adornment of their gardens. It seems likely that they brought in sweet as well as sour oranges.

Sweet oranges were undoubtedly cultivated in southern Europe long before Vasco da Gama reached India in 1498. The most direct evidence is a letter written in 1483 in which Louis XI of France asked that sweet oranges be sent him from Provence, but there is also considerable indirect evidence. It is well known that Columbus took orange, lemon, and citron seeds from the Canary Islands with him to Hispaniola on his second voyage in 1493; and while there is no statement as to whether the oranges were sweet or sour, we do have Oviedo's testimony that barely thirty years later sweet orange trees were abundant in Hispaniola. Furthermore, on the return of da Gama from India, his men reported that the sweet oranges they found were superior to those they had at home. These superior types of sweet orange, when brought back to Portugal, made cultivation of this fruit much more worthwhile than it had previously been considered. Henceforth the sweet orange took the lead, and with the development of special houses (later called "orangeries") for growing sweet oranges where cold made their outdoor culture impossible, their cultivation was extended into northern Europe in the seventeenth century.* It may be noted, incidentally, that when the Portuguese finally introduced oranges directly from China to Europe in 1640, these were again so much better in quality than the type brought from India that "China" oranges soon replaced "Portugals" as the preferred type.

---

* There is evidence of such culture of citrons, in houses using mica glazing, in Italy as early as the first century A.D.; in the fourteenth century, such orangeries became popular in northern Italy.

The Sweet Orange in Florida

The introduction of sweet oranges into Florida probably coincided with the establishment of the colony at St. Augustine in 1565, since we know of no earlier permanent settlement anywhere in the state. By 1579 Menéndez could report that oranges were becoming abundant there. Thus our Florida citrus industry is over four centuries old. From the trees cultivated by the Spaniards, Indians carried fruit to their villages and scattered the seeds widely as they ate the oranges. This resulted in the many scattered thickets of wild orange trees of which remnants—all of them of the hardier sour type—may still occasionally be found around the lakes and rivers in some sections of the state. Urbanization and freezes have destroyed most of these thickets. The orange proved so well adapted and flourished so well as a naturalized tree, escaped from cultivation, that William Bartram in his exploration of Florida in 1773–74 found great areas covered by apparently wild trees. His uncertainty as to whether they were wild or escaped is shown when he wrote: "Whether the orange tree is an exotick, brot in here by the Spaniards, or a Native to this country, is a question. I have inqu[ired] of some of the old Spaniards at Augustine, who tell me that they were first brot in by the Spaniards and spread over the country by the Ind[ians]." It is only in relatively recent times, however, that the citrus fruits have taken a prominent place in our diet, not only as valuable sources of health-giving vitamins and minerals but also as welcome and useful additions to the pleasure of eating.

Plantings of the sixteenth and seventeenth centuries were limited to the few areas along the coast where Spanish colonies were established and were not at all commercial. Not until Spain ceded Florida to England in 1763 was there any commerce in oranges; but, under English rule and with English colonies to trade with, export of sour oranges assumed some importance to St. Augustine, and orange plantings were made in several areas of East Florida. With the cession of Florida to the United States in 1821, the development of sweet orange groves moved rapidly ahead, especially along the St. Johns River and its tributaries, which provided transportation to northern markets. Introduction of the insect pest known as long scale in 1838 and its subsequent spread to all citrus groves in the state caused a serious decline in citrus growing between 1840 and 1870, until the pest ceased to be a serious problem.

The first big expansion came in the 1870s as growers realized the size of the potential market and the possibility of satisfying it with Florida fruit. In the years 1874 to 1877, about two hundred million oranges with a value of over $2 million were imported annually into the eastern United States, mostly from the Mediterranean area but partly from the West Indies. Imports of lemons were almost as large. All of these could have been grown in Florida, the leading growers urged, and so plantings were made to achieve this objective. In this period there was extensive replacement of wild sour orange trees with sweet orange trees in the hammocks of north-central Florida, and this area became the center of the citrus industry. The "big freezes" of 1894–95 and 1899, however, caused this center to move south a hundred miles or so.

The change from growing citrus on a small scale, often as a crop of secondary interest to the grower, to its production on the large commercial scale now characteristic of Florida has occurred since 1900. Several factors have influenced this phenomenal change. There is a very large area with satisfactory climatic and soil conditions for successful citrus production. Populous areas are in and near Florida's groves, making for easy marketing of the crop. The development of three major rail systems out of the many short lines built during the nineteenth century provided more efficient transportation for the crop than the earlier water routes afforded. More recently the availability of good roads has enabled transportation by truck to open new markets and reduce hauling costs to many points. Due tribute must also be paid to the enterprise of the growers of the last century who pioneered in the change from seedlings to budded varieties and to the wisdom shown in selection of seedlings that have become important to our industry. Finally, the fortunate choice of adopting rough lemon for use as a stock must be credited with much of the amazing citrus development of Florida, for without this stock the rapid industry expansion in the sandy hills of central Florida would have been much more difficult.

Change is the character of human existence. Florida, during the decades of the 1950s and 1960s and continuing to the present has become a mecca attracting large influxes of new residents; to the pressures they create have been added the impacts of tourism stimulated by space exploration from Cape Canaveral and the development of Disney World and numerous other tourist attractions, particularly "theme parks." Vast acreages have been devel-

Table 1-1.
Citrus production in Florida
(in thousands of 1⅗ bushel boxes)

Citrus type	1973–74	1978–79	1983–84	1988–89
Oranges—early/mid.	92,100	91,000	69,700	85,300
Oranges—late	73,700	73,000	47,000	61,300
Grapefruit—seedy	10,000	7,300	4,500	3,350
Grapefruit—white seedless	25,900	29,400	23,000	27,700
Grapefruit—colored seedless	12,200	13,300	13,400	23,700
Tangerines[a]	2,800	3,500	2,975	2,900
Temples	5,300	4,700	2,900	3,750
Tangelos	3,700	4,200	3,600	3,800
Limes	1,050	720	1,440	1,250
Total	226,750	227,120	168,515	213,050

SOURCE: Florida Agricultural Statistics Service, *Citrus Summary 1988–89*.

a. Honey tangerines ("murcotts") not included prior to 1981–82.

oped to accommodate people, especially in the better-drained areas of the state. Land values and taxes have increased to cause the ultimate abandonment of many acres of groves. Previously, citrus plantings were expanded to the poorly drained areas until a total of almost one million acres of groves existed in the late 1960s. However, in the 1970s the number of acres being planted did not keep pace with removals required by urbanization so that the total as of 1973 was an estimated 877,000 acres. Due to a series of disastrous freezes during the late 1970s and early and mid 1980s, Florida citrus acreage was further reduced. It bottomed out at 624,500 acres in 1986. As Florida lost its distinctive agricultural character of earlier years due to increasing population, the citrus industry was faced with problems of labor shortages and restrictions on road, land, and chemical usages. In many counties, it has been relegated to a secondary position. The previously mentioned freezes had a profound impact on many of the more northerly citrus counties, particularly Lake, Marion, and Volusia.

Successful development of a fruit industry, however, requires more than a tasty product, favorable growing conditions, and facilities for marketing it. It must be possible for the grower to offer a product that will consistently merit favor by the purchasing public, to produce it at a profit, and to distribute it to a wide market in orderly fashion. Research by state and federal agencies as well as by private organizations and individuals has been an important element in the growth of a sound industry by overcoming many production and marketing difficulties. And the various inspection agencies, regulatory bodies, and trade organizations have helped assure a more orderly flow of high-quality fruit to market.

Modern Florida citrus production, distinct and vastly different from that of the nineteenth century, is the result of the influence of all these—at times totally unrelated—factors. Today citrus fruits are no longer a luxury; they are essential components of a modern diet all over this country.

Citrus Growing in Other Parts of the World

In the United States, the citrus industry of California is second only to that of Florida, with Arizona in third place and Texas in fourth. Texas and Arizona's relative positions in the U.S. citrus industry have been swapped as a result of freezes in the early 1980s. Both Arizona and Texas are heavily committed to grapefruit and have considerable interest in oranges. Arizona also grows a fair quantity of lemons. There is a very small satsuma and orange industry in southern Louisiana. California produces the bulk of the lemon crop of this country, has a very important production of sweet oranges, a small grapefruit crop, and a very small production of mandarins and limes.

Mexico has considerable production of oranges and leads the world in limes. Cuba and Puerto Rico have important commercial crops of oranges and grapefruit, and all the other islands of the West Indies grow oranges and limes in abundance for their own use or for minor export. The same may be said of the Central American countries.

Italy and Spain lead European production and have considerable orange, lemon, and tangerine production. Turkey and Greece also have small but important orange and lemon plantings.

Brazil is the world leader in orange production and is increasing its lead as its fairly young plantings begin to mature. Ar-

Table 1-2.
Principal citrus fruits—production by states
(in thousands of tons)

State	1973–74	1978–79	1983–84	1988–89
Florida[a]	10,088	10,101	7,485	9,457
California	2,285	2,189	2,783	3,108
Texas	709	632	235	271
Arizona	330	407	329	296
Total U.S.	13,412	13,329	10,832	13,132

SOURCE: Florida Agricultural Statistics Service, *Citrus Summary 1988–89.*
  a. Does not include Florida lemons or K-Early Citrus Fruit.

gentina has important crops of oranges and lemons. Paraguay, Bolivia, and Peru grow oranges on a large scale, while Uruguay and Chile produce small amounts of grapefruit as well. Every country in South America has good supplies of citrus fruits for home consumption.

Among Asiatic countries, China may have the largest production of sweet oranges, but mandarins are grown in far larger amounts there. Shaddocks and lemons are also produced in large amounts. Unfortunately, accurate production figures are not available. Japan has a substantial mandarin industry and leads the world in reported production. India has considerable commercial production of citrus fruits, and an even larger production by small growers. The mandarins are more popular there than oranges, and both limes and lemons are also very widely grown. Throughout the Asiatic islands, from Taiwan and the Philippines to Sri Lanka, and in the countries from Vietnam to Burma, citrus fruits play an important part in the food supply of the people, but production is not found on a large scale.

In the Near East, Israel and Egypt have large industries, producing both oranges and grapefruit for the European market. Lebanon, Syria, Cyprus, and Iran all have some commercial growing of oranges and lemons.

Algeria and Morocco both produce large quantities of oranges for export. At the lower end of Africa, South Africa has developed an important export industry in oranges and to a lesser extent in grapefruit and lemons.

On the far side of the world, Australia has commercial production of oranges, lemons, and grapefruit, and so does New Zealand on a smaller scale, although both countries import some citrus to fill their domestic needs. All the islands of the Pacific grow various citrus fruits, but not on a commercial scale.

Table 1-3 shows the known production of different kinds of citrus fruits in major countries of the world for which records are available.

Table 1-3.
Citrus production by selected countries, principal types
(in thousands of metric tons)

Country	1984–85	1985–86	1986–87	1987–88	1988–89
[Oranges]					
Brazil	11,715	11,015	10,975	10,500	12,150
U.S.	6,241	6,912	7,121	7,896	8,191
Mexico	1,000	1,410	1,683	1,942	2,268
Spain	1,365	1,942	2,059	2,442	2,225
Italy	1,960	2,257	2,424	1,400	2,020
Egypt	1,182	1,168	1,235	1,387	1,390
Morocco	686	841	650	913	890
[Grapefruit]					
U.S.	2,046	2,122	2,330	2,523	2,602
Israel	375	371	392	317	373
Cuba	155	237	250	284	300
Argentina	157	178	165	160	145
[Lemons]					
U.S.	889	632	986	712	751
Italy	744	800	813	660	750
Spain	325	482	613	760	679
[Tangerines]					
Japan	2,344	2,870	2,542	2,941	2,390
Spain	947	1,050	1,164	1,307	1,120
Italy	360	500	531	336	510
Brazil	668	486	479	453	460
Morocco	244	347	290	300	390
U.S.	273	290	363	364	356

SOURCE: U.S.D.A. Foreign Agricultural Service.

2 /
The Kinds of Citrus Fruits

The Orange Subfamily

Citrus fruits and their relatives, some close and some distant, constitute the Orange subfamily, Aurantioideae, of the great and diverse Rue family, the Rutaceae. This subfamily is entirely Old World and is mostly limited to the tropics and subtropics of southeastern Asia and the southern Pacific, although a few genera are African. The fruit in this subfamily is a specialized berry called a *hesperidium,* usually with a leathery rind but with a hard woody shell in one small group of genera. Leaves and the bark of twigs and young branches contain oil glands, as do the leathery rinds of some fruits.

This subfamily, Aurantioideae, was divided by the late W. T. Swingle, an eminent citrus taxonomist, into two tribes, Clauseneae and Citreae, the latter including *Citrus* and *Citrus*-like genera. The tribe Citreae is further divided into three subtribes of which the Citrinae contains the Citrus Fruit Trees. This in turn is separated into three groups: Group A, the Primitive Citrus Fruit Trees (including the ornamental shrub *Severinia*); Group B, the Near-Citrus Fruit Trees; and Group C, the True Citrus Fruit Trees. This last group contains six genera that possess the typical citrus fruit characters of leathery rinds with oil glands and of pulp vesicles filling the interior of the fruit. Three of the six genera are of little or no commercial importance while the other three include all citrus fruits grown commercially.

The three unimportant genera occur only in Australia and some of the southwest Pacific islands. *Eremocitrus,* native to southern Queensland and northern New South Wales, is the only distinctly xerophytic form in the whole subfamily and is called the "desert lime" because it thrives in semiarid regions. It has great tolerance for saline soils and may be of value as a stock for citrus trees in areas where the soil has a high salt content. It has been used as a parent in some rootstock breeding programs in an attempt to capture some of its desirable traits. *Microcitrus* is also native to eastern Australia, and one species is native to adjacent New Guinea. Some species show some adaptation to low rainfall, but others are found in areas of high rainfall. The fruits are known as wild-limes, and they are quite acid. Some of the species may have value as stocks for commercial citrus fruits. The third genus, *Clymenia,* is known only from the island of New Ireland, in the Bismarck Archipelago northeast of New Guinea, and has not been extensively studied.

The three genera of commercial significance are *Poncirus,* the trifoliate orange; *Fortunella,* the kumquat; and *Citrus* itself (see table 2-1). These will be discussed in more detail below. All these genera possess certain characters in common:

1. The plants are thorny shrubs or trees with fragrant white flowers.

2. The leaves are compound in nature, still retaining this visibly in *Poncirus* with three leaflets, but reduced to a single terminal leaflet in the other genera. While appearing to be simple leaves at first glance, their compound origin is shown by the joint where the blade attaches to the petiole. Except in *Poncirus,* also, the leaves may be persistent for two years or more, making the trees evergreen.

3. The petiole is often bordered lengthwise by bladelike extensions called wings, and their size and shape, when present, are characters useful in identifying certain species.

4. The typical citrus fruit, the *hesperidium,* is spheroidal or oblong in shape, with leathery rind, which is green when immature and at maturity is green, yellow, orange, or red. This rind possesses abundant oil glands, which are developed by the separation and breaking down of some of the subepidermal cells. The oil contained in these glands at fruit maturity is an essential oil and differs characteristically between species. Oil from the rind of orange, lemon, and lime is commercially important. The inner portion of the rind (mesocarp) is a whitish, spongy material known as "albedo," while the outer, colored portion (exocarp) containing oil glands and color bodies is called the "flavedo."

5. The interior of the fruit, within the rind (endocarp), is divided into several segments by thin membranous walls, the number of these segments having some species diagnostic value at times. Each segment is packed full of juice vesicles except for the space occupied by the seeds (when present), and these vesicles normally have thin, easily ruptured walls.

6. The juice in the vesicles contains sugars, organic acids (including ascorbic acid, or Vitamin C), pigments, glucosides (which are often characteristic of species), carotene (forming vitamin A) in some species, and inorganic salts as well as traces of other

Table 2-1.
Classification of commercially important citrus types

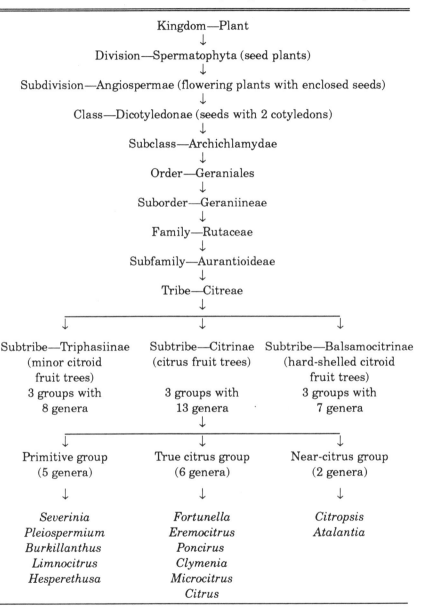

Kingdom—Plant
↓
Division—Spermatophyta (seed plants)
↓
Subdivision—Angiospermae (flowering plants with enclosed seeds)
↓
Class—Dicotyledonae (seeds with 2 cotyledons)
↓
Subclass—Archichlamydae
↓
Order—Geraniales
↓
Suborder—Geraniineae
↓
Family—Rutaceae
↓
Subfamily—Aurantioideae
↓
Tribe—Citreae
↓

↓	↓	↓
Subtribe—Triphasiinae (minor citroid fruit trees)	Subtribe—Citrinae (citrus fruit trees)	Subtribe—Balsamocitrinae (hard-shelled citroid fruit trees)
3 groups with 8 genera	3 groups with 13 genera	3 groups with 7 genera

↓

↓	↓	↓
Primitive group (5 genera)	True citrus group (6 genera)	Near-citrus group (2 genera)
↓	↓	↓
Severinia	*Fortunella*	*Citropsis*
Pleiospermium	*Eremocitrus*	*Atalantia*
Burkillanthus	*Poncirus*	
Limnocitrus	*Clymenia*	
Hesperethusa	*Microcitrus*	
	Citrus	

organic substances. Taken together, these constituent compounds are called the soluble solids of the juice; sugars form by far the largest part of the soluble solids.

7. Seeds often contain embryos formed from the nucellus in addition to the usual embryo formed by fertilization following pollination. These nucellar embryos are derived wholly from the mother plant and reproduce it vegetatively as buds or grafts do. Apparently the stimulus of fertilization is needed for them to begin development, but the sexually derived embryo may fail to develop in many cases.

8. Both bud and seed mutations are known to occur with some frequency, giving rise to "sports," which may possess new and distinctive characters. Sometimes these are desirable changes and give rise to valuable new forms.

9. The species of these genera can hybridize freely with each other. Many hybrids have doubtless been formed naturally during thousands of years of wild development, and they often cause problems in estimating relationships among naturally occurring forms. Many other hybrids have been created deliberately by man, some of them having commercial value.

10. Budding and grafting are easily done reciprocally among these genera, so that a wide range of stock-scion combinations is possible. Many have been used for a long time and others seem certain to be tried in the future.

The Genus *Poncirus*

The genus *Poncirus* was separated in 1815 by Rafinesque from the genus *Citrus,* but the Linnaean name *Citrus trifoliata* continued in use by all citrus writers until Swingle called attention in 1915 to the need for transfer to another genus. It has only one species, *P. trifoliata,* and is distinguished from all other true citrus fruits by being deciduous and having trifoliolate leaves. It is also distinct in having flower buds formed during the summer previous to their spring opening, as is common in apples and peaches, and in having the fruit covered with fine hairs. Since all other citrus fruits and their close relatives are tropical or subtropical, it seems likely that this species is derived from a primitive tropical form that migrated northward long ago when the climate was warmer and managed to adapt to the change of climate by developing the deciduous habit. The 3-foliolate leaf is undoubtedly a very primitive character, and it is somewhat surprising that no other species have been differentiated during the extended period that it has been in existence in northeastern China. Long cultivated as an ornamental tree in China and in Japan, which received it in the eighth century, it came to the United States in 1869 as an introduction by William Saunders for the U.S. Department of Agriculture. It is so cold hardy that it can be grown in the open as far north as Washington, D.C., enduring temperatures as low as 0°F when dormant. This cold hardiness seems to be a dominant character, which is transmitted to hybrids of it with more tender types. It is unfortunate that the name "orange" was attached to this species on its introduction to this country because the fruit bears only the most superficial resemblance to an orange. The pulp is not only acid but also contains a very bitter oil, which makes it inedible. (Nevertheless, both immature and mature fruit were utilized, along with powdered rhinoceros horn, in classical Chinese medicine.) The fruit itself is small, round, yellow at maturity, and has a distinct pubescence and numerous seeds.

The trifoliate orange is known in two very similar forms, distinguished only by the size of the flowers as large-flowered and small-flowered. The species finds commercial use as a rootstock, either directly or in its hybrid progeny, and has minor significance as an ornamental and as protection for wildlife.

Poncirus trifoliata has been valued in Florida since 1892 as a stock for citrus fruits because it is able not only to endure uninjured as much cold as ever is known in this state but also to confer some degree of cold hardiness on the scion top. In Florida, as in Japan, it is the only stock that is regularly used for satsumas, which are somewhat dwarfed by it, and the one often used in the northern part of the state for kumquats, oranges, or mandarins. It is now being used in a limited way as a stock in the central citrus area of the state. Scion varieties on this stock apparently are hardier to cold because of the tendency of this stock to keep them dormant during the period when *Poncirus trifoliata* would be without its leaves. When tops are not dormant, they are no hardier than on other stocks, which is a distinct disadvantage in years of early cold weather following a warm fall period. The trifoliate orange is subject to exocortis, a viral disease that seriously impairs the vigor of the stock.

This species readily forms hybrids with species of *Citrus*. Most important of the hybrids are those resulting from crossing trifoliate orange with sweet orange and with grapefruit. The first *Poncirus* × sweet orange hybrids were produced by Swingle in 1897, working at

Eustis, Florida, and named "citranges" by Webber and Swingle in 1905. The citranges usually come true from seed because they rarely develop a true embryo but form several nucellar embryos. They show quite a range of variation in degree of deciduousness, of leaf compounding, and of cold tolerance, being somewhat intermediate between the two parents in these characters. Usually they are tardily deciduous, trifoliolate, and hardier to cold than sweet orange.

Citranges inherit the acidity of trifoliate orange but have less bitterness, so that with liberal addition of sugar they supply a very good substitute for lemonade in regions farther north than lemons can grow. The fruits are juicy and presumably as rich in vitamin C as lemons. The varieties Rusk (from the first crosses in 1897) and Troyer (from a cross by Swingle in 1909 at Riverside, California) attracted attention as possibly valuable stocks, were extensively tested, but were never widely used in Florida. The Carrizo citrange is currently very popular in many areas to replace older types that have fallen into disfavor due to disease complexes. Some other citranges are also being investigated as stocks.

Several *Poncirus* × grapefruit (citrumelo) hybrids have been produced and have been of little value. In recent years, however, there has been considerable interest in the Swingle citrumelo as a rootstock.

The trifoliate orange has been used as an ornamental for centuries in northern China and Japan. The white flowers and yellow fruits are rather showy, and the twigs and thorns are dark green when the leaves have fallen, making the tree attractive at all seasons. The heavy armament of thorns makes a hedge of trifoliate orange quite impenetrable, thus affording good protection, but these same thorns may be a serious hazard if the plants are used around a playground. On the other hand, the thorns help make this an excellent species for wildlife protection. Thickets of trifoliate orange trees give splendid cover for ground-nesting birds, rabbits, and other animals and have often been planted as game refuges by wildlife associations.

The Genus *Fortunella*

Cultivated in China for at least a thousand years and in Japan for several centuries, the kumquats somehow escaped notice by early European plantsmen. Ferrari, in his account of citrus fruits in 1646, mentioned them as Chinese fruits on secondhand acquaintance, and Kaempfer included them briefly in his 1712 account of the plants cultivated in Japan, but no introduction to Europe was made until 1846. In that year, Robert Fortune brought a plant of the oval kumquat back to England from China, where he had been collecting plants for the London Horticultural Society. It may be that attempts had been made earlier to introduce the kumquat by seed, but it does not thrive on its own roots, and such introductions may have died before they fruited. Thunberg named the common oval-fruited species *Citrus japonica* in 1784, and this name continued in use until 1915 when Swingle decided that it was too different from all known species of *Citrus* to fit in that genus and designated the new genus *Fortunella* in honor of its introducer to the Western world.

A specimen of this kumquat was brought to America within three or four years of its reaching England and probably was introduced to Florida very soon afterward. In 1885, however, both the Glen St. Mary Nursery and the Royal Palm Nursery made importations directly from Japan of the oval and small, round kumquats under their Japanese names "Nagami" and "Marumi," respectively; and most of the specimens growing in Florida derive from these introductions.

Kumquats are shrubby evergreen trees, rarely over ten feet high, with dense branching and small, apparently simple leaves with hardly any petiole wings. Most kumquats are nearly or quite thornless. Trifoliate orange is the most commonly used rootstock. The fruits are small, ovoid, or globose in shape, less than two inches long or wide, and have very thick, sweet rind and mildly acid pulp. The seeds are distinctive in having green cotyledons, which are white in most other citrus fruits. Kumquats are hardier to cold than any species of *Citrus*, being able to endure temperatures down to 10°F when fully dormant, especially on trifoliate orange stock. In part this cold hardiness is due to the fact that they have less tendency to start growth during warm periods of the winter than do *Citrus* species. Another factor is that they delay blooming until late in the spring, long after danger of frost is past. They are probably native to southern China, but are known only in cultivation.

The fruits are very showy, being borne in large numbers and brilliant orange in color. The name "kumquat" is an English form of the Chinese words for "golden orange." No citrus fruit except possibly the calamondin exceeds it in ornamental value, and the kumquat is slower growing and more suitable to landscape usage as a specimen shrub. Since the fruit color is fully developed by December, the kumquat is well suited for use as a living Christmas tree.

Three cultivars of kumquat are grown most commonly: Nagami, Marumi, and Meiwa. Nagami, the oval kumquat, is considered a species, *F. margarita,* separate from the Marumi or small, round kumquat, *F. japonica,* though the differences are not easily noted. The large, round kumquat Meiwa was not introduced to Florida from Japan until 1911. Swingle named it *F. crassifolia* in 1915, but in 1943 decided that it was a hybrid between the other two species and withdrew the specific name although it still persists in horticultural writing. Nagami is the most popular kumquat, being vigorous and prolific. Its fruits are oval, from 1¼ to 1¾ inches long and about two-thirds as wide, and have two to five seeds; it is pleasantly flavored. Meiwa has globose fruits, from 1 to 1½ inches in diameter, and is often nearly seedless. Its rind is much thicker than the rind of the other two forms, and it has a somewhat sweeter taste. Marumi fruits are also globular but smaller, rarely over an inch across, and have one to three seeds. The flavor is good but often is considered a little less pleasing than Nagami; the rind is thinner, and the trees are slightly thorny instead of practically thornless. However, Marumi is a little hardier to cold than Nagami, which is slightly hardier than Meiwa. Nagami is the form best known in China, while Meiwa and Marumi are known only from Japan, although undoubtedly they were introduced there long ago from China.

The Hongkong wild kumquat, *F. hindsii,* is not cultivated in Florida, although specimen plants exist in the state. It is worth growing for its bright scarlet-orange fruits, which are hardly over one-half inch in diameter. The shrubby tree is spiny, and the abundant fruits have a spicy flavor but are palatable only when cooked with sugar.

The fruits are used chiefly for decorating gift boxes of oranges and grapefruit and for making preserves, even though the fresh fruits are quite palatable raw. For gift-box usage, twigs are cut with both leaves and fruit, the oval kumquat being preferred because it is more showy. Judicious pruning methods are used by gift-fruit shippers to assure continued production of fruit. Kumquats are excellent for making marmalade or for making candied fruits, but most varieties are quite seedy and the seeds are somewhat of a drawback for this usage. Kumquats are popular also as decorations for buffet and dinner tables.

The cold hardiness of kumquats suggested they would be useful in trying to develop hardy acid fruits since lemon and lime are less cold hardy than orange. Swingle first made such crosses in 1909 using the small, round kumquat and the Key lime and coined the name "limequats" for the resulting hybrids. Two cultivars (cultivated varieties), Eustis and Lakeland, have been sparingly planted to extend lime culture for home use into north-central Florida. They are less hardy than the calamondin, however.

The Genus *Citrus*

Commercial production of citrus fruits is limited to certain species of the genus *Citrus*, which had its primary center of origin in northeastern India and a secondary center in southern China but became widely diffused throughout southeastern Asia and the adjacent island chains. An amazing diversity of forms has developed in this area over thousands of years, and authorities differ dramatically regarding which of these forms are to be considered true species. Just as in oaks, blackberries, and hawthorns in the United States, the bewildering number of different types undoubtedly has arisen as the result of much crossing between original species. Most botanists recognize these resultant forms as species, for they have been able to perpetuate themselves naturally. Most of the varied forms of *Citrus* are known only as cultivated plants. Swingle very conservatively accords species status to only sixteen of these forms and considers all the others to be hybrids of varying complexity.* Yet very few of his accepted species are known as wild plants, and two or three of them are almost certainly of cultivated origin, so that his classification scheme is not consistent. Tanaka very liberally recognized 145 species of *Citrus*, accepting in this category most (but by no means all) distinctive forms regardless of the theoretical possibility of a hybrid origin so long as

---

* Walter Tennyson Swingle spent sixty years studying the citrus fruits for the U.S. Department of Agriculture and was recognized as the leading world authority. He had no peer in his knowledge of citrus relatives and in his production of hybrids by interspecific and intergeneric crosses in *Citrus* and related genera. The rich variety of forms so produced, however, led him to suspect nearly all the forms of citrus fruits found wild or cultivated of being hybrids—on purely theoretical and often ingeniously suspected grounds—and to deny species status to them on this account. Particularly in the mandarins was he blinded by this prejudice from noting valid differences.

such origin was not proven.* Undoubtedly Swingle's is much too narrow and Tanaka's is much too broad in the number of forms to which they assign specific rank. If Swingle's classifications are used, the mandarins and tangerines become an area of great confusion. In this work we have accepted some of Tanaka's species as valid but by no means all of them. There is need for much more taxonomic study in the very complex and confused genus *Citrus*.

Characters

The following characters are common to all *Citrus* species:
   1. Trees evergreen, small to medium in size, more or less thorny.
   2. Leaves 1-foliolate, the petioles with or without wings, the blade jointed to the petiole (except in the citron).
   3. Flower buds without protecting scales, formed just prior to the advent of a growth flush, normally in early spring, sometimes in summer.
   4. Flowers usually large, fragrant, white mostly but in a few species white tinged with pink or purple; both stamens and pistil normally present in the same flowers.
   5. Fruits small to very large, typically with leathery rind, the color at maturity varying from yellow through orange to a deep orange-red (in tropical areas the fruit may be fully mature but still green); the pulp varying from insipidly sweet to very acid, with droplets of oil in the juice vesicles, which are acrid in some species but not in any of commercial interest; segments eight to eighteen, usually ten to fourteen.
   6. Seeds none, few, or many (there may be from four to twelve in each segment), the cotyledons usually white but pale green in the mandarin group.
   7. Resistance to cold variable, with definite specific differences in hardiness when fully dormant. In order of decreasing hardiness to cold the sequence is: sour orange, mandarins, sweet orange, grapefruit, lemon, lime, citron. All species are easily damaged by cold when in active growth. (In a climate of widely fluctuating winter

---

   * Tyozaburo Tanaka spent a long life studying citrus forms and investigating them intensively all across southern Asia. His knowledge of these forms from firsthand study was unrivaled. For many years a protege and colleague of Swingle, he has opposed him bitterly since 1930 for his ultra-conservatism in citrus taxonomy. Tanaka made a particularly strong case for recognizing several species of mandarins instead of only one.

temperatures, the strong tendency to resume growth prematurely is a big problem for growers.)

Uses

The various *Citrus* species are suited to a variety of uses around the home, although most trees by far are planted for commercial utilization. All species are handsome in foliage, flowers, and fruit, and may be used in warm areas for landscaping where any other evergreen tree of similar size would be suitable. The useful fruits are an added bonus and may be consumed fresh, juiced, or made into various types of preserves, marmalades, crystallized fruits, etc.

Commercial citrus production until 1920 was concerned only with fruit to be used fresh. Canning of citrus fruit begin in 1921 and ultimately utilized a considerable part of the grapefruit crop as well as a small part of the orange crop. The advent of frozen concentrate processing in 1945 led to spectacular changes in the disposition of harvested oranges, limes, lemons, and, to a lesser extent, mandarins.

The processing of citrus fruits created a problem of what to do with the residue of rind, expressed pulp, and seeds. This problem has been solved by researchers, and valuable by-products are now derived from these former wastes. The principal by-products are dried citrus pulp (actually consisting mostly of rind) for cattle feed, molasses from the waste juice, and citrus peel oil from the oil glands of the rind; less important are citrus seed oil, pectin from the inner rind (albedo), bland syrup, and feed yeast.

The sweet orange, grapefruit, mandarins, lime, and lemon are cultivated commercially in Florida in that order of importance. Citron, shaddock, and sour orange are grown commercially in other parts of the world for their fruit, but not in Florida. The characteristics of the various commercially important species of *Citrus* and their varieties will be considered in turn, and also the varieties of hybrid origin that are grown in Florida.

The Sweet Oranges

Both in Florida and in the world generally, the sweet orange, *Citrus sinensis,* is the leading citrus fruit, far exceeding in value all other citrus fruits combined. Indeed, the orange comes second only to the apple as the leading tree fruit in the world. The typical sweet orange tree is upright in growth with branches nearly horizontal, of medium large size except on dwarfing stocks. The leaves are medium in size among *Citrus* species, the petioles with rather narrow wings, which may flare out somewhat at the upper end but never overlap the blade. Fruits vary from oval to flattened-globose, with thin, smooth rind, tightly appressed, not bitter in taste, and with the pulp solid without a hollow core. Rind color ranges from light to deep orange at full maturity with cool temperatures, but with warm weather the rind may remain green or become green again if previously orange.

The great popularity of the sweet orange may be attributed to the following factors:

1. The pleasing flavor resulting from satisfactory balance of sugars and acids. Fully mature oranges are of dessert quality in competition with any other fruits, yet they do not cloy the appetite of the consumer.

2. The relative ease of production of the fruit, within the climatic and soil limitations, and the possibility of both satisfactory yields and a choice of cultivars covering a very long marketing period.

3. The suitability of the fruit not only for fresh use but for a variety of types of processing, including frozen concentrate juice, canned single-strength juice, frozen and canned sections, frozen salads, marmalades, wines, etc.

The sweet orange will likely remain the principal citrus fruit in Florida in the future as it has always been in the past. Most of the new citrus plantings in the state are of this species, in large part because net returns to the grower average higher for sweet oranges than for other citrus fruits. The name "sweet orange" is used advisedly: while "orange" means the fruit of *C. sinensis* to most people, it is often applied to fruit of other species that may resemble sweet oranges. The unfortunate use of the term "trifoliate orange," in which the resemblance is definitely minimal, has already been mentioned. More confusing are such terms as "Temple orange," "King orange," "Orlando orange," "satsuma orange," "mandarin orange," and others, all of which are usually accepted as "oranges" by the general public and compete with the sweet orange for the consumer's dollar but none of which belongs to the species *C. sinensis*. Only the term "sweet orange" refers unequivocally to this species and its varieties.

Four groups of sweet oranges are recognized when the varieties are classified by fruit characters: normal, navel, blood, and acidless oranges. The normal, or common, orange has the characteristics cited for the species without navel development or red pigmentation in the flesh, and its cultivars constitute by far the largest part of the Florida citrus industry. Navel oranges are distinguished by fruit showing a peculiar development at the stylar end (actually an aborted secondary fruit), called a "navel" for obvious reasons. Blood oranges develop red coloring throughout the flesh or in streaks under certain climatic conditions, and sometimes they show red color of the rind. Under Florida conditions, the blood oranges may not develop much, if any, red color in mild winters. Acidless oranges are a curiosity in Florida and have no commercial value. They are cultivated to some extent in some other countries.

The Florida citrus industry also divides orange cultivars into three groups based on season of maturity: early, midseason, and late. Early oranges are those maturing from late September through November. Midseason oranges mature primarily in December and January, and late oranges mature from February through August. The number of cultivars grown in the state has been much higher than is needed or desirable for usual commercial marketing purposes; only a few are of large commercial importance. A great many cultivars have been selected and named in the past only to be discarded entirely. There are also many variant types, producing fruit slightly different from the variety proper—or sometimes distinctly "off-type"—which are marketed under the variety name, although they constitute only a small part of the total crop. Citrus trees are quite subject to bud mutations, and these may be propagated by the unwary nurseryman who checks only to be sure of the variety and not to see if the fruit is characteristic.

Sweet oranges are also classed as seedy and seedless, the latter term including varieties with only a few seeds (commercially seedless) as well as those with no seeds (strictly seedless). If there are more than ten seeds in any fruits of a variety, it is considered seedy; usually the fruits classed commercially as seedless have six or fewer seeds.

The important commercial orange cultivars of Florida, in order of current popularity as indicated by nursery sales, are listed in table 2-2. These cultivars are described in detail in subsequent text.

Any variety that is to supersede one of the varieties listed in table 2-2 must represent a distinct improvement upon it since the large investment in the established cultivars creates a hurdle that a new variety cannot leap if it is only slightly superior in some respects. Florida still has too many commercial cultivars, and whoever proposes to add to the number must offer a great deal more than mere novelty. Yet there is a place, for example, for a good navel va-

Table 2-2.
Important Florida sweet orange cultivars

Commercial importance	Cultivar	Maturity season	Seediness
Major	Hamlin	Early	Seedless
Major	Valencia	Late	Seedless
Major	Pineapple	Midseason	Seedy
Secondary	Parson Brown	Early	Seedy
Secondary	Washington navel[a]	Early	Seedless
Secondary	Queen	Midseason	Seedy
Secondary	Jaffa	Midseason	Seedless
Secondary	Pope Summer[b]	Late	Seedless

a. Many different cultivars of navel oranges have been and continue to be grown. Most new selections are unnamed, numbered selections obtained through the Florida Department of Agriculture, Division of Plant Industry Budwood Registration program.

b. Several cultivars, commercially indistinguishable from Valencia, have been identified but probably do not deserve varietal status. The Pope, Lue Gim Gong, Hart's Late, and others are in this group.

riety bearing heavy crops regularly, or for a midseason variety of Pineapple quality and productivity that is commercially seedless.

In selecting cultivars for large-scale planting, the grower is usually guided by market returns for the crop in the preceding year—or still better, over a period of years. Cultivars that year after year bring good prices are those that have found favor with the public and will probably continue to do so. Another factor of equal importance is, of course, the size and regularity of the crop, for total returns depend both on price per box and productivity. One uncertainty that can hardly be guarded against is always present. Selections that are profitable one year may not be the most profitable in future years when the planting comes into full production. The needs of the processing industry are not the same as those of the fresh fruit industry, although this difference has in the past had its effect on cultural practices rather than on cultivars. Even with this uncertainty, it is safer to plant with an eye to proven consumer acceptance than to plant on the basis of personal satisfaction with the performance of a particular cultivar.

In selecting new orange varieties, the demands of both fresh-fruit shippers and processors must be kept in mind. The commercial packinghouse and the gift-box shipper desire oranges with attractive color of both rind and flesh, smooth and thin rind, rather fine flesh texture, pleasantly tart flavor, good shipping qualities, and optimum fruit sizes. The canning and concentrating industries care little about rind color, texture, or fruit size, but want high juice content with good color, high solids content, a fair degree of acidity, good aroma, and freedom from any off-flavor.

Orange Cultivars

Valencia—This is the leading cultivar in the world. While all oranges probably originated in China, the immediate origin of the Valencia cultivar is uncertain beyond the fact that it was sent out by the Rivers Nursery in England around 1870. Since Rivers obtained his plants from Mediterranean sources, it is probable that he obtained this cultivar in Spain or Italy, where it had long been grown. Attention was first drawn to it in the United States in 1877 when E. H. Hart of Federal Point, Florida, announced that he had a tree with unusually late maturing fruit. The tree had been imported from Rivers Nursery by S. B. Parsons of Parsons Nursery, Long Island, who planted it and several other cultivars at his orange grove and nursery at Federal Point in 1870. When the tree came into bearing, Mr. Hart noticed its unusually late season and found it had no label of identification. The Pomological Committee of the Florida Fruit Growers Association examined specimens of the fruit, confirmed its remarkable lateness of maturity, and named it "Hart's Tardif" ("tardif" meaning "late").

Another importation, also unlabeled, was made from Rivers Nursery to California in 1876. After this tree had attracted attention, it was recognized by a visiting Spanish citrus expert as the variety known in Spain as "naranja tarde de Valencia," and the name "Valencia Late" was soon adopted (1887) in California. It was not until 1914 that Hart's Late and Valencia ceased to be considered as different cultivars in Florida, although by 1893 many citrus authorities in California considered them identical.

Valencia has prime quality in Florida from late March to June, and it remains on the tree in fairly good condition all summer although considerable fruit drop, regreening of the rind, and drying of the flesh may occur under certain conditions. There are usually five or six seeds. The quality is excellent. Several strains of Valencia have arisen by bud mutation and not all are equally desirable. Only one strain is propagated by name in Florida, but several have been recognized and named in California. The Florida strain is "Rohde

Red," a Valencia type very similar to typical, but with improved juice color. It was released in 1975 and has achieved some commercial popularity since the color is such a desirable character. The Budwood Registration Program of the Florida Department of Agriculture's Division of Plant Industry is evaluating many strains of Valencia and other citrus cultivars to determine the best types.

Pineapple—This is the leading midseason cultivar and is of even more obscure origin than Valencia. About 1860 Rev. Dr. J. B. Owens moved from South Carolina to Florida and settled near Sparr, a community north of Ocala. He planted orange seeds, which W. J. Crosby said he had obtained in Charleston from an English vessel, probably from China. When Rev. P. P. Bishop was looking for desirable trees from which to bud wild sour orange trees around Orange Lake (between Ocala and Gainesville) in 1873, he was told of the Owens trees and bought the tops of nine trees that Dr. Owens wanted to move. One of these trees had been named "the pineapple tree" by one of the Owens girls, and when Mr. Bishop's budded trees came into fruit, the budlings from this tree had fruit superior to the other. He budded the rest of his large tract of sour oranges from the "Pineapple" variety. There is disagreement among men who knew the original tree at the time it was first propagated as to the origin of the name "pineapple" in the Owens family. One says it was because the fruit had pineapple flavor; another that the aroma of the fruit, not the flavor, was like pineapple; and a third says it was the shape of the tree, with cylindrical sides and bushy top, which resembled a pineapple fruit. Since no one seems able to detect any flavor except that of orange in the fruit and the marked aroma is noted only in a packinghouse full of this cultivar (such as the Owens never had), the third explanation is the most reasonable. The Pineapple oranges from the Bishop Hoyt (later the Crosby-Wartmann) grove found good market reception but were propagated by the other growers only slowly. After the freeze of 1894–95, however, when extensive replanting had to be done, this cultivar was widely budded. It has prime quality during January and February and has a very fine and distinctive flavor when well grown and properly mature. The number of seeds varies from ten to twenty.

Hamlin—This is the principal early orange of Florida and is of Florida origin. The parent tree was a seedling in a grove planted in 1879 by Judge Isaac Stone a few miles northwest of DeLand. Later this grove was bought by A. G. Hamlin while he lived in DeLand, and so the cultivar was propagated under his name when extensive budding was undertaken following the "big freeze" to take advantage of its unusual earliness of maturity. Its season is from late October to January, and the seed numbers rarely exceed six. While the quality never equals Pineapple, it has a notably smooth, thin rind and as good quality as any early orange. Under comparable conditions, the Hamlin variety produces higher yields per acre than any other cultivar of sweet orange, although the individual fruits are often quite small. As with Valencia, evaluation of several strains of this cultivar is currently underway.

Parson Brown—Before 1920 this was the leading early orange, but it has given place to Hamlin largely because of Parson Brown's seediness. The original tree of the cultivar was one of five seedlings at the home of Rev. Nathan L. Brown near Webster, Florida. These had been given to him as small seedlings in 1856 by a man who said they grew from the seeds in an orange brought to Savannah from China on an English ship. When Capt. J. L. Carney in 1874 was looking, like P. P. Bishop, for a source of budwood for the wild sour orange trees on his island in Lake Weir, the fruit of one of the Brown trees took his special favor because of its fine quality before fruit of the other four trees was mature. He bought the rights to the budwood of this tree and propagated it as the Parson Brown variety. The other four trees were the source of budwood for many groves following the freeze of 1894–95 because it was believed that all of Parson Brown's trees were the same, and this gave rise to much variation in the fruit and trees sold as this variety. The Carney strain represents the true Parson Brown cultivar and matures first in October and November. It has from ten to twenty seeds and a thick, slightly pebbled rind, which loses the green color very slowly. The quality is good.

Lue Gim Gong—At the time of its introduction in 1912, this was believed to have originated as a hybrid of Valencia and Mediterranean Sweet, made at DeLand in 1886 by a Chinese gardener after whom it was named. It was also considered to be even later maturing than Valencia. Few would claim today to be able to tell any difference between Lue Gim and Valencia in season of maturity or in fruit or tree characters, and it is now considered simply a nucellar seedling of Valencia. The cultivar is properly the Lue Gim Gong strain of Valencia.

Pope Summer (Glen Summer)—For over seventy years, varieties of sweet orange that can be held on the tree a little later than Valencia and Lue Gim Gong without excessive dropping have been marketed as summer oranges. They are always similar to Valencia and may represent mutant strains. The parent tree of the Pope

Summer was found in a forty-acre planting of Pineapple near
Lakeland by F. W. Pope about 1916. Evidently one tree was budded
in error. The contrast between the very late season of maturity of
this one tree and the surrounding Pineapple trees was very striking,
for the fruit held well into August. Commercial propagation began
in 1935, and the name "Pope's Summer" was trademarked in 1938.
On sour orange or sweet seedling stocks, especially on hammock
soils, the fruit is good quality in July and August, though mature in
May. The same cultivar was propagated by the Glen St. Mary
Nurseries Company as Glen Summer.

Queen—The parent tree of this cultivar was a seedling of unknown origin in the King grove on Lake Hancock, near Bartow,
which survived the freeze of 1894–95. In 1900 buds from this tree
were obtained for use in the planting of the Perrin and Thompson
grove at Winter Haven because it seemed to have fruit of unusually
good qualities. At first C. H. Thompson called the variety "King," to
honor the man in whose grove the parent tree grew, but later he
changed the name to "Queen" to avoid confusion with the well-established King mandarin. Commercial propagation was begun by
Lake Garfield Nurseries in 1915, and the cultivar has had modest
popularity. The fruit is much like Pineapple in season and quality
with fewer seeds, but it tends to be higher in juice solids on rough
lemon stock and to hold better on the tree during periods of deficient
soil moisture. The trees grow vigorously, yield well, and are slightly
more cold hardy than Pineapple.

Jaffa—Introduced by General Sanford in 1883 from Palestine,
where it was reputed to be a very fine cultivar, the Jaffa soon became popular in Florida because of its few seeds and good quality.
After 1895 its popularity declined in favor of Pineapple because of
its erratic bearing habit. It has not been extensively planted since
except for a brief period of interest following World War II. The fruit
ripens in midseason, is of medium size, and has from six to ten
seeds. Quality is very good and the yields are satisfactory in many,
but not all, groves.

Ruby—This is the only one of several "blood" oranges, once popular in Florida, that is still propagated commercially; demand is
small for it. General Sanford introduced it from the Mediterranean
area about 1880. The quality of Ruby is very good but not more so
than Pineapple and Jaffa, which mature in midseason with it. The
streaks of red color in the flesh develop only with quite cool
weather, and in southern Florida many growers have been disap-

pointed in the failure of the fruit to show the "blood" character. Fruit exposed to light on the tree develops more color than well-shaded fruit. The cultivar is grown chiefly for home use and gift-box shipments, where its novel coloring combined with high quality (well-matured fruit has more color) makes a big appeal. Seeds number about ten.

Navels

Several cultivars of navel oranges are propagated and planted in Florida, but planting of unnamed navel types considerably exceeds that of named varieties. Most of them—named or unnamed —are of the same general type as the famous Washington cultivar grown so extensively in California, but none of them is anywhere nearly so important in Florida—nor are all of them taken together—in Florida as Washington is in California. Navels as a group make a small but increasing fraction of the orange trees in Florida, and the fruit often commands a premium early in the season as a "salad" fruit. Washington itself was introduced to Florida soon after it proved so successful in California, whither budded trees were introduced from Brazil via Washington, D.C., in 1873. Indeed, some trees seem to have been sent by the U.S. Department of Agriculture directly to Florida at the same time as to California, but real interest developed only after the California success, from 1880 on. Although its quality was good, this cultivar proved a shy bearer in Florida and consequently has never been extensively planted, although still propagated on a minor scale. Washington tends to make very large, coarse fruit when the crop is very light, often with early dryness and an unsightly navel. Current interest centers on numbered selections from the Florida Budwood Registration Program. Some of the more popular old-line navel types are discussed in the text that follows.

Summerfield is one of the popular old-line navel cultivars in Florida. Several old trees have been found in groves south and southwest of Lake George on the St. Johns River; they were probably derived from nucellar seedlings from the navel orange introduced from Brazil in 1835 by D. J. Browne and planted for him on Drayton Island by Zephaniah Kingsley. This was the same Bahia navel type introduced and named Washington. Studies of Washington in California have shown that a large number of slightly different strains have arisen there by bud mutation. Summerfield may represent a strain of the same original stock as Washington but one better adapted to Florida conditions; it bears somewhat heavier crops, and its fruit size is smaller in proportion to crop. The fruit is otherwise very like that of Washington.

Glen Improved navel represents another strain, this time derived from Washington itself. The parent trees were noted in a planting of Washington in a Polk County grove belonging to W. G. Roe of Winter Haven. These trees, evidently budded from an unrecognized mutant branch, were bearing good crops of normal-sized fruit. Good results are obtained only on heavier soil types where sour or sweet seedling stocks can be used successfully.

Dream is a navel strain that was found as a budded tree in a grove in Seminole County by D. J. Nicholson in 1939. In 1944 he took out plant patent No. 625 on this cultivar and began commercial propagation. It undoubtedly represents another bud mutation from Washington, although an unusually favorable one. According to the originator, it matures in early October, which is quite early for a navel, and can be held on the tree for several months without drying out—whereas the large scanty fruit of the typical Washington tends to dry out badly in a couple of months after being mature. Like the Glen Improved, the variety is not very successful in deep sandy soils on rough lemon stock, but it yields beautiful and high-quality fruit when properly grown. This strain has fallen out of popularity due to the presence of viruses in the budwood.

Orange Cultivars

There are many other sweet orange types. Some of the more popular (but now uncommon) cultivars include Delicious, Enterprise, and Homosassa. Some very new sweet orange cultivars have been released in 1987, including Sunstar, Gardner, and Midsweet. These are U.S. Department of Agriculture introductions and are all classified as midseason. Since they are so new there is no commercial production, but each cultivar offers some advantages over old-line types. Grower and consumer acceptance will determine whether these new cultivars will be commercially grown.

Grapefruit

Grapefruit is considered a distinct species (*Citrus paradisi* Macf.), although it is known only in cultivation. It appears to have arisen, probably as a mutant of the shaddock (*C. grandis* Osbeck [also known as pummelo]) in the West Indies during the eighteenth century; it was first heard of in Barbados in 1750 under the name "forbidden fruit." In 1789 the "forbidden fruit or smaller shaddock" was reported common in Jamaica, and in 1814 it was called "grapefruit" there, the name being given because the fruit hung in small clusters, like some grapes, instead of one to a twig as is common with oranges and shaddocks. The specific epithet *paradisi* reflects the early name "forbidden fruit." During the first quarter of the present century, horticulturists made determined efforts to have the name "pomelo" adopted for this species instead of grapefruit, but the latter name was too well fixed in the minds of growers and the buying public. Pomelo is still the common name in Brazil. *Toronja* is the common name in Spanish, but it is practically never used anymore in the United States.

Grapefruit not only originated in the Western Hemisphere but is little cultivated anywhere in the Old World, although Israel and South Africa have some commercial plantings. The United States currently produces about 74 percent of the world crop. The introduction of grapefruit to Florida took place in 1823 when Dr. Odette Philippe, a French count, settled near Safety Harbor on Tampa Bay, bringing with him seeds or seedlings of grapefruit and other kinds of citrus fruits from the Bahamas. So far as we know, all of our present cultivars are descended from this introduction by seedling variation, mutation, or hybridization.

The new fruit attained popularity very slowly. It was chiefly a curiosity until about 1885, usually being considered merely a variation of shaddock, although considerable quantities were imported from the West Indies (78,000 fruit into New York in 1874). In 1875, Florida nurseries offered only grapefruit seedlings, and a book on Florida fruits in 1886 mentions grapefruit only as the best of the shaddocks and unworthy of commercial cultivation. Yet in 1884 a New York fruit dealer was quoted in a Florida newspaper as saying there was a considerable demand for the fruit. Evidently some shipments were being made already, for in 1884–85 J. A. Harris reported he had shipped 1,500 barrels from his Citra grove. But in 1889 W. S. Hart considered that there was still no commercial production. He noted that several improved varieties were being offered by nurseries, but at the State Horticultural Society meeting that year there was a premium only for the best plate of grapefruit (no cultivars) while premiums were offered for about fifty named orange cultivars. The first named grapefruit cultivars appear in the horticultural literature only in the 1897 list of the American Pomological Society even though nursery catalogs had been listing some cultivars for several years.

Grapefruit ranks behind the sweet orange in production and consumer acceptance. World production of grapefruit equals only about 10 percent of the production of oranges, and Florida produces more than 69 percent of the global crop. In addition, Florida can claim credit for originating many of the important varieties (and many more unimportant ones), except for Redblush, which appeared first in Texas. The first planting of grapefruit trees in the United States, the first shipment of grapefruit to northern markets, and the first commercial plantings of grapefruit also took place in Florida.

In spite of an auspicious beginning, grapefruit growers in Florida have had many difficult years. Often during the 1950s and 1960s, the fruit was simply left on the tree (economic abandonment) because the prevailing prices would not pay for picking, hauling, packing, shipping, and selling costs, let alone return any profit to the grower. The immediate cause of this situation was, of course, production far in excess of consumer demand. But the basic factor in small demand is that the "tonic" flavor of grapefruit is relished by fewer persons, generally of middle age or above, than those who enjoy oranges. The tendency to market grapefruit prematurely has not improved the situation. Furthermore, although canned grapefruit segments and juice proved a more satisfactory product than canned oranges, the frozen orange concentrate is far more popular than either canned or frozen grapefruit.

For many years, few plantings of grapefruit were made in the state because of the above-mentioned possibility of economic abandonment. Since 1968, however, growers have begun to make new plantings with the realization that the older plantings of this fruit were gradually being exhausted. This took on greater proportions with the increased demand and better prices for grapefruit occasioned by consumer interest in the diet value of the fruit. Plantings are continuing, especially in the Indian River area and the southern Florida flatwoods to satisfy this market.

The original grapefruit trees and the ones first planted in Florida had yellow rinds at maturity and flesh of pale ivory-yellow, usually spoken of as white. By rather infrequent mutation this color may become pink, and the pink form may mutate to produce one with red flesh. So far as is known, the naturally occurring pink and red colors have appeared only as bud mutations, where a single bud on a tree develops into a branch bearing fruit of a color different from that on all the other branches. Buds taken from this mutant branch will produce trees with fruit exactly like that borne by this branch, and the new form can therefore be propagated as a cultivar.

(At least one cultivar, Star Ruby, is the product of seed irradiation and will be discussed later in the text.)

While the earliest known mention of grapefruit in Florida, by Atwood in 1867, refers to the red flesh of the fruit, all the seedlings known in the 1880s seem to have borne fruit with white flesh. It was not until 1906 that a pink-fleshed sport (Foster) was found, and only in 1929 that one with red flesh (Ruby) was discovered. While pink, or especially red, flesh may have eye appeal for the buyer, it should be emphasized that there is no correlation between color and taste. The color sports taste like the varieties of which they are mutants. Starting in about 1935 there was quite a vogue in Florida for planting pink, seedless grapefruit, followed in about 1945 with similar heavy planting of red, seedless forms. Since 1954, however, there has been a notable decrease in enthusiasm for red grapefruit, and there has even been extensive topworking (see chapter 3) of these types to other citrus forms, sometimes even before they were mature enough to bear. This was in large part due to the inability to produce a satisfactory juice product from pigmented cultivars with the technology available at that time. Many new plantings are again being made of the various colored types.

The seedless condition, by which is meant that very few or no seeds develop beyond a very early stage, has also arisen in grapefruit by mutation, but in this case by seed mutation, not by bud mutation. This simply means that the genetic change occurred during the formation of the embryo of the seed, and that all branches of the resulting tree are alike. At least four instances are known of seeds from normal seedy grapefruit producing trees with seedless fruit, and four seedless cultivars—Cecily, Davis, Marsh, and Star Ruby —have been propagated in consequence. Only Marsh, however, has been grown to any considerable extent, although Star Ruby is being planted in some areas. While Marsh is now the leading grapefruit variety of the world as well as of Florida, it is the convenience of not having seeds rather than superior quality that has put the seedless varieties ahead. It is generally conceded that the seedy varieties excel the seedless ones in taste. For canning, also, the white flesh is most desired.

The color mutation is quite independent of the mutation for seedless condition, and pink and red forms of both seedy and seedless types are grown. Since the Duncan cultivar was a seedling of the original tree introduced to Florida in 1823, we may consider that all other cultivars have arisen from it. The relationship of the color mutants to their parents is shown in table 2-3.

Table 2-3.
Grapefruit cultivar relationships

	Fruit Characteristics		
Seediness	White flesh	Pink flesh	Red flesh
Seedy	Duncan →	Foster →	Hudson
			↓
Seedless	Marsh →	Thompson →	Star Ruby (seedless irradiation mutant) Ruby Redblush Burgundy Ray Ruby Henderson Flame

Red, seedy grapefruit have been propagated in Florida, but no varieties have been described and the possible relation to Foster (no other pink, seedy variety has been recorded) cannot be determined. The Hudson, a red-fleshed, seedy bud sport of the Foster, was named and described in Texas. From irradiated seed of this cultivar arose the Star Ruby, which is red-fleshed and seedless. In the seedless cultivars, the sequence is clearly established as indicated. Many seedy types with white flesh are so similar to Duncan that they are practically indistinguishable, and they are all sold on northern markets as Duncan. Some distinct cultivars have arisen by natural seedling variation since only about nine out of ten grapefruit seeds reproduce the parent tree exactly. Others have appeared that lack the slightly bitter taste that is characteristic of grapefruit, and while seeming otherwise to be true grapefruit are considered possibly to be hybrids. These include the Royal and Triumph of Florida, the Imperial of California, the Isle of Pines from Cuba and the Chironja of Puerto Rico, which appear to be a natural group of orange-grapefruit hybrids (orangelos). It is also possible that the loss of the bitter principle is due to a gene mutation.

Grapefruit cultivars, like oranges, may mature early, in midseason, or in some cases late when allowed to develop normally. Commercially the differences are small, and most grapefruit are considered early-midseason. Considerable differences in maturity dates between similar cultivars may be due to bloom dates and fruit age, selection of rootstock, and latitude. Generally speaking, grapefruit grown in the southern portion of the state mature before similar fruit in the northern portion because they accumulate more heat units and, of course, usually bloom earlier.

The various markets for grapefruit do not all want the same fruit characters. The fresh-fruit and gift-box shippers demand a regularly oblate shape, which can be cut into two symmetrical halves for serving at the table. Fruit should have a rind that is smooth and uniformly yellow or blushed, without any green. Seedless fruit is preferred, and pink or red flesh color is usually an advantage, although white flesh sometimes brings better prices. Desirable sizes are large to medium—from 27 to 48 per standard carton (four-fifths bushel).

The producer of canned sections and citrus salads is concerned with having pleasant tasting fruit and segments that are intact after processing. Pink and red flesh colors do not usually look attractive after canning, and seedy fruit has better section stability than seedless, as well as higher solids content; so seedy varieties with white flesh are used generally.

For canned juice and frozen concentrate,the important qualities are attractive juice color, high juice content, high solids, a fair degree of acid, and low bitterness. Again the seedy, white-fleshed varieties are preferred, although much of the seedless crop is also processed. Recent innovations in processing technology now allow the use of pigmented juices. Older methods of processing often yielded a brown, muddy-looking product.

In 1989 some 88 percent of the grapefruit trees in the state were seedless varieties. The fresh market is made up almost exclusively of seedless varieties. Most of the processed products are now seedless although seedy fruit is desired for sectioning.

Grapefruit Cultivars

Duncan—The oldest commercial grapefruit cultivar, Duncan was not the first to be named and propagated. Its parent tree was planted around 1830 near Safety Harbor and lived to be nearly a century old. About 1892 it was introduced and propagated by A. L. Duncan of nearby Dunedin. It has been the standard of quality in grapefruit ever since its introduction. It is probably the grapefruit cultivar hardiest to cold, but it has from thirty to fifty seeds per fruit. It matures normally from December to February and has white flesh. While Duncan is still propagated and planted in small numbers, any seedy, white-fleshed grapefruit may sell on northern markets under this name since it is the prototype of this common sort of grapefruit.

Foster—The first cultivar with pink flesh to be discovered, Foster arose as a bud sport of the Walters cultivar and was first noted in 1907 by R. B. Foster of Manatee in the old Atwood grove near Ellenton. It was first propagated by the Royal Palm Nursery at Oneco in 1914. Its rind is also flushed pink, so that the fruit as it hung on the parent tree was quite in contrast to the yellow fruit of the Walters. The season of normal maturity is November and December. Quality is good, but the number of seeds is as large as or larger than in Duncan.

Marsh (Marsh Seedless)—The original Marsh tree was a seedling supposedly planted about 1860 near Lakeland. It was first noticed with interest in 1886 by E. H. Tison, who began propagation and offered it in 1889 for the first time simply as "budded seedless grapefruit (very choice)." A few years later, C. M. Marsh bought this nursery and named this variety "Marsh's Seedless," but the name was long ago shortened to "Marsh." The fruit is smaller than fruit of Duncan and Foster, normally matures a little later, and can be held longer on the tree without excessive dropping. Flesh color is white, and the seeds range from six down to none in the best strains. Marsh has long remained a very popular grapefruit cultivar in Florida and the world.

Redblush or Ruby—The first grapefruit with deep red flesh originated in a planting of Thompson made at McAllen, Texas, in 1926 by A. E. Henninger. When the trees first fruited in 1929, one branch had fruit with a crimson blush, and on cutting it open the flesh color was found to be ruby red. Plant patent No. 53 was issued to Mr. Henninger in 1934, but several similar mutations of Thompson with pink to red flesh and rind, which cannot be distinguished from Ruby, have appeared in both Texas and Florida. Many nurseries now simply propagate them as Red Seedless or Red Marsh. Season and quality of these red sports are the same as for Thompson. The name Redblush is widely used in Texas, where the variety originated, and is more descriptive than Ruby due to the blush on the rind occasioned by the red albedo. Furthermore, this name avoids the confusion with the much older Ruby orange variety. The name

Red Marsh is often used in the fresh-fruit trade. This red-fleshed cultivar is second only to Marsh in grapefruit plantings in Florida in 1989.

Thompson—Originated in 1913 as a pink-fleshed bud sport of a Marsh tree in the grove of W. B. Thompson at Oneco, the Thompson cultivar was not propagated until the Royal Palm Nursery of Oneco introduced it in 1924. It is seedless, just as Marsh is, and of the same quality and external appearance, for no pink shows on the rind. Thompson matures earlier than Marsh when the fruit develops normally but is like it in holding the fruit well without dropping for several months, although the pink color fades with age.

Triumph—While not of commercial importance, Triumph is one of the best cultivars for home planting because of its unusually fine flavor and freedom from bitterness. It is very seedy but also very juicy. It was the first cultivar to be named and propagated, having been offered to the public in 1884. Nothing is known of its origin except that the parent tree was growing on the grounds of the Orange Grove Hotel in Tampa. The cultivars Royal and Isle of Pines are very similar to Triumph, and all mature naturally in November. As mentioned previously, this variety, as well as the Imperial and the Chironja, may be rightly called an orangelo (orange × grapefruit hybrid).

Burgundy—The parent tree was found about 1948 in a grove of Thompson near Ft. Pierce, probably originating as an undetected bud sport. It was patented in 1954 and introduced commercially in 1956. The fruit is red-fleshed, seedless, and late-ripening with white albedo similar to the Thompson. Known locally in the Indian River citrus area, it has not been widely planted.

Star Ruby—Developed by the Texas A & I University Citrus Center from an irradiated seed of the Hudson grapefruit, Star Ruby differs from the seedy, red-fleshed Hudson in being commercially seedless with zero to nine seeds. Similar to its parent, it often shows a reddish tinge of wood and bark at the cambial layer. Leaves, narrower than those of other grapefruit, often exhibit chlorotic patterns. The tree is bushy and compact, blooms profusely, and bears some fruit in clusters. The original tree has produced substantial crops of good-sized fruit with red albedo. The Star Ruby may find a use in the sectionizing industry since segments hold together well; it is suitable for juicing, too, since at single-strength it retains its color well. Introduced in Texas in March 1970, it was officially released in Florida on 15 November 1973. The previously mentioned chloroses and other problems, which are probably a result of genetic charges due to the radiation treatment, make this cultivar more difficult to grow than most other grapefruit types.

Other Grapefruit Cultivars—While many other grapefruit cultivars have come and gone over the years, the ones listed are among the most popular over time. Recent interest in red-fleshed grapefruit types had resulted in the recent release of three new red grapefruit cultivars—Henderson and Ray Ruby from Texas and Flame from Florida. All appear to be somewhat superior to the industry standard Redblush. Since these are very new types, little is known about their commercial acceptance at this time.

The Mandarin Group

The name mandarin, or "mandarin orange," is applied to a number of citrus fruits that have as their common characters distinguishing them from oranges a peel that is quite free from the flesh, green seed cotyledons, and flowers singly or in clusters that never form a branched inflorescence. The term "kid-glove orange" was at one time applied because it was said that a lady could eat one while wearing kid gloves without getting them wet; and mandarins have had some publicity as "zipper-skinned oranges." The mandarin group as a whole is one of specialty fruits with rather short season and some marketing difficulties for distant shipment because the soft, loose rind is easily injured, with resultant development of diseases and postharvest disorders.

Three species are grouped under the mandarin name—the satsumas, the King and kunenbo, and the tangerines (or mandarins proper), though Swingle put them all in one elastic species, *Citrus reticulata* Blanco.

Satsumas (*Citrus unshiu* Marc.) (*C. reticulata* of Swingle)

The satsuma originated in Japan in about A.D. 1600 from seed brought from China, much as the grapefruit did in the West Indies. Its Japanese name, unshiu, is a corruption of Wenchow, the area of China from which the seeds came. It represents a mutation in all probability, again resembling grapefruit in origin, for no similar citrus fruit is known in China. In Japan the satsumas are the most important fruit grown on a commercial scale. The fruit is exported to the United States and Canada, although the bulk of the crop is consumed at home. There are several satsuma cultivars in Japan, and while at least four of these are known to be in cultivation in this country, only one—Owari—is at all common.

The Owari satsuma was first introduced to Florida in 1876 by Dr. George Hall and in 1878 by Gen. George Van Valkenburg, both importations being of budded trees. It is notably more resistant to cold than the sweet orange and has been successfully cultivated all around the Gulf Coast from Florida to Texas. It is usually considered most satisfactory when grown on trifoliate stock, on which it makes a small tree, and is cultivated almost entirely north of the main citrus belt. However, there have been cases of vigorous growth and fruiting on sour orange stock. The trees bear heavy crops; the fruit, which has a distinctive flavor and attractive appearance, matures in October and November with the earliest oranges. Both rind and pulp are deep orange in color when fully mature, but rind color may be quite green early in the season even though fruit is mature. If left on the tree after they reach maturity, the fruits become puffy and lose their sprightly taste. Normally they are seedless.

King (*Citrus nobilis* Lour.) (*C. reticulata* × *C. sinensis* of Swingle)

The King "orange" of Indo-China and the closely related kunenbo of Japan are the only representatives of this species. They may have arisen many hundreds or thousands of years ago as hybrids, but they have maintained a distinctive existence since then and have never been duplicated in any man-made crosses, so they seem entitled to species recognition.

The King was introduced as fruit from Saigon to California in 1880 and thence as small seedling trees to Florida in 1882, fruiting here first in 1884. The fruit is the largest, with the thickest rind, of all the mandarin group. It has never been important commercially because of a tendency to overbearing, with resultant breakage of limbs, and to sunscalding of fruit because of upright branches with relatively sparse foliage. Furthermore, the rough rind is unattractive, with no sales appeal except to the few who know the fruit's superb flavor. The season of maturity is March to June, and the fruit has several seeds that, unlike all the other seeds of the mandarin group, have white cotyledons.

Tangerines (*Citrus reticulata* Blanco)

There is no satisfactory distinction in meaning between "mandarin" and "tangerine." The former word is of older usage, and the earliest use of "tangerine" (1841) is as a synonym for mandarin. The name was originally spelled "tangierine" because fruits were imported from Tangiers in Morocco to England. At one time it was customary to separate the varieties with yellow-orange rind as mandarins and those with reddish-orange rinds as tangerines, but this does not accord with Florida practice of recent years. Yellow Oneco and red Dancy are alike called tangerines here. It seems desirable to let the word "mandarin" be the group name, as is widely done, for all the loose-skinned, sweet citrus fruits, and to refer to all mandarins except satsumas and King as "tangerines."

The first mandarins (tangerines) introduced to Florida must have arrived about 1825, for the village of Monroe on the St. Johns changed its name in 1830 to Mandarin, which must have been the result of pride in possessing this novel citrus fruit. We know nothing of the source or the cultivar introduced, though the Ponkan was available in England after 1805, nor do we know the source of the second importation in 1838. This came from China, however, by way of Parson's Nursery on Long Island, and on its leaves came the long scale that nearly wiped out all the citrus trees of the state. Perhaps all the tangerine trees were killed, for in 1877 Major Atway was given credit for introducing this type of citrus fruit to Florida from Louisiana. The Read and Hartley groves at Mandarin survived the long scale, but they may have had no tangerine trees. But what Major Atway introduced is somewhat uncertain. Usually he is credited with bringing in the Willowleaf ("China") variety, which originated in Italy and was well known there long before 1840. It is supposed to have been introduced to New Orleans from Italy between 1840 and 1850. The Atway grove at Palatka was bought by Dr. N.-H. Moragne in 1843, and his daughter has stated that a mandarin tree was growing there at that time. This could have been the Willowleaf, though this is unlikely. But the fruit that the Pomological Committee of the Florida Fruit Growers Association described from the Moragne grove in 1877 as "Tangerine Orange (synonyms: Mandarin, Kid Glove, Tomato Orange)" and ascribed to Major Atway's introduction was definitely not the Willowleaf but was very similar to the Dancy. It seems that either the committee erred or Major Atway did not introduce the Willowleaf. In 1885 Colonel Dancy, who was then a neighbor of Dr. Moragne, stated that the Moragne tangerine had been introduced from Tangiers about 1850.

The only Willowleaf tangerine known to have been in Florida

in 1877 was one small tree in the grove of E. H. Hart at Federal Point, a few miles downriver from Palatka. This had been obtained from England by S. B. Parsons in 1870. Since this type was not known in China, it could not have been imported from China in the 1830s, and it almost certainly was the type introduced to Louisiana in the 1840s. If Major Atway brought it to Florida, it must have died before 1877, for Hart certainly knew the trees in the small Moragne grove, and his tree was unique. Much mystery surrounds the supposed Atway introduction, but in any event it was definitely not the first introduction of mandarins in Florida. The first mention of Willowleaf by name (as "China") was by A. H. Manville in 1883, and it was Pliny Reasoner in 1887 who erroneously made it a synonym of the Moragne tangerine.

The name *Citrus reticulata* Blanco was originally applied to the tangerine known in Formosa as "ponkan" and in India as "suntara." Tanaka would limit its use to this important and widely distributed form and apply separate specific names to each of the many other types of tangerines. Undoubtedly the differences between Dancy and Ponkan are much greater than those between Parson Brown and Valencia and might well justify specific distinction, for they seem comparable to the differences between Nagami and Marumi kumquats. Some of Tanaka's species, however, seem based on rather trivial differences, and some of our cultivars do not fit into any of his species. For this reason, *Citrus reticulata* is used in this book to include all the tangerines, although the authors recognize that several possible species may well be included therein.

Some tangerines are native to India, some to Malaya, several to China, and one (as above noted) is of Italian origin. All the types grown on even a small commercial scale in Florida are marketed as tangerines, but until about 1945 the only tangerine of real value was Dancy because it is the only one that had been marketed for a long period in large quantity. (Several other tangerine types are currently grown and marketed commercially as tangerines. These are man-made citrus hybrids that closely resemble tangerines and usually have the tangerine as a parent plant. These types are discussed in the section on citrus hybrids.)

As specialty fruits, tangerines have long been popular for home use and for gift boxes. The attractive color of rind and flesh, the ease of removing the peel and separating the segments of the flesh, and the sweet taste with pleasant flavor make them desirable as dessert fruits. But as fruits for large commercial production they have several disadvantages in comparison with oranges. If left on the tree after becoming mature, the fruit suffers a rather rapid loss of acidity, which leaves it insipidly sweet, and the segments dry out. With shrinkage of the segments from drying out, the space between flesh and peel increases, causing "puffiness." Tangerines tend to overbear, producing in one year a large crop of uneconomically small fruit that so devitalizes the tree that only a very light crop (of desirable large fruit!) is borne the following year; and the alternating cycle is repeated. Fruit produced inside the canopy of foliage is much less well colored than that borne on the outside and may also have poorer internal quality. Loss of green color and development of red is often slow, and since attractive color is an important factor in selling price, it is necessary to make a series of spot-pickings for size and color. Even after several pickings, much fruit may still remain on the tree, especially in a mild winter.

In the early days of the citrus concentrate industry it was hoped that tangerines of undesirably small size and poor color for fresh shipment might be utilized as frozen concentrate. This hope has not yet been fulfilled to any great extent, but some tangerine juice is sometimes blended (up to 10 percent) into orange juice for concentrate to increase color of the finished product.

The shipping season for (Dancy) tangerines is short, the best market being in the period from Thanksgiving to Christmas for the holiday trade. There is a secondary period of demand in spring that can only be filled by late-bloom fruit. In transit, tangerines are highly susceptible to injuries that permit rapid invasion by rots and molds.

The price per box "on the tree" for tangerines is often higher than that for oranges, but the number of boxes of marketable fruit per acre is lower and the net return per acre is usually lower for tangerines. Many shipping organizations refuse to handle tangerines, although when sales efforts are specifically directed to this fruit, satisfactory market arrangements are possible.

At one time, tangerines were very extensively planted in Florida, the only state that markets a large crop. Since 1930 new plantings of all tangerines have been relatively small until the 1980s. Renewed interest in specialty fruit of all kinds was rekindled following serious freezes early in the decade. Some of the citrus hybrids (tangerine types, tangors, and tangelos) that will be discussed later have some of the desirable qualities of tangerines without some of the serious disadvantages. They are often marketed as competitors of oranges rather than of tangerines, although they should be considered specialty fruits.

Tangerine Varieties

Dancy (*Citrus tangerina* of Tanaka)—This is the cultivar that is usually thought of when the word "tangerine" is heard, and until 1945 it was almost exclusively the one planted for commercial production. The original tree of Dancy developed in the grove of Col. F. L. Dancy at Orange Mills from seed of the Moragne tangerine. The cultivar is typical of the tangerine type native to the Foochow area of southern China and introduced to Japan in the sixteenth century probably, where it is known as Obeni-mikan. This variety reproduces practically 100 percent true from seed unless a mutation occurs, which is very rarely, and the source of the seed is known in this case. The first mention of the cultivar is in the report of the Pomological Committee in 1877, which considered this a new fruit similar but slightly superior to the fruit of Dr. Moragne's tangerine. Various opinions have been expressed on its origin, but Colonel Dancy himself stated in 1885 that it arose from a seed of the Moragne tree planted in 1867. Commercial propagation began about 1890 by the Rolleston Nursery at San Mateo. In bright color and pleasing combination of sweetness and sprightly acidity, Dancy is typical of most tangerines and has the typical defects also. It matures in December and January and has from seven to twenty seeds.

Ponkan (Chinese Honey orange, Warnurco tangerine) (*Citrus reticulata* of Tanaka)—This cultivar is of Indian origin but has been popular in southern China for many centuries and also in Formosa and Japan, where it is called "Ponkan." Two fruits of this cultivar were sent about 1892 to J. C. Barrington of McMeekin (near Hawthorne) by Dr. Parks, a medical missionary in China. He gave some of the seedlings raised from the seed of these fruits to Frank Jenkins of Melrose, and one of them survived the 1895 freeze, as did two seedling planted by Mr. Barrington. Dr. Parks apparently sent them as "honey oranges," and the fruit attained some small fame as Chinese Honey orange. In the 1920s the Wartmann Nursery Company at Ocala propagated this fruit under the name Warnurco tangerine. Under its proper name, Ponkan, it has been planted sparingly since 1945 and has never been prominent in the market.

The fruit of the Ponkan is more nearly globose than most tangerines and is heavy and soft, with very sweet, melting pulp. The rind color is orange, not reddish like the Dancy, and the seeds are few. The season of maturity is November and December, and fruit left on the tree does not hold its quality long.

Oneco—Introduced from India in 1888 as seed by P.W. Reasoner of Royal Palm Nurseries, Oneco, this cultivar was identified by Tanaka in 1929 as merely a strain of the Ponkan. Certainly it resembles the Ponkan closely except that it matures first in January and holds its fruit in good condition until late in the spring, much like the Murcott. It has never been planted on a large commercial scale, and as a consequence is not well known.

Cleopatra (*Citrus reshni* of Tanaka)—This handsome, small, red tangerine is far more important as a stock for other citrus fruits than as a fruit tree even though it was originally introduced for its fruit. Native to India, it had somehow reached the West Indies a century ago and was introduced to Florida about 1875 from Jamaica as the Spice tangerine by Col. C. Codrington, who had formerly lived there. The origin of the name Cleopatra is entirely obscure. It first occurs in horticultural literature in 1887 in Pliny Reasoner's report, in which he says that Cleopatra probably is a synonym of Spice. H.J. Webber considered it "probably the most ornamental of all citrus types" because of the symmetrical tree shape, the dense, dark-green foliage, and the brilliant red fruits. The fruit is of good quality, but rather tart, and is too small and seedy to be worth cultivation except as an ornamental or as a source of stock seeds. It matures in January and February.

Lemons

The true lemon, *Citrus limon* Burm., seems to have had its origin in northwestern India. It is not known in wild form and may have arisen thousands of years ago under cultivation. It reached southern Italy by A.D. 200 but may have failed to survive the Dark Ages following the overrunning of Italy by the Goths and Vandals. Tolkowsky has shown that the lemon was introduced again to Sicily before 1000 by the Moslems, if it was not still surviving there, and that it was being cultivated in Iraq and Egypt by 700. With nearly a millennium of culture in Sicily, it is not surprising that this has traditionally been the source of commercial varieties. Apparently the true lemon did not reach China until around 1200, the "lemon" mentioned earlier in Chinese literature being a related species, *C. limonia* Osbeck, from Tanaka's careful investigations. By 1100, lemons were widely known in Italy, Spain, and Portugal.

Lemon seeds were brought to Hispaniola by Columbus in 1493, and while they are not specifically mentioned, the importance of lemons in the Spanish diet suggests strongly that they might well have been included among the fruits listed in 1579 as flourishing at St. Augustine. Little mention is made of lemons in records of colonial Spain, but in 1839 Williams noted that lemons were increasingly being planted in northeastern Florida. Grown entirely as seedlings, lemon trees would often recover from the occasional freezes of this area.

Commercial lemon culture in Florida was begun only after 1870 and was spurred by the extensive importation of lemons to the United States from Sicily. Florida orange growers (and likewise those in California) felt that this market could profitably be supplied with homegrown fruit. They recognized, however, that the seedling types already growing in this country could not compete with the superior types coming from Italy and so set about obtaining equally good varieties with which to supply the market. Several varieties resulted simply from planting seeds of good Sicilian lemons and selecting among the seedlings for superior quality and performance. Budwood was also imported in a few cases. An industry rapidly developed in both Florida and California, but in addition to the handicap of a freeze in 1886, the lemon suffered two additional disadvantages in Florida. In the humid climate of this state, the lemon scab disease was hard to control, and proper curing of lemons was difficult. After the freeze of 1894–95, lemon culture was almost wholly abandoned as a commercial proposition in Florida, although a small lemon culture for home and local use was continued.

After 1953 there was a renewal of interest in growing lemons in Florida, and several large plantings were made. This interest was chiefly in the production of lemons not for shipment fresh to the market but for making frozen lemonade concentrate. This use involved no need for curing the fruit, and control of lemon scab was not a real problem with the fungicides and spray equipment then available. Florida growers were confident that they could produce lemon juice at a lower cost than their competitors. However, cured Florida lemons were well accepted by the housewife, and the demand within the state is large. It was felt that it might prove profitable to make spot-pickings for the fresh market early in the season (August–September), while fruit harvested later would go to processing plants. The tendency for the size of Florida-grown lemons to be too large for the grocery trade is no disadvantage in producing them for processing. The processor asks only for (1) high juice content, (2) high acid content, and (3) absence of any unpleasant aftertaste. These are qualities Florida lemons can provide. The only real problem is the somewhat greater cold hazard for lemons than for oranges, which limits the area suitable for lemons.

Plantings of lemons in the southern portion of the state gradually increased to about 10,000 acres, and for a time there was continued interest in further development. Most of the acreage was located near Lake Okeechobee in Martin and Palm Beach counties, an area that is relatively frost-free. Smaller plantings were also located in Hillsborough County and other locations that could afford the proper climatic protection. Production has exceeded 1 million boxes in the early 1970s. The freezes of 1977 and the 1980s reduced lemon plantings to less than 1,300 acres by the 1988–89 season, and there appears to be little interest in large-scale replanting at this time.

Lemon Cultivars

There are basically only two types of commercial true lemons, and these were apparently selected long ago in Sicily and in Portugal. The various named cultivars are selections within these two types, represented by Eureka and Lisbon. As analyzed by H. J. Webber, the Eureka type is rather sturdy, characterized by an open, spreading tree habit with relatively few branches and twigs and leaves that are dark green and rather blunt-pointed. The Lisbon type makes a rather dense tree with many slender, upright branches and leaves that are light green and acute at the tip.

Eureka—This is the principal lemon cultivar of California. It is not grown under that name in Florida to any extent. It originated as the best seedling from seeds of a Sicilian lemon planted in California in 1858 and was introduced as a cultivar in 1878 by T. A. Garey of Los Angeles as "Garey's Eureka." Within two years, however, the name had been shortened to "Eureka" alone. Thorns are few, acidity is high, and seeds are few, but fruit is mostly borne on the tips of the branches, so that it is somewhat subject to damage from wind and sun. The tree is more subject to injury by cold than most other lemon cultivars. The major portion of the fruit matures in Florida from August to December, although some fruit may mature all year long due to the ever-blooming nature of the plant.

In California, the Eureka has yielded heavy crops but tended to have a short bearing life because of susceptibility to shell-bark and dry-bark diseases. However, Dr. H. B. Frost has developed a nucellar strain that is free from these viral infections, and this strain has been widely planted. Many clonal selections are now being used in California.

Lisbon—This cultivar remains in second place in California. It was considered the best lemon grown in Florida, although it was not known as Lisbon here. It had its origin in Australia from the seed of lemons from Portugal and was introduced to California from Australia in 1874 as budwood. Like Eureka, it was first propagated commercially by Garey around 1880. Trees are much more thorny than are Eureka trees but are more vigorous and productive. Acidity is as high, there are usually more seeds, and the fruit tends to be produced mostly inside the tree canopy where it is better protected from sun, wind, and cold than in Eureka. Selections of outstanding trees for propagation by nurserymen in California have given rise to many clonal types.

Sicily—The cultivar planted under this name in Florida since 1953 is apparently not the Sicilian type at all. It somewhat resembles the strain of Lisbon known in California as "Short-thorned Lisbon." The cultivar Sicily that was imported from that island by General Sanford in 1875 has apparently disappeared from Florida culture. The presently planted Sicily was found about 1952 as an old seedling tree in the Bearss grove near Lutz, Florida. The parent tree is believed to have been planted about 1892. A selection was made and planted extensively near Babson Park in 1953 by Libby, McNeill, and Libby. This grove was sold in the late 1960s and is no longer in production, although it supplied budwood for the company's later plantings in Palm Beach County. This cultivar is now referred to as the "Bearss" lemon. Large plantings were made in Martin, Palm Beach, and Hendry counties in the mid and late 1960s.

Avon—This cultivar originated as a budded tree of unknown origin at Arcadia. A tree budded from this about 1934 by Mr. J. H. Jones in the Alpine grove near Avon Park attracted the attention of Mr. W. F. Ward by its heavy production of high-quality fruit for frozen juice. The variety has been propagated since 1940 by Ward's Nursery as the Avon.

Harvey—About 1940 Harvey Smith discovered the parent tree growing in the home grounds of George James in Clearwater. It was already there when he bought the property, and the original source is unknown. Because the trees budded from this tree fruited well on several stocks and stood up well in a freeze, the Glen St. Mary Nurseries Company began commercial propagation in 1943, calling it "Harvey." It is apparently very similar to Eureka.

Villafranca—Introduced into Florida in 1875 from Sicily by General Sanford, this cultivar has been grown continuously since that time. It is very similar to Eureka, distinguished by greater vigor and thorniness while trees are young, but almost impossible to differentiate by fruit characters or mature tree habit.

Ponderosa—Not a commercial cultivar, this has been a favorite for home planting since around 1900. It originated around 1886 as a seedling of unknown source grown by George Bowman of Hagerstown, Maryland, and was first propagated as a greenhouse plant under the name "American Wonder" lemon. The fruits resemble ordinary lemons except for being much larger and are grown more for the curiosity of their size than for the juice they produce; the juice is abundant and of good acidity, although seeds are numerous. The tree is small and fairly thorny. This is probably not a true lemon, but if it is a hybrid, the experts do not agree on its probable parents. It is more tender to cold than true lemons, although not more so than limes.

Meyer (Citrus meyeri Tanaka)—Definitely not a true lemon and not even looking very much like a lemon, this cultivar is commonly called a lemon because the juice tastes much like lemon juice. It was introduced in 1908 by Frank N. Meyer for the U.S. Department of Agriculture from China, where he found it cultivated near Peking as an ornamental pot plant. The mature fruit greatly resembles an orange in both external and internal appearance, although it may possess a low nipple at each end; it is very juicy, with smooth, thin rind and about ten seeds. Juice quality is good but acid content is lower than the true lemon, and the rind lacks the lemon aroma. Indeed, the different character of the peel oil is the biggest handicap to larger use of this lemon for concentrate. Even a small amount of Meyer peel oil gives an undesirable flavor to the juice, though this can be masked, if not too intense, by adding peel oil of true lemon. Some fruit matures at all seasons, but the main crop is from December to April. The tree is small and bushy, nearly thornless, and much more resistant to cold than any true lemon. It was planted on a rather large commercial scale in Texas and has been commercially planted on a small scale in Florida since 1930. Because this variety carries the tristeza virus, it should not be planted on sour orange stock or in areas where tristeza is active. It is prohibited by law in some areas of California. By reason of its cold hardiness it is popular throughout the orange belt of Florida as a lemon tree for the home grounds, since it bears heavily and needs a space only about eight or ten feet square. Undoubtedly the Meyer is a hybrid, but the other parent besides lemon is entirely unknown, although the color suggests orange or mandarin.

Rough—Used in Florida only as a stock, this lemon does not belong to the same species as the true lemon but is *Citrus jambhiri* Lush. Native to India, where it is the most important citrus stock, this lemon must have reached Florida early in the nineteenth century, but no record exists of its introduction. H. J. Webber thinks it was introduced to the West Indies in the seventeenth century, but there is no known mention of its existence there or in Florida until the last quarter of the nineteenth century. By that time, it had escaped from cultivation and become widely naturalized, being known as "Florida Rough" and as "French." In southern Africa it became wild along the banks of the Mazoe River in southern Rhodesia, and so is known as "Mazoe" lemon in the citrus industry of South Africa, where it is the principal stock. It is also the principal stock used in Florida, but while it was already so used in 1876, it was not until the extensive planting of the deep sandy soils of central Florida that this usage became dominant. With the appearance of blight in Florida, especially on trees budded to Rough lemon, this stock has been severely restricted in new plantings. Only a minuscule amount is currently being used by nurserymen. The tree is very thorny, and the fruit is much flattened, with very thick, bumpy rind. The juice is much like that of true lemon, though lower in acidity, and the mature fruit is lemon-colored.

Limes

The true lime, *Citrus aurantifolia* Swingle, is a small, thin-skinned, very acid fruit native to the Malaysia area. It does not occur in China at all, being too tender to cold, but it is found in many forms in eastern India and perhaps is truly wild in northern Malaya. This species is not mentioned in early citrus literature, whether because it was confused with the lemon or because it was less hardy to cold is uncertain. Not until the thirteenth century do we find the lime recorded in Italy, and until the seventeenth century it was no more than casually mentioned in northern Europe.

While Las Casas does not specifically include the lime among the seeds brought by Columbus to Haiti in 1493, he does not pretend to give an exhaustive list. Since Oviedo reported limes as plentiful there in 1520, it is quite probable that Columbus did bring lime seeds from the Canaries. The lime soon became naturalized on some of the West Indies, on the coast of Mexico, and ultimately on some of the Florida Keys. The first mention of it in Florida is by Williams in 1839, who noted that planting of limes was increasing. In 1838 Dr.

Henry Perrine planted a few lime trees from Yucatán on Indian Key and perhaps some adjacent islands, and naturalized lime trees found on many of the Keys at the turn of the century have often been considered as having resulted from his plantings. However, in 1876 his son was unable to find any trace of those plantings still in existence. Throughout the nineteenth century, the common lime, variously known as "Key," "Mexican," or "West Indian," was primarily a home fruit in Florida, although there was some small commercial culture by 1883 in Orange and Lake counties.

After the culture of pineapples was abandoned on the Keys in 1906 as the combined result of depletion of organic matter and the 1906 hurricane, there developed slowly a lime industry in its place. Plantings increased rapidly after 1913 on the Keys and on islands near Fort Myers, with production reaching a peak in 1923. The hurricane of 1926 gave this industry a reverse from which it never recovered.

Meanwhile the so-called Tahiti or Persian lime had entered the picture. This is not a true lime, being probably a hybrid of some sort, and is called *Citrus latifolia* by Tanaka. Undoubtedly it is a hybrid resulting under cultivation, for it is known only as a garden plant appearing in California about 1875. From 1850 to 1880 oranges and limes were imported in great numbers to San Francisco from Tahiti, and seeds of these fruits were sometimes planted. The parent tree of the Tahiti type of lime must have arisen from such a seed, representing a chance cross that occurred in Tahiti. The variety is triploid in chromosome number, a condition usually producing sterility. No one seems to have recorded anything about this tree, and our first record is the statement by Garey in 1882 that the Tahiti lime is worthless in California. The next year, Rooks noted that the Tahiti lime was growing in Florida and that he knew by report of the Persian lime. For many years, Tahiti and Persian appeared as distinct types, with one sometimes rated inferior to the other, but the two names have long been considered synonymous. No explanation has ever been offered for the origin of the name Persian for this type of lime, which is now known in Florida chiefly by this name and is called Bearss in California. Obviously, Tahiti should be the preferred name.

Reasoner in 1887 reported that the Tahiti lime was planted in grove form in "the lake country," but the lemon was considered a more promising commercial fruit of acid type and plantings of Tahiti lime increased only slowly. Along with the decline of Key lime plantings in the late 1920s, however, much interest developed in groves of Tahiti lime in the southern orange belt. Since 1930 Florida limes have been almost wholly of the Tahiti type, with Dade County far in the lead.

Key limes were so much smaller and seedier than lemons that there was never any confusion between them in the market. Tahiti limes are seedless, as Eureka lemons tend to be, and are of lemon size, so that confusion is easy. The lime grower has preferred to put his fruit on the market green as an easy means of separating it in the mind of the buyer from lemons. Like lemons, Tahiti limes are largely picked by size. Very few Tahiti limes are grown in California because of the cooler climate, and so this lime is almost wholly a Florida industry. The volume of Florida limes is far smaller, however, than the volume of California lemons. Tahiti limes, like common limes, mature at all seasons of the year, but the peak of production is during the summer months.

Most of the limes grown in the world are of the common, true lime type, and these are grown in far larger amounts in other countries than are Tahiti limes in Florida. Florida produces about 95 percent of the limes grown in this country. Florida limes are largely shipped to the fresh-fruit market, but since 1949 a considerable amount of the crop has been processed as frozen concentrated limeade, the volume thus used varying from one-fourth to over one-half of the crop.

Three other citrus fruits are called limes or resemble them greatly—the sweet lime, the calamondin, and the Rangpur lime. None of these is a true lime and none is of any commercial importance in the United States. The sweet lime, often called sweet lemon, is widely but not commercially grown around the shores of the Mediterranean and is used as a stock for oranges in Brazil and Israel. It has been tested as a stock in Florida but abandoned because of its great intolerance to xyloporosis, a viral disease. However, there is some lingering interest in the sweet lime as a rootstock with budwood free of damaging viruses. The Palestine sweet lime, *Citrus limettioides* Tanaka, is common in India. It is not the same as the Mediterranean sweet lime, *C. limetta* Tanaka, of Spain and Italy. This latter species was responsible for British sailing ships of the eighteenth century being known as "lime-juicers" and British sailors as "limeys." The lime juice carried to prevent scurvy was not the acid West Indian lime but the sweet lime with a higher content of ascorbic acid.

The calamondin, *Citrus madurensis* Lour., is a small seedy lime with thin, red rind and soft, juicy, red flesh. Native to the Philippines, it was named *Citrus mitis* by Blanco, but Loureiro had seen and named it earlier in Madura, an island near Java. It is sometimes given as *C. microcarpa* Bunge, but this is a different fruit, the musk lime. The calamondin was introduced to Florida as an "acid orange" in 1899 by Lathrop and Fairchild from Panama and was early called "Panama orange." It had come to Panama from Chile, and to Chile from China, where it has long been cultivated both as an ornamental and as a stock for mandarins.

Hardier to cold than any true citrus species, the calamondin is popular as an attractive home fruit to provide a lime substitute. The tree is dwarf and bushy and is quite showy for months when the mature fruit is hanging on it, being everbearing with the heaviest crop in winter. The acid content is high, the flavor is distinctive, and juice color is attractive. Seed propagation is used, inasmuch as no seedling variation has been observed. Various hypotheses have been put forward as to the possibility of the calamondin being a hybrid of lime and mandarin or lime and kumquat, but these are highly speculative. It is a species that has made its own way for centuries.

The Rangpur lime and its near relative the Kusaie lime are considered by Tanaka as lemon relatives and belong to *Citrus limonia* Osbeck. They are always called limes in the United States and are used like true limes and calamondins. They have thin rinds easily separated from the soft, juicy flesh, the rind and flesh both being red in Rangpur and yellow in Kusaie, and are often thought to represent hybrids of mandarin with lime or lemon. Rangpur was introduced to Florida as seed from India in 1887 by Reasoner Brothers. It matures fruit in the fall and winter. It has been sparingly grown as a yard tree for ornament and acid juice, but has been of more interest in recent years as a stock species for possible commercial use. Kusaie lime is not known to be cultivated in Florida, though it is popular in Hawaii.

Citrons

The citron, *Citrus medica,* has already been discussed as the citrus fruit first known to Europeans and has been grown in the warmest areas around the Mediterranean for at least two thousand years. Commercial culture today is mostly limited to Sicily, southern Italy, Corsica, Crete, and a few small Greek islands in the Cyclades. The pulp and juice are useless, but the thick rind is preserved in brine for use in making candied peel for fruitcakes and confections. There is a small inedible type of watermelon that is also called citron because its rind is used similarly.

It was among the citrus species brought to the New World by Columbus, but it has never had extensive culture here. It was probably introduced to Florida when St. Augustine was settled, but also probably did not survive winters there. There is no commercial production in Florida today, although a few specimen trees may be found in collections of citrus fruits. No variety is grown as such, although the common large-fruited form grown commercially in Italy is similar to what has long been seen in Florida. It is propagated readily by cuttings, or may be budded. A few seedlings may be seen of the small-fruited form with persistent styles called "Etrog," which is used in the Jewish ceremonies of the Feast of Tabernacles.

Citrus Hybrids

All species of *Citrus* will cross with one another, and even with species of the closely related genera *Fortunella* and *Poncirus*. Undoubtedly such crossing had a part in the development of some of our present species in the past, for that is a normal method of origin of new species, but nobody can say with certainty which species are primitive and which are derivative. There are several cultivated forms such as the Temple and Murcott, and Meyer and Tahiti —none of them known to exist outside of gardens—which are universally conceded to have arisen from crossing of established species, although there is not such uniform agreement on the exact species involved. Unless exactly the same form is produced by a known cross made by man, opinions as to the crosses that produced these forms remain speculative.

Many hybrids have been produced by man through controlled (guarded) crosses in which both parents are known with certainty. The first hybrids of this kind were produced by W. T. Swingle for the U.S. Department of Agriculture in 1897, and most of the numerous early citrus hybrids that have been knowingly produced were the work of Swingle and his associates in the succeeding fifteen years. No one can predict the fruit characters that will result from any given cross, and each seed in a single fruit produced by hand-pollination may develop into a seedling with fruit and tree characters different from the others. This is true, however, only if a true hybrid embryo matures. As stated previously, the only embryos that mature in a high percentage of citrus seeds are nucellar ones, which are derived wholly from the mother plant and reproduce it exactly.

In some crosses, the hybridizer may never be able to produce a hybrid or must make dozens of crosses and grow the seedlings to fruiting before a single hybrid is obtained. Thus it has only recently become possible to produce a hybrid using Dancy tangerine as seed parent. Removal of young developing embryos from immature seeds and culturing them on nutrient gels (a technique known as "embryo" rescue) has made heretofore impossible citrus hybridizations possible. In other crosses, a large percentage of seedlings will be hybrids. Another very new innovation in producing hybrids involves the combination of genetic material at the cellular level. This technique, known as protoplasmic fusion, can be used to make hybrids between two widely separated species that could not be made with conventional breeding methods. Once a hybrid has been obtained, however, it can be maintained permanently as a variety by budding.

Hybrids may show characters intermediate to those of their parents, some characters of each parent, new characters that are not exhibited by either parent, or characters once present in an ancestral form. Only hybrids that represent definite improvements over the parents in some quality should be propagated as varieties. Some such hybrids have been developed and others are possible. Qualities to be considered are flavor and taste, disease resistance, vigor, productivity, adaptation to climate, and ease of handling and shipping. Some hybrids have merit as stocks because of superior adaptation to soil conditions or climate, resistance to soil diseases or insects, and ability to enable the scion variety to produce fruit of high quality.

Citrus hybrids are classified as:

1. *Intervarietal*—crosses made between cultivars of the same species. These are not properly called hybrids and usually result in little or no more variation in seedling characters than self-pollination gives. They are of no importance in production of new varieties.

2. *Interspecific*—crosses made between species of the same genus. These are easily produced, except for the possible small number of hybrids that may be found in the resulting seedlings when they bear fruit; and most of the interesting and valuable citrus hybrids have arisen in this way, notably tangelos and tangors.

3. *Intergeneric*—crosses made between different genera, which must usually be very closely related and must always be within the same family. Intergeneric hybrids are more difficult to obtain than interspecific hybrids, and many attempts have resulted in failures.

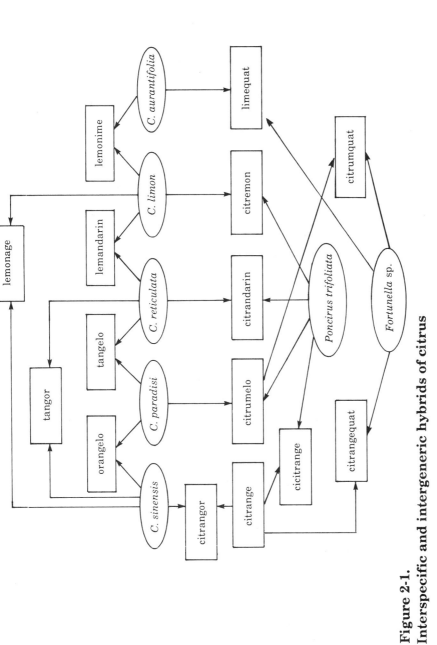

Figure 2-1.
Interspecific and intergeneric hybrids of citrus

When the crosses are successful, vigorous hybrids have resulted, some of which show promise as rootstocks. Citranges and citrumelos are good examples of intergeneric hybrids.

4. *Complex*—crosses made between interspecific or intergeneric hybrids and another species or genus. These are the result of two or more crosses. The difficulty of making such hybrids is even greater than for simple bigeneric hybrids, and only recently have any commercially promising forms arisen in this way.

Citrus hybrids are known by class names, such as tangelo or citrange, and such class names are sometimes tongue twisters. In practically all instances, they were coined by W. T. Swingle to identify the types of hybrids he had developed. The names consist of portions of the name of each parent, though sometimes these are difficult to recognize. Class name derivation can be followed in figure 2-1. Cultivars of hybrids, like cultivars within a species, are individual seedlings (or sports) propagated by vegetative means.

Classes and Varieties of Hybrids

Tangelos—These are interspecific hybrids resulting from crossing tangerines with grapefruit (*C. reticulata* × *C. paradisi*). When the name was coined in 1905, horticulturists were trying to establish "pomelo" as the accepted name for grapefruit so that *tang*(erine) and (pom)*elo* were combined into *tangelo* to indicate this cross. The first tangelos, Sampson and Thornton, were named and released in 1905 and were quickly planted on a small commercial scale. They did not prove very successful and are uncommon today. In 1931 Lake, Minneola, and Seminole tangelos were released and have proven more satisfactory. Minneola and Lake (Orlando) are still widely planted today. Certain marketing groups have worked diligently to maintain quality in shipments and to stimulate market demand. The Tangelo Act of 1955 placed these cultivars under maturity regulations for the first time and was a further aid to orderly marketing of fruit of good quality.

Orlando (Lake)—The result of Dancy tangerine pollen on Duncan grapefruit pistil, a cross made by W. T. Swingle in 1911, Orlando has little resemblance to either parent. It was to be accepted by the market as an orange under the name "Orlando orange," which replaced its original name, "Lake tangelo." Tangelos are a recognized entity today, and this cultivar is known commercially as Orlando tangelo. Size and shape are tangerine-like, but the color and texture are orange-like. Rind color is deep orange as is the pulp color, and the rind adheres firmly to the pulp. It is variably seedy (depending on pollination) and matures in November and December. It was planted on a large commercial scale, totaling some 20,000 acres in 1970, but in 1985 only 10,000 acres remained. Temple and/or Robinson trees are usually interplanted with Orlando for satisfactory crops since it requires cross-pollination for maximum fruit size and production.

Minneola—This cultivar resulted from the same cross as Lake, but shows much more evidence of its tangerine parentage, although it also does not have the loose-skin character of the mandarins. Minneola has a delicious flavor and aroma when fully mature, is strikingly handsome with dark reddish-orange rind and dark orange flesh, and is also very juicy. It has been handicapped somewhat by low productivity, but optimum care can help keep production commercially acceptable. It is also subject to attack by citrus scab, and the fruit shape does not lend itself to easy packing. (The fruit has a ridged "neck" at the stem, giving rise to another common name "Honeybell.") Seeds average less than ten, and the season is late, January to March. The fruit is grown primarily for the local retail and gift-box trades.

Seminole—The third cultivar from the cross producing Lake and Minneola, this one has been planted much more sparingly than Minneola, which it resembles greatly. It differs from Minneola chiefly in having a more easily peeled rind, less susceptibility to scab, a much larger number of seeds (twenty-two), and a later season of maturity (February to April). Flavor, aroma, and juiciness are good, though the taste is considered by most to be somewhat tart. It is not a commercially important fruit today.

Sampson—The result of using Dancy pollen on an unnamed grapefruit in 1897 by W. T. Swingle, this was the first tangelo developed. Like the tangelos described previously, it is very juicy, highly colored, and moderately seedy (about fifteen seeds), but it is quite tart and is best suited to making an -ade. There is also a trace of the bitterness characteristic of grapefruit but absent in the previously described tangelos. The combination of high acidity, very thin rind, and easy bruising, together with high susceptibility to scab, made Sampson unsatisfactory commercially. Its season of maturity is February to April.

Thornton—This cultivar resulted from the same type of cross as Sampson but was made two years later. It differs markedly from all the above tangelos in having a thick rind, easily separated from the flesh, which becomes quite loose when overmature, making puffy fruit. Rind and pulp are both light orange in color and seeds number about fifteen. The pulp is soft, juicy, and sweet, being insipidly so when overmature. The season of maturity is December to February. Thornton has never been planted on a commercial scale.

Nova—This cultivar, released by the U.S. Department of Agriculture in 1964, is a hybrid of Clementine tangerine × Orlando tangelo. It resembles Orlando in most respects and likewise requires a pollenizer for maximum productivity. Seed numbers in the fruit are a function of cross-pollination. The cultivar has been sparingly popular among growers of fruit for the fresh market but has never achieved the popularity of Orlando.

Lee—Like Nova, this cultivar is a hybrid of Clementine × Orlando. However, this cultivar was released by the U.S. Department of Agriculture in 1959. While the fruit most closely resembles a tangelo, it has been described (and sold) as both a tangelo, and at times, a tangerine. Lee matures in November-December, and is slow to develop good peel color, often leading to degreening problems. It has never achieved significant commercial importance.

K-Early—This cultivar was a product of some of the early breeding work of Swingle and Webber and not deemed worthy of introduction. This is a tangelo that most closely resembles the grapefruit and is plagued by fruit quality problems. However, the early maturity has intrigued some growers, who have planted it in spite of the quality problems in an attempt to get early fruit to market.

Tangors—These are interspecific hybrids between some type of tangerine and the sweet orange, the name being a combination of tang(erine) and or(ange). Of the tangors produced by known crossing, only the Murcott has attained any commercial importance, but the creation of these hybrids has made it practically certain that some hybrids that have occurred by chance under cultivation are natural tangors. Notable among these is the Temple, which is an important cultivar, usually sold as an orange. The Umatilla tangor is a known hybrid that has been planted to a small extent. Some authorities believe the King mandarin is a tangor, but if so it is a very ancient one that has persisted for many centuries on its own, whereas all of the above have arisen in recent times. In general the tangors have flesh texture and flavor more like oranges than mandarins, but have rinds separating fairly readily from the flesh, though less so than do mandarins. Sugar content of juice and juice content of tangors are often greater than is usual with oranges, but fruit cannot be held on the tree as long as can oranges.

Temple—By far the best known and most important tangor is marketed as "Temple orange." It originated in Jamaica sometime late in the nineteenth century, but first came to horticultural attention in a small way about 1896. A fruit buyer named Boyce, who usually obtained his supply for northern markets in the Oviedo area, went to Jamaica for oranges following the big freeze of 1894–95 because there were none in Florida. Here he ran across a seedling orange that pleased him greatly, and sent budwood to friends at Oviedo. Several trees were propagated and budwood was shared among other friends. The fruit caught the attention of W. C. Temple, formerly manager of the Florida Citrus Exchange; and Mr. Temple, in turn, called the attention of M. E. Gillett, his associate in the Exchange and one of the leading citrus nurserymen, to the unusual qualities of the new variety. After testing it out on several stocks, Mr. Gillett signed a contract in February 1916 for the exclusive propagation of this variety, not yet named. It was Mr. Temple's desire to have it called "Winter Park Hybrid," although editor Edgar Wright of the Florida Grower urged that it be named Temple. After propagating a large supply of nursery trees, Buckeye Nurseries, of which Mr. Gillett was president, first announced this cultivar publicly in May 1919 under the name Temple as a posthumous honoring of W. C. Temple.

The Temple was not the overwhelming success that had been anticipated, in part because of propagation in considerable measure on rough lemon stock, under inadequate mineral nutrition. The fruit proved somewhat hard to ship when given the same packinghouse treatment as oranges. The quality is exceptionally fine with proper fertilization, however, and well-grown fruit usually commands a good premium over oranges. The season of maturity is January to March, or sometimes April. Planting of Temple has been heavy since 1940, and in 1970 there were more than 20,000 acres of this variety. Freezes in the late 70s and early 1980s have reduced the current (1988) tree acreage to just under 10,000.

Temple fruit is highly colored and handsome, a deep orange or reddish orange with about twenty seeds. It is somewhat subject to citrus scab. Quality of flesh is slightly better on Cleopatra than on other commonly used stocks, but color is not so high. Good quality is obtained on all of the standard stocks with good fertilizer programs.

Murcott—This old cultivar has been planted extensively only since 1952. The parent tree was sent for trial from the U.S. Department of Agriculture nursery at Little River (Miami), Florida, to R. D. Hoyt of Safety Harbor about 1913. Undoubtedly it was a tangor from the breeding work being carried out by Swingle and his associates at that time, but the identification label was lost. A neighbor, Charles Murcott Smith, obtained a bud of this tree from Mr. Hoyt and propagated a few trees about 1922. Small-scale commercial propagation was undertaken in 1928 by the Indian Rocks Nursery under the name "Honey Murcott," and several other nurseries on the West Coast propagated the variety in a limited way prior to 1950. In 1944 J. Ward Smith (no relation to C. M.) became interested in commercial production and made near Brooksville the first planting for commercial shipment. He used the name "Smith Tangerine," apparently unaware that the name "Murcott" had previously been approved by C. M. Smith. The cultivar is also known as the "Honey Tangerine" in the fresh-fruit trade.

The fruit is yellow-orange, smooth and glossy with an oblate shape. The pulp and juice is quite orange and richly flavored. Seeds number 18 to 24 and the season of maturity is January to March.

Murcott is somewhat subject to scab and also to xyloporosis. The tree is bushy, with willowy branches, and fruit is sometimes wind-scarred because it is borne mostly near the ends of the branches. This position also makes fruit more subject to frost injury and sunburn. Like Temple, the Murcott runs higher in soluble solids than sweet oranges of comparable maturity. The trees tend to bear heavily in alternate years, which may result in nutritional stresses to the tree that can be debilitating. Careful attention to pruning, irrigation, and nutrition are essential to successful cultivation.

Umatilla—This cultivar came from pollination of Ruby orange by Owari satsuma in 1911 by W. T. Swingle, but was not offered for propagation until 1931. The fruit is the size and shape of a King mandarin and matures about the same time, although the rind is redder orange than King and quite smooth. Quality is excellent but the variety has never been planted on a commercial scale. It is a fine late variety for home use and gift-box shippers. Because of its general similarity to the tangelos, it is sometimes known, incorrectly, as Umatilla tangelo.

Orangelos—This is a group of varieties that have the general appearance of the grapefruit without its bitterness and aroma and are considered to be natural interspecific hybrids of *Citrus paradisi* × *C. sinensis*. The Triumph, discussed under grapefruit as the first named cultivar, along with the Imperial and Royal should probably be so classified.

Limequats—These are intergeneric hybrids, produced by pollinating Key limes (*Citrus aurantifolia*) by kumquats (*Fortunella* spp.). Two of these hybrids, from crosses made by Swingle in 1909, have been sparingly grown in Florida. It was hoped that they would extend lime culture farther north by adding some of the cold hardiness of the kumquat to the usual fruit qualities of the lime. This hope has been realized to some degree, but the hybrids are about like Temples in hardiness and not quite equal to sweet oranges. They are very resistant to the withertip disease, which has seriously limited growing of common limes on the mainland, and they are quite prolific producers of a fruit that closely resembles limes. Yet they have never become very popular and are planted solely as home fruits.

Eustis—The result of Key lime pollinated by Marumi kumquat, the fruit is nearly oval, about 1¾ by 1¼ inches, light yellow at maturity, with around eight seeds. The main crop is borne in late fall and winter, but there is some at most any season. The distinctive feature from the lime parent, besides greater hardiness to cold and disease, is the sweetness of the rind instead of the bitter flavor of lime rind. Trees have abundant small thorns.

Lakeland—This cultivar was developed from another seed of the same fruit as Eustis. It has much larger fruit than Eustis, 2¼ by 1¾ inches, and is a slightly deeper yellow color, but similar in shape and acidity. Seeds are fewer (about five) and larger, and the twigs are nearly thornless.

Citranges—Webber and Swingle described the first crosses between *Poncirus trifoliata* and *Citrus sinensis,* naming them "citranges," in 1904. Their desire was to impart the cold hardiness of the trifoliate orange to a hybrid with the delectable qualities of the sweet orange. The fruits fail to come up to the standard of quality of the sweet orange, although they retain some of the cold hardiness of the trifoliate parent. The Rusk and Troyer citranges have been given consideration as rootstocks, along with other named types. In Florida, the Carrizo citrange has been used as a rootstock to overcome the difficulties besetting some of the more common rootstocks that have had long usage in the state. Some evidence indicates that the Troyer and the Carrizo are of a single clone that resulted from the same cross (Washington navel orange × trifoliate orange), made under the direction of Dr. W. T. Swingle in 1909.

Citrumelos—These intergeneric hybrids resulted from crosses between *Poncirus trifoliata* and *Citrus paradisi.* They are very similar to citranges and, like them, hold the principal interest as possible rootstocks for other types of citrus. The Swingle citrumelo is enjoying considerable popularity as a rootstock although it is quite susceptible to a strain of citrus bacterial canker known as "nursery canker" (not to be confused with the serious Asian strain of canker).

Citrangequats and **Citrangedins**—These are examples of the numerous classes of complex hybrids created by Swingle and his associates, none of which has any commercial importance. Citrangequats represent crosses of the kumquat (*Fortunella* spp.) with the hybrid citrange and are trigeneric crosses. Citrangedins result from crossing citrange with calamondin (*Citrus* madurensis) and so are bigeneric only, although complex. The "Thomasville" citrangequat and the Glen citrangedin have both been described and propagated in a very limited way for use as lime substitutes in areas like Georgia that are too cold even for the calamondin. Several other citrus hybrids have achieved varying degrees of commercial success.

Other Citrus Hybrids

The U.S. Department of Agriculture breeding programs has developed many hybrids; and the Orlando, Minneola, Nova, Lee, and several others have been discussed earlier in this chapter. All but Nova and Lee were simple crosses of one species by another. Nova and Lee are distinctive because they had a hybrid as one parent (Clementine × Orlando tangelo). Descriptions of other citrus hybrids that follow are presented here since they are similar complex hybrids with one or more of the parents hybrids themselves. These cultivars are in effect second-generation hybrids.

Robinson—Known commercially as a tangerine, this citrus hybrid is a Clementine × Orlando cross that was released in 1959. Harvested October–December, this cultivar is one of the earliest and has achieved some importance because of this character. Maximum production occurs with good cross-pollination and Orlando, Temple, and Lee work very well. Seed number varies with pollination received. The tree is brittle and may break with heavy crop loads and is susceptible to limb and twig dieback problems. It is a cultivar that has considerable cold hardiness.

Osceola—Another Clementine × Orlando citrus hybrid that was released in 1959, this cultivar most closely resembles a tangelo. It has a highly colored fruit with fifteen to twenty-five seeds and matures in October–November. It is scab susceptible and has a rather tart flavor. It has never achieved significant commercial production levels.

Page—This Minneola × Clementine citrus hybrid most closely resembles an orange. The cultivar was released by the U.S. Department of Agriculture in 1963. Seed number varies with pollination, and fruit quality is considered to be among the best of all citrus cultivars. However, the Page is plagued with a problem of commercially unacceptable small fruit sizes; and, as a consequence, has not been well received by commercial producers. The fruit does have potential for dooryard fruit producers.

Sunburst—Commercially marketed as a tangerine, this cultivar is a Robinson × Osceola hybrid; it most closely resembles the latter. Sunburst was released in early 1979 and has become fairly popular in the early 1980s. The cultivar will produce larger crops when cross-pollinated, but extensive field data on production is not available at this time since this is such a new release. Interestingly, Sunburst appears to be resistant to citrus snow scale but highly susceptible to citrus rust mite. The main period of fruit maturity is November–December.

Fallglo—This 1987 release was made by crossing Bower citrus hybrid × Temple, and it most closely resembles the latter but matures two months earlier. Field production and commercial acceptance are untested at this time.

Ambersweet—This new orange hybrid was released in early 1989. It is a complex hybrid of Clementine × Orlando tangelo, which was crossed with a seedling midseason sweet orange. It is an early variety, maturing most years in late October. It shows promising cold hardiness, good fruit size (3–3½-inch diameter), and good juice color. It is few-seeded but may have up to fifteen seeds per fruit in mixed plantings. Very few field data are available, and commercial acceptance is unknown at this time.

3 /
Propagation of Citrus Trees

The first citrus trees grown in Florida were seedlings since seeds were far easier to transport on long sailing voyages than budded trees. For two and a half centuries thereafter, it seems unlikely that any method of propagation other than by seed was practiced here. Budding was apparently standard practice in Europe during the sixteenth and seventeenth centuries, but during the eighteenth century there came a realization that seedling orange trees were larger and more productive, whereupon budding went out of fashion in Spain and Italy. This was undoubtedly largely responsible for the delay in using budding to propagate citrus trees in Florida.

Historical Background

The first budding of which we have record was used in developing the Dummitt grove on the upper end of Merritt Island in 1830. Zephaniah Kingsley had imported budded orange trees from Spain in 1824 for a planting later known as the Mays grove at Orange Mills, a few miles north of Palatka. Buds from this grove were taken, according to E. H. Hart in 1877, for budding the wild sour orange trees of the Dummitt grove. Thereafter we read of occasional groves being budded, but far more were planted by seed. The phenomenon of nucellar embryony* in citrus seeds was another potent factor for delaying recognition of the superiority of budded trees. Seedling apple trees bear fruit almost always

---

* The term *nucellar embryony* refers to the production of extra embryos within a seed. Most seeds contain a single embryo (one grain of corn, for example, is a single embryo), but some plants and most citrus plants produce seeds with multiple embryos. A sexual embryo is usually formed following pollination and sexual fertilization, but within the developing seed, extra vegetative embryos may arise from nucellar tissue found within the seed. Thus a single seed may give rise to several plants, most from nucellar embryos and occasional ones from sexual embryos. Plants produced from nucellar embryos are exactly like the parent plant since they have been formed vegetatively and not by sexual fertilization.

much inferior to the parent tree, but a high percentage of orange seedlings come from nucellar embryos, which reproduce the parent exactly. There are always some variant trees in a seedling grove, however, and all trees are usually more thorny when grown from seed and require much longer to come into commercial production.

In the 1870s there began to be really large-scale development of orange groves around Orange Lake and Lake Weir by budding wild sour orange trees, and for this purpose budwood was carefully selected from a very few trees. Citrus growers began to be interested in clonal* varieties derived from one parent rather than in seedling types, and budded nursery trees of various named varieties were imported from Europe. Mostly these came from the Rivers Nursery in England, but some were brought by Gen. H. S. Sanford from the Mediterranean area. In 1877 the short list of such varieties with descriptions was drawn up by a committee for the Florida Fruit Growers Association. Thereafter the varietal list grew apace, and more and more groves tended to be budded trees rather than seedlings, although many growers continued to argue the merits of the seedling grove. Around 1880 several treatises on orange culture appeared in both Florida and California, all stressing the superiority of budded trees, and thereafter few seedling groves were planted.

Any method of propagation other than by seed will assure the advantages of early bearing, few or no thorns, and uniform fruit season and quality that distinguish the budded tree from the seedling. While stem cuttings or layers may also be used, only budding or grafting can give the additional advantage of having a root system that is better adapted to soil conditions than the scion roots are, or that can confer greater hardiness to cold on the aerial part of the tree. Grafting was long ago found much

---

* *Clone*, or *clonal variety*, is a term introduced by the late H. J. Webber to denote plants derived by asexual (vegetative) propagation from a single original plant. Thus, all trees of the clone Pineapple sweet orange may properly be considered as branches of the original Pineapple tree. In recent years, the term *cultivar* (abbreviated "cv."), for "cultivated variety," has been promoted in horticultural literature internationally to distinguish horticultural from botanical varieties. All clones are cultivars, but by no means are all cultivars clones. It is quite correct to write "sweet orange cv. Pineapple" or "variety Pineapple"; it is also correct to write "sweet orange 'Pineapple,'" the single quotes indicating that the name is that of a variety (cultivar).

less satisfactory than budding for propagating citrus trees, except for topworking old trees in some situations; and budding is universally employed for all kinds of citrus fruit except citrons and some limes, which are often grown from cuttings. Over 95 percent of all Florida citrus trees are budded, the great majority of seedling trees being quite old remnants of early plantings.

Stocks

Stocks for budding citrus varieties are practically always grown from seed today. In the case of a variety that produces few seeds, such as the Rusk citrange, cuttings may serve in place of seedlings. Thanks to the high percentage of seedlings of any of the common stocks that develop from nucellar embryos, there is a high degree of uniformity in a bed of seedling stocks. The few seedlings that show variation (usually less vigorous) can be rogued out easily. Several different species or hybrids have been used as stocks, each having some merit under certain conditions. Commercially only a small number have proven desirable. A satisfactory stock must be congenial with the top budded on it; that is, the two must form a union that permits good growth, long life, good yields, and good fruit qualities of the scion variety. Any dwarfing effect may be an indication of a certain degree of uncongeniality, or of the presence of a systemic disease, although yield may be good for the tree size and fruit quality excellent.

Besides compatibility with the scion, the stock must possess certain abilities to adapt itself to the various factors of its environment if it is to be successful. Among these are: (1) *Nursery adaptability*—ease of handling from the nurseryman's standpoint. This includes ready availability of seed, high percentage of nucellar embryos, vigorous seedling growth, relative freedom from pest attacks, and easy budding. (2) *Soil adaptability*—the relative vigor of growth on soils of varied depth, texture, structure, pH, salinity, moisture, and nutrient supply. (3) *Climatic adaptability*—the degree of hardiness to cold conferred by the stock. (4) *Biotic adaptability*—(a) the degree of freedom from or resistance to various soil pests and diseases or (b) the effect of the stock in its relation to the scion on the resistance of the system to various disease complexes.

Some stocks are superior in one or more of these qualities but inferior in others, and none is outstandingly superior on all counts. The same stock may be superior for one scion variety under given environmental conditions and inferior for another variety, although usually all varieties of a species will give similar responses on the same stock in the same environment. The choice of a stock, therefore, must be made for a particular scion-stock combination in a particular environmental condition. All of the stocks commonly used in Florida have satisfactory nursery adaptability. The six stocks discussed below have been used by the Florida industry over long periods of time. Researchers and commercial growers have been able to determine, with a good deal of assurance, the responses that may be obtained from these stocks with various scion varieties and under different environmental conditions. Three of them, rough lemon, sour orange, and Cleopatra mandarin, formerly accounted for 90 percent of the plantings in the state. Several other stocks are becoming increasingly popular over time, and the old standbys are falling into disfavor. These new stocks will be discussed in a section following the information on the six historically significant stocks.

Rough lemon (*Citrus jambhiri*)—This stock is especially suited to deep, well-drained, sandy soils. On these soils it has produced large trees in relatively short times. Its use has been restricted generally to areas south of a line running from Leesburg to Sanford by its tenderness to cold and to properly drained soils by its susceptibility to foot rot. It is tolerant of the tristeza and exocortis viruses. It forms a normal union with all scion varieties, develops a deep root system, and produces high yields of fruit. Longevity of trees on this stock is limited in many areas by blight. Fruit quality is a little lower on this stock than on other common ones. Often the higher yield more than compensates for this effect, but not when the scion is a fresh-fruit type where the low quality may affect maturity.

Prior to 1865, apparently only sour orange and sweet orange were used in Florida as stocks. Soon thereafter the "native" rough lemon attracted attention as a stock giving faster growth and earlier bearing for oranges and lemons. As the high pineland soils were planted more extensively in the southward development of the citrus industry, rough lemon more and more replaced older stocks for use on these soils.

Rough lemon was the rootstock used on about 70 percent of the citrus acreage of Florida in groves planted from the 1920s to the 1960s. However, in 1964, at Wauchula (Hardee County), a six-year-old grove of Pineapple orange on this stock began to show symptoms of a decline that was subsequently called "young tree decline." During the intervening years, this decline (discussed more fully in chapter 7) weakened many young trees in the flatwoods; and then a similar type of decline, called "sand hill decline," was noted in the well-drained areas in the southern portion of the citrus belt. Because this decline appears most prevalent on rough lemon budded with sweet oranges, it has also been called "lemon root decline." Although further observations indicated that other stocks were also affected, growers have been reluctant to continue the use of this stock after losses of more than 80 percent in some groves on rough lemon. This decline has been a serious blow to the citrus industry, and no solution is available at present. These declines are now known to be so similar that they share a common name, "blight," and the malady will be referred to hereinafter by that name. The gravity of this problem is evidenced by the fact that citrus nurseries have reduced propagations on rough lemon stock from 60 percent of total nursery inventories in 1960 to less than 10 percent in 1973 and less than 1 percent in the late 1980s.

Sour orange (*Citrus aurantium*)—This species is the preferred stock for the low hammock and flatwood soils with fine texture and high water table, where its resistance to foot rot gives it a real advantage. It is sufficiently hardy for use in all sections of the state where oranges are grown commercially. Trees on sour orange are of standard size, in spite of a slight tendency for the scion to overgrow the stock, and produce good crops of excellent quality. The sour orange is, unfortunately, very much affected by the presence of the viral disease tristeza, with almost all scions except lemons. The citrus industry of Brazil, with nearly all trees on sour orange, was literally wiped out in the 1940s by a severe form of this virus. The disease is present in Florida in forms of varying virulence. Tristeza has been quite troublesome in some areas and is now widespread in the state. It is spread by budding and also by aphid vectors and represents a serious threat to trees on sour orange stocks. The stock remains fairly popular with growers because of its good horticultural characteristics. However, the specter of the virus must not be overlooked, and the use of sour orange should be discouraged.

Cleopatra mandarin (*Citrus reshni*)—This species came into use in Florida rather late, having been first used by Reasoner about 1920 as a stock for Temple oranges on highly sandy soil. It attained a small success as a producer of good quality in Temples and tangelos on sandy soils and as a substitute for sour orange with kumquats on low ground, but it remained a very minor stock until the discovery of tristeza in Florida in 1952. In the search for a stock to replace sour orange for general use, Cleopatra was perceived to be a possible substitute, and is still fairly popular among Florida stocks. It is nearly as cold hardy as sour orange and is fairly tolerant to foot rot.

It is also tolerant of tristeza, xyloporosis, and exocortis. It makes good unions with all kinds of citrus scions and produces on them fruit of high quality. It is slower growing in the nursery than other common stocks, trees on it come into bearing a little more slowly, and fruit size is usually reduced; but, by the time the trees are ten years old, they have made up the difference in both size and yield, even on deep sandy soils, except possibly with Valencias. (Valencia on Cleopatra has a bad reputation that may be undeserved. Some of the newer Valencia selections do quite well on Cleopatra, but some old lines did very poorly indeed.) In many ways, Cleopatra seems to combine several of the good features of both rough lemon and sour orange and may represent a good compromise for some growers, especially those growing tangerines or hybrids.

Sweet orange (*Citrus sinensis*)—This stock was extensively used in the first big expansion of the citrus industry after budding became standard in the early 1880s, but it gave rise to much trouble from foot rot. This was particularly a problem on the low, fine-textured soils but was encountered even on high pineland. By 1890 sweet orange was no longer in favor as a stock, and when the second big expansion took place on the sand hills of southern central Florida after the big freeze in 1894–95, hardly any stock but rough lemon was used. When not attacked by foot rot, sweet orange stock produces orange, grapefruit, and tangerine trees larger than on sour orange, though not so large as on rough lemon, and with fruit quality almost as good as on sour orange. Union of stock and scion is good with all kinds of citrus, but scions are delayed a little in coming into bearing as compared to rough lemon. The stock is resistant to common scab and tristeza and tolerant of xyloporosis and exocortis; it lies between Cleopatra and rough lemon in cold hardiness.

In the early 1920s, when there was a big postwar expansion of plantings on deep sands, several citrus leaders urged the substitution of sweet orange for rough lemon stocks on these soils because many old groves on sweet stock were producing good yields of fine fruit. Their arguments made few converts, however. Sweet orange has never been widely accepted nor is it being propagated in nurseries to any extent today. In theory, the seeds of any sweet orange variety may be used with equal satisfaction, but in practice only the seedy varieties produce enough seed to be useful.

Trees on sweet orange stock appear to be much less likely to be affected by blight than those on rough lemon stock. This stock should be considered in spite of the threat of foot rot. Many groves exist with only minor foot rot problems; furthermore, there is a feeling that after the first few years of the grove's life the problem is lessened to the extent that commercial results can be obtained, especially when good sanitation methods are used. There are also chemicals available today that offer excellent control of the disease. Indeed, a fresh look at sweet orange stock is probably in order.

Trifoliate orange (*Poncirus trifoliata*)—Trifoliate orange is by far the most cold hardy of the citrus stocks in northern Florida, where the stock becomes dormant early and holds the scion dormant better than other stocks. Trifoliate orange does not confer exceptional cold hardiness in central and southern Florida. Here the warm weather in early winter may delay the dormancy of the stock, and the scion may be even more hurt by cold than on other stocks. It is usually reported as unsuited to deep sands and does poorly on calcareous soil, but it is well adapted to low, fine-textured soils. It is resistant to tristeza and xyloporosis viruses and quite resistant to foot rot, but it is attacked by scab and is the most susceptible of all stocks to exocortis viroid. It is highly resistant to the citrus nematode although susceptible to the burrowing nematode. Blight is a problem in many groves on this stock. So far as is known, trifoliate orange stock always overgrows the scion markedly, but while some kinds of citrus are dwarfed on it, other kinds make standard trees in spite of what seem to be poor bud unions. Infection with exocortis almost always induces dwarfing. Growth is slow in the nursery, but trees on trifoliate orange stock start to bear early and produce fruit of excellent quality. Yields are good for the tree size attained. In the past, it has been used little in Florida except for satsumas and kumquats; now it is used for other types of citrus in restricted numbers. In California and Australia, it has been valuable on certain fine-textured soils for oranges. Because exocortis can easily be avoided by careful budwood selection, the resistance to tristeza and the high quality of fruit make it of interest as another possible replacement for sour orange on low soils.

Grapefruit (*Citrus paradisi*)—Rarely or never used today as a stock, grapefruit was considered promising at one time because trees budded on it grew vigorously on low, fine-textured soils and seedling grapefruit trees bore large crops. Interest declined rapidly because yields on this stock too often were disappointingly low. Few orange and grapefruit groves on this stock are still in production, and the stock has only historic interest today. "Yellow spot," a symptom of molybdenum deficiency, is sometimes found in groves on grapefruit stock on acid soil, although spraying with sodium molybdate can be used to correct this symptom.

Other Stocks

Many other types of citrus are being tried as stocks in the hopes of avoiding virus, mycoplasma, and nematode problems and of finding a solution for blight. In the 1950s, through extensive field search, three trees were found that showed resistance or tolerance to burrowing nematodes. These were named: Milam, a resistant citrus hybrid of unknown parentage; Estes, a tolerant rough lemon type; and Ridge Pineapple, sweet orange, which showed resistance. Milam, the only one of the three that has been used with any frequency, has a small and steady interest from growers (see further discussion in chapter 7).

Rusk, Morton, and Troyer citranges have been used very sparingly, while today Carrizo citrange is a favorite of many nurserymen and growers in Florida, accounting for a substantial portion of nursery trees at the present time. Budwood used on the citranges, as with their trifoliate parent, must be free of the exocortis viroid. Swingle citrumelo is becoming increasingly popular, although its susceptibility to a nursery strain of citrus canker has created some problems. Rangpur lime is gaining more attention as exocortis-free budwood becomes available. Palestine sweet lime (sometimes called sweet lemon) is deserving of attention for its yield potentials on sandy soils with xyloporosis- and exocortis-free budwood. *Citrus volkameriana* is a stock that also has generated some interest. *Citrus macrophylla* is susceptible to tristeza and xyloporosis viruses, but this has not been a deterrent to its widespread use in California and Florida as a rootstock for lemons, even though most of the commercial lemon budwood in Florida carries xyloporosis. Unfortunately, wide testing in commercial groves will be needed before complete recommendations can be made concerning these rootstocks. Carrizo citrange is one stock that has emerged as one of the better ones and has found widespread acceptance. Swingle has become quite popular as well. In fact, the widespread use of both Carrizo and Swingle today will necessitate a complete rewriting of this section in future editions of this publication. Other stocks will no doubt emerge in time. In summary, it should be remembered that while the stock does not bear a single fruit, its selection is just as important to the grower as is the selection of the scion variety. No better evidence can be given of the worth of a given combination of stock and scion than the appearance and productivity of a grove of this constitution that has survived the nursery and early growth periods and is in its prime fruiting condition at fifteen to twenty-five years of age.

A rootstock quick-reference chart is provided in table 3-1. It summarizes in a general way, across all scion cultivars, the relative ranking of various rootstocks for the listed characteristics. The chart is helpful as a guide for learning or reviewing basic rootstock responses but should not be relied upon for rootstock selection without consulting more detailed information.

Budding Procedures

Two important phases of successful budding are choice of a suitable stock and selection of satisfactory budwood. Since the factors influencing stock have been discussed above, this section will deal only with budwood. Under the Citrus Budwood Registration Program of the Division of Plant Industry, it is now possible to obtain budwood (and stock seed) that is certified free from most of the viral diseases and true to type for the variety. In this program, the Division has had the cordial cooperation of state and federal research workers, as well as the backing of progressive citrus growers; and this cooperative effort has brought a new era to the Florida citrus industry. No person now entering the nursery business on either a home or commercial basis needs to face the uncertainties that were unavoidable to nurserymen of the past or earlier generations. One only need take advantage of available help.

In selection of budwood, there are two important steps: the selection of the tree from which scions are to be taken and the selection of bud sticks on that tree.

The following points should be considered in selecting the parent tree:

(1) It should be true to the variety, or strain of the variety, in fruit characters, and should be free from any indication of chimeric development, indicated by the appearance in the same tree of two types of foliage, fruit, or growth resulting from a mutation that produces, in the same tree, two or more genetic constitutions.

(2) It should have a record of satisfactory production over a period of at least five years, to even out any difference from year to year due to alternate bearing.

(3) It should be free from systemic (viral) diseases such as psorosis, xyloporosis, tristeza, and exocortis. Absence of visible symp-

Table 3-1.
Rootstock quick-reference chart

Rootstock (Characteristic)	Phytophthora tolerance	Flood tolerance	Drought tolerance	Cold tolerance	Blight tolerance	Tristeza tolerance	Exocortis tolerance	Xyloporosis tolerance	Burrowing nematode tolerance	Citrus nematode tolerance	Yield/tree	Brix	Fruit size	Tree vigor	High calcium tolerance	Salt tolerance
Rough lemon	S	G	G	P	P	T	T	T	S	S	H	L	LG	H	H	I
Volkamer lemon	S	G	G	P	P	T	T	T	S	S	H	L	LG	H	H	?
Citrus macrophylla	R	G	G	P	P	S	T	S	S	S	H	L	LG	H	H	G
Palestine sweet lime	S	G	G	P	P	T	S	S	S	S	H	L	LG	H	I	P
Rangpur	S	?	G	P	P	T	S	S	S	S	H	L	LG	H	H	G
Milam lemon	S	G	G	P	P	T	T	T	R	S	H	L	LG	H	?	?
Sour orange	T	I	I	G	G	S	T	T	S	S	I	H	I	I	H	I
Cleopatra mandarin	T	P	I	G	G	T	T	T	S	S	L-I	H	SM	H	I	G
Sweet orange	S	P	P	I	G	T	T	T	S	S	I	I	I	I	L	I
Ridge pineapple	S	P	P	I	G	T	T	T	R	S	I	I	I	I	L	I
Carrizo citrange	T	P	G	I	P	T	S	T	T	T	H	I	I	H	L	P
Swingle citrumelo	R	G	I	G	I?	T	T?	T	S	R	I	H	I	I	I?	I
Trifoliate orange	R	I	P	G	P	R	S	T	S	R	L-I	H	SM	L	L	P
Rusk citrange	T	?	P	G	?	T	T?	T	S	T	L-I	H	I	I	L	P
Grapefruit	S	?	P	I	?	T	T	T	S	S	H	L	SM	H	L	I

Key to symbols:

G = good	LG = large	SM = small
H = high	P = poor	T = tolerant
I = intermediate	R = resistant	? = inadequate information
L = low	S = susceptible	or rating unknown

SOURCE: W.S. Castle, D.P.H. Tucker, A.H. Krezdorn, and C.O. Youtsey. 1989. *Rootstocks for Florida Citrus.* University of Florida IFAS Publication no. SP-42.

Fig. 3-1a. Preparing inverted T on rootstock.

toms is not sufficient evidence of freedom, for many scion varieties may carry infection without showing any evidence of it on one stock and give abundant evidence when worked on another stock. This is where the above-mentioned Registration Program plays such an important role. (There are limitations such as in the case of tristeza. The disease is so widespread that indexing for the virus is no longer done. Therefore tristeza-free budwood cannot be ensured.) It should also be free of propagatable malformations such as witches' broom.

(4) It should have attained maturity, be in apparently good health and vigor, and have reached a normal size for its age, stock, and soil type.

In selecting budwood from the chosen tree, the following points should be taken into account:

(1) The bud stick should be all of one growth flush, usually the second one back from the tip of the twig, and should have five to nine good plump buds, not yet starting into growth.

(2) The bud stick should consist of strong, well-matured wood, which is free from scale. Well-rounded twigs are much easier for the novice to cut buds from than angular wood, although the experienced budder will have equally satisfactory results with either.

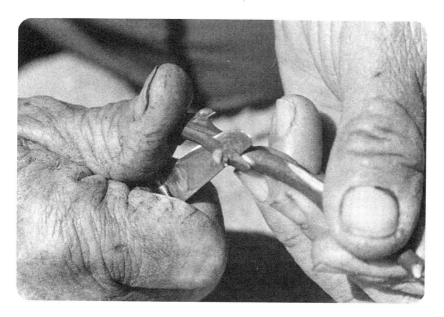

Fig. 3-1b. Removal of bud from budstick.

Leaves should be cut off at once to conserve moisture in the bud stick.

(3) Budwood should preferably be cut just prior to use and protected from drying out by keeping the sticks in damp sphagnum or peat moss. However, for budding in early spring, when buds may start into growth on the twigs as soon as the bark will slip, it is advisable to assure a supply of unsprouted buds by cutting budwood before any buds begin growth. The bud sticks should be put at once into polyethylene bags, such as those used for freezing vegetables, and stored in a household refrigerator at between 40° and 45°F. In commercial practice, quantities of budwood may simply be stored in a cool place in damp peat moss or sawdust wrapped in burlap.

(4) Bud sticks should be labeled at once after cutting them, if more than one variety is used, for it is impossible to identify the variety after it is cut from the tree.

Techniques used to produce citrus trees are very similar for all nurseries, but there are now two main types of nurseries and some intermediate ones. The two nursery types are those that produce container-grown plants (usually in a controlled environment) and those producing field-grown trees that may either be sold as bare-

Fig. 3-1c. Inserting bud into inverted T.

root plants or dug, potted up, and sold in containers at a later date. The intermediate nursery types usually grow seedlings in a greenhouse and produce the budded plants under field conditions but many combinations exist.

Containerized trees produced under controlled conditions are usually ready for sale in about one year from seed but are usually smaller than bare-root trees sold for planting in the field. There is a divergence of opinion as to which tree is best, and both types have demonstrated good success in the field. The key to good performance for any tree is careful attention to planting and aftercare, and bad results are more often than not the result of grower carelessness.

The text that follows describes in some detail the procedures for a field nursery with comments added for a similar greenhouse operation.

The development of a budded nursery tree, ready for planting in a grove or in the home grounds, may be conveniently considered in five phases:

(1) *The seedbed.* This should be established on well-drained soil free from disease organisms, and should be located conveniently for watering and other maintenance. The site must also be approved by

Fig. 3-1d. Bud ready for wrapping.

the Division of Plant Industry. After clearing, plowing, and harrowing, the seedbed should be made smooth and level. Fumigation with appropriate chemicals is desirable to kill weeds, diseases, insects, and nematodes before seeds are planted. For large numbers of seedlings, where mechanical cultivation is important, seeds should be planted in rows from one to three feet apart (depending on the cultivating instrument), spacing the seeds about an inch apart in the row and planting them an inch deep. When rather small numbers are involved, seeds may be sown fairly thickly in a solid block. No shading of the seedbed is needed in Florida. Trifoliate seed, which is hardy to cold, is usually planted in the fall, but seed of all other citrus is usually planted in spring as soon as danger of frost is past. The soil should be kept moist, but not wet, until the seedlings appear, which should be in about a month; thereafter, water should be supplied as needed to prevent wilting. Maintaining too moist conditions in the seedbed may encourage fungal diseases.

Citrus seeds are unlike seeds of deciduous fruits in that once they have become thoroughly dry they are no longer able to germinate. It is necessary to use seeds that have not been out of the fruits for more than two or three weeks, unless special storage

Fig. 3-1e. Wrapping with budding tape.

precautions have been observed, and seeds planted within a few days of extraction will be best. Freshly extracted seeds may be stored for a few weeks by washing them, drying them in thin layers in the shade for a day or two, and then mixing them with clean sand in boxes kept in a cool place; or the surface-dry seeds may be stored in a plastic bag in the household refrigerator at around 40°F. A hot water treatment or a fungicidal dip is recommended to keep fungal diseases at a minimum.

The developing seedlings should be kept free of all competition from weeds, and should receive frequent (bimonthly), light applications of a good garden fertilizer with a 1-1-1 or similar ratio. (Fertilizers such as 6-6-6 or 8-8-8 would be ideal.) Spraying is rarely needed in the seedbed. If the seedlings are at least the thickness of a lead pencil at the base by the end of the growing season, they may be lined out in nursery rows. No fertilizer application should be made to the seedbed after 1 October.

Containerized plants grown in a controlled environment would necessarily be handled differently. In this system, seeds are sown into a commercially prepared medium that has been placed in reusable plastic tubes or trays. One or two seeds are placed in each cell or tube, and a single plant is allowed to grow in each con-

Fig. 3-1f. Budding completed and wrapped.

tainer until it is ready to be transplanted, and budded soon afterward.

(2) *The nursery row.* Preferably the nursery should be located on soil of the same type as that in which the trees will be set out, although this is not essential. The commercial nursery should be on virgin soil, if possible, or at least on soil that has not previously been used for citrus. If the same site is used for a nursery again, it should be fumigated to eliminate fungal disease and nematode problems. Like the seedbed, the nursery soil should be well plowed, harrowed, leveled, and cleared of pieces of roots.

Before the seedlings are transplanted, the seedbed should be well watered. Not more than a foot of taproot can easily be transplanted, so the seedlings should have their roots cut at a depth of ten to twelve inches with a long-bladed spade. Only vigorous plants of about the same size should be transplanted, with all weak plants or those with undesirably crooked roots discarded. Twice as many seeds should be sown in the seedbed as the number of seedlings desired in the nursery rows to allow rigorous culling in transplanting.

Nursery rows are spaced three or four feet apart for mechanical cultivation, and the seedlings are spaced one foot apart in the row. Care should be taken in transplanting not to let the seedling roots

dry out and not to permit taproots to be bent over. Furrows should
be deep enough to allow the shortened taproot to be in vertical position. Seedlings should always be set at the same depth in the soil at
which they grew previously since the root system is adapted to conditions at that depth. Thorough watering immediately after lining-
out the seedlings is essential to settle the fine soil particles in close
contact with the fine roots. Fertilizing, watering, and cultivation for
weed control should be continued as for the seedbed, so that rapid,
vigorous growth may be made. Spraying for control of mites and
scale insects or of scab on susceptible species will likely be needed.
By the end of the next growing season, the seedlings should have
attained a diameter of at least one-half inch and be ready for
budding, although seedlings of Cleopatra and trifoliate orange may
not reach desirable size in the first season and must be left another
year in the nursery.

For containerized production where climate is carefully controlled, seedlings are ready for transfer to larger containers within
three to six months. Seedlings are usually budded shortly after this
transfer operation and allowed to develop in the new and larger containers.

(3) *The budding operation.* A diameter of one-half inch at the
base is considered desirable for citrus stocks to be budded, although
seedlings of diameters from one-fourth to one and one-half inches
can be worked. Budding is usually done when the bark will "slip,"
meaning that because of active cambium division the bark can
easily be separated from the wood. Budding may be done at any
time when the bark slips and unsprouted buds are available, but
most budding of citrus in Florida is done in early fall—September
and October. Early spring is the next most favorable time for
budding. If temperatures are above 50°F, seedlings can usually be
induced to make active cambial growth when the bark sticks tightly,
that is, to change to a slipping bark condition, by applying nitrog-
enous fertilizer and water.

Budding in very late summer or early fall is called "dormant"
budding not because the stock is dormant (for budding would then
be impossible) but because the scion bud will stay dormant all winter if the budding is not done too early. If one waits until too late in
the fall before budding, the stock will be dormant and the bark will
not slip. If budding is done too early, the bud will start into growth
in the fall and be very susceptible to cold injury. Buds inserted in
spring will have a fairly long growing season ahead before cold
weather and should be well matured by that time. The dormant

buds, however, can start growth at least a full month before the spring buds because the dormant buds will have united with the stock in the fall whereas the spring buds will need a month or so for union to form before they can grow.

The type of budding most widely used for citrus in Florida is called "shield budding" because the scion piece is cut in an oval or shield shape. This shield of bark plus a little sliver of wood bears the bud proper in its center. A T-shaped incision is made in the stock bark to receive this shield. In most citrus-growing areas of the world, including Florida, the cut is made to form an inverted T so that the shield is pushed up from below. The upright T is used in California and some other areas, however, and there seems to be no inherent superiority of either method. A skilled budder can attain as high a percentage of success with one as with the other, if he is equally skillful in using both. There is some variation in different citrus areas also in the height at which the bud is inserted, but in Florida it has long been considered best to make the stock incision only two or three inches above the ground. Current research has shown, however, that less foot rot will occur on a susceptible scion variety when the bud is placed at a height of six inches above the soil line. The vertical cut should be an inch long.

The shield should be about one-half to three-fourths inch long, cut from the bud stick so that the inner face is nearly flat and not tapering greatly toward either end from the center. Lifting the corners of the bark at the bottom of the stock incision, gently force the bud up under the bark, taking care that the shield is not doubled back on itself, until it is wholly within the incision. If the bark does not "slip" easily enough for the bud to enter the incision readily, it is often possible to lift the bark and open the incision for its whole length with the budding knife or a probe, and then to insert the bud. The cambium tissue of the stock is now in intimate contact with the cambium tissue around the wood sliver on the inner face of the shield. For successful union, and to prevent drying out of the bud, it is necessary to maintain this intimate contact. Both needs are met by wrapping the stock tightly with a waterproof material. Formerly, waxed cloth strips were the usual wrapping material, but strips of polyethylene plastic are often used now. Wrapping is started at the base of the bud and carried upward in a spiral so that each successive turn overlaps slightly the one below it. At the top of the incision, the wrap is secured by slipping the free end under the last lap. Excessive pressure of the wrap on the bud should be avoided, but there should be no slack in the wrapping ma-

Fig. 3-2. Field citrus nursery with young budded trees.

terial, for the bark must be held firmly against the bud. When
budding is done in late spring or summer, it is better to leave the
bud itself uncovered since it may start growth within two weeks
and be injured if covered.

Another method of budding that has rather recently gained
some popularity in Florida is the use of a so-called hanging bud or
chip bud. Instead of the usual T-shaped incision, a piece of bark
about an inch long and one-fourth inch wide is lifted by a single upward cut with a knife held almost parallel to the bark surface. The
lower half of this flap is cut off, and the usual shield bud is inserted
under the remainder. The bark flap should cover the shield as far
down as the bud itself, which should not be covered, and the
pressure of the bark on the upper part of the shield holds it in place
so that it "hangs" with the lower end free. Wrapping is done in the
usual manner for standard shield budding. The advantages of this
method are that making the incision and inserting the bud may be
done slightly faster, and failure of the bark to slip is of slightly less
importance than in the standard method.

Fig. 3-3. Young budded citrus trees in the nursery row (note bud union).

About three or four weeks after budding, (two weeks if budded during the summer period), the wrap may be removed and the bud examined. If it is still green and callus tissue has formed, the bud has "taken." If the shield has turned brown and slips easily out of the incision, a new bud may be inserted at another place if the bark will still slip, or rebudding may be done in the spring. If these are the usual dormant buds, the stocks on which the buds have taken may be banked, after unwrapping, with clean soil for the winter about the end of November to prevent injury of the bud by cold. This bank will be removed again in spring after the last danger of injurious cold. Of course, the stocks budded in spring have no need of banking.

Containerized trees grown under greenhouse conditions could be budded at any time of the year since they are not subject to the vagaries of the weather. The budding techniques used are exactly the same as for field-grown trees, but budding is often done with smaller plants since they are easier to handle and this will cut down on the length of time required to produce a finished plant.

Fig. 3-4. Potted citrus nursery tree.

Cold protection should not be a problem since they are in a climate-controlled situation.

(4) *The budlings.* After removal of the banks from dormant-budded stocks, or as soon as union is sure in stocks budded in spring or summer, the stocks should be cut off just above the bud. A sloping cut is made from a point just above the bud downward at about a 45-degree angle across the stem of the stock. This assures the starting into growth of the bud and conserves for its development all of the water and mineral nutrients taken in by the roots. Amateurs may find it easier to make this cut in two steps, first cutting squarely across the stock an inch above the bud, and then making the finish cut as above. A clean cut, with no ragged edges, will permit more rapid healing of the wound. As soon as the bud pushes out, the stock and scion constitute a "budling," or young budded tree. Another widely used practice or an alternative to lopping is "looping" or "rolling over" the seedling by tying down the top so that the bud is forced. The top is then cut off after the bud begins to grow.

A stake should be provided for each budling, so that the developing shoot can be given support and assured of upright habit. This stake, about four feet long and an inch square, should be placed close against the stock adjacent to the bud, and be driven a foot or so into the ground. Heavy galvanized wire (No. 8) may be used instead of the stake. When the budling shoot has reached a length of four or five inches, it should be tied to the stake with soft, heavy twine, fastened loosely enough so that the expanding stem tissue will not be constricted. As the budling continues to grow, additional ties should be made at about ten and fifteen inches above the union. By the end of the growing season the scion will no longer need support and the stake can be removed before digging.

Care of the budling should be the same as has been discussed for the nursery already, with watering, fertilizing, cultivating, and spraying carried on as needed for healthy, vigorous growth. The budlings should be examined quite frequently for stock sprouts so that these may be removed before they have a chance to compete seriously. Quite young, tender sprouts can simply be rubbed off; older ones should be cleanly pruned off.

Container-grown plant material will be handled much in the same way as field-grown trees. Stakes (usually bamboo) should be provided as the buds emerge, and the new plant should be tied to the stake at regular intervals. Unlike field-grown plants, these plants are usually sold in the container with the stakes as part of the completed package.

(5) *Digging the budling.* At the end of one growing season after budding, the budling should be ready for transplanting to the grove, with a diameter just above the union of at least five-eighths inch. If this caliper has not been attained, the tree may be left for another season. The first step in digging is to "top" the tree; that is, cut off the top, at a height of about two feet. If the tree has already formed branches from about a twenty-inch height upward, these may be cut back to six- or eight-inch stubs. Then the lateral roots are cut at about a foot from the trunk all around the tree with a shovel, except that the cut must be made midway between adjacent trees in the row. Finally the roots are undercut below the tree at a depth of twelve to eighteen inches with a long-bladed nursery spade. Using this as a lever with one hand, one pulls the tree from the ground with the other.

The greatest hazard in transplanting citrus is drying out of the roots. The excess soil clinging to the roots in digging is shaken loose and the roots are at once covered with wet sawdust, peat moss, or other water-holding material. The top of the tree, devoid of leaves or retaining only a few, is then covered with a tarpaulin or similar material to cut off sun and wind and maintain a humid atmosphere. The budling can now be taken to the planting site. Avoid injury from cold winds during the winter season by use of covered conveyances.

Trees grown in containers, whether they were produced in containers from seed to finished product, or dug bare-root and finished in a container are handled much differently from bare-root stock.

Trees that were dug and potted are often fairly large and are sold in
three- to five-gallon containers. Trees produced from seed under
controlled conditions are sometimes sold as single-stemmed plants
in a container or plastic sleeve of approximately one gallon size, but
most are headed prior to shipment to assure proper future growth.

Topworking

The term *topworking* refers to the operation of changing the scion
variety of a tree that has already formed its scaffold branches, by
budding or grafting these with another variety. Either a seedling or
a budded tree may be topworked, although there is rarely occasion
to topwork seedling citrus trees. The process is mostly employed to
change an undesirable variety or strain to a desirable one, without
losing the advantage of its established root system. The topworked
tree can be in production in two years and will be much larger than
would be the case if the old tree were pulled out and a new nursery
tree planted. A variety may be undesirable because it was unwisely
selected in the first place or because changing market conditions
make it less profitable than was anticipated. Or the grower may
discover that the desired variety is of a poor strain; it may simply be
unproductive, or it may bear fruit of poor quality. In either case, the
tree can be topworked without sacrificing more than two or three
crops. In the home planting the owner may wish to have several varieties of fruit borne by a single tree, to conserve space. It is only
feasible to grow a single variety in the nursery row, but once well
established in the grove, more varieties can easily be added by topworking. Thus, early, midseason, and late oranges may be produced
on the same tree, or grapefruit and tangerines may be borne also on
an orange tree.

Topworking can be done in several ways, using budding or
grafting as the situation warrants. The easiest way is to cut back
the tree to short stubs of its scaffold branches and to bud the shoots
that develop from these branches as if they were seedling stocks in
the nursery. A second possibility is to insert buds into bark incisions
on the branches just below the points where they will later be cut off
after the buds have "taken" satisfactorily. With older trees, it is usually necessary to thin the bark by paring or scraping it before
budding can be done, and a larger bud shield is preferred than for
nursery budding.

Either the usual T-incision (inverted or upright) can be made, or
a single oblique cut made from one side, the side- or hanging-bud

technique. In the latter case, the flap of bark must have a notch cut to avoid covering the bud proper, or "eye." Wrapping of buds is carried out as for nursery budding.

Another method is to cut off the scaffold branches as above and then insert scions at once, instead of waiting for sprouts to reach budding size. The branch stub may be split clear across and a cleft graft made, or if the bark will slip, the scion may be inserted under the bark in a bark graft. If the grafting is successful, a season of growth may be saved over budding sprouts; if it fails, the sprouts can still be budded.

In cleft-grafting it is of utmost importance that the cambium layers (the point where bark meets wood) of stock and scion should match exactly. The bark of a three-inch stub is sure to be much thicker than that of a one-fourth-inch scion, so that the latter must be set slightly inward from the edge of the stock. Of course, only the cambium on one side of the scion can be matched. Scions should be chosen of well-matured twigs, usually not the last flush of growth, with plump but dormant buds, and should be five or six inches long and from one-fourth to one-half inch thick.

After the stock is split to a depth of three or four inches, the cleft is held open by a wedge (either the one provided for the purpose on a grafting iron or a special one) in the center of the stem to the necessary width to allow easy insertion of the scion. The sides of the cleft should be carefully trimmed to a smooth, even surface. Then the basal two inches of the scion are cut to a tapered wedge, very slightly thicker on one side than the other. This wedge is inserted in the cleft at one side of the stock, with the thicker edge next to the periphery, so that cambium layers match. If the stock is less than one inch in diameter at the cut surface, only a single scion is likely to be used. With larger stocks, a second scion is inserted on the other side of the stock similarly. Then the center wedge holding the cleft open is carefully removed, allowing the pressure of the stock to hold the scions firmly in place. In the case of large stubs, either sturdy scions must be used or this wedge only partly removed so that it prevents crushing of the scions. After completing the graft, the stub is wrapped with tape and the cut ends of stock and scion are covered with grafting wax or asphalt emulsion to prevent drying out of cambial tissues and entrance of disease organisms.

Two other possible methods are both rather unsatisfactory. They involve cutting the tree to the ground and either crown-grafting the stump or budding sprouts after they have developed. In both cases, the scaffold structure of the old tree is lost, the healing of the one big stump is slower and less certain than that of several branch stumps, and the chances of developing a satisfactory new tree are reduced.

Trees seriously hurt by cold may be killed well below the forks, perhaps even below the bud. Such trees must often be cut off close to the ground. Either cleft-grafting, bark-grafting (usually called crown-grafting in this case), or budding of sprouts may be employed to make a new top, but serious consideration should be given to removing and replacing trees so seriously hurt. While several scions may be inserted, it is best to select the strongest one after they have made some growth and use it to form the new top as if it were a nursery budling, pinching back and eventually eliminating the other scions. If all are allowed to grow, they usually form very acute crotches, which permit the whole limb from one or more scions to split off under a heavy load of fruit. A tree should be cut below the main forks only by necessity.

The new growth developing naturally from latent or adventitious buds on branch stumps, or from buds inserted under the bark of these branches, is exceedingly lush and soft because of the very large amount of food and water supplied by the old stock. This growth is not very firmly attached to the old branches for two or three years and is easily broken off at its point of origin by wind. To prevent this, the bud growth should be supported by being tied to stout stakes driven into the ground beside them or nailed to the old branch stubs. If budding is done before cutting back the scaffold limbs and new shoot growth has pushed out from the buds, too, special care is needed in cutting off the limbs. A preliminary cut can be made several inches beyond the new shoot, and then a second cut made close to it more easily.

No tree should be topworked unless it is vigorous and healthy. If the trunk and limbs show evidence of disease or serious injury, they cannot be expected to produce a vigorous new top or to give it a long life. Grapefruit trees are topworked very successfully because they make sturdy and well-formed scaffold branches. Usually all varieties of sweet orange can also readily be topworked. Tangerine trees, however, have not proven very satisfactory for topworking since the new top often breaks off at the point of union with the old trunk when the first heavy crop is borne. As a rule, it is better to remove tangerine trees and replace them with nursery trees than to topwork them.

When a tree has been topworked by budding to another variety of the same species, it is often very difficult to distinguish the shoots of inserted buds from shoots developing from the old branches or trunk. For this reason, it is important to inspect the topworked trees at frequent enough intervals to remove stump sprouts while they are still very small. Leaves of orange can easily be distinguished from leaves of grapefruit, but there will be no way of telling one variety of orange or grapefruit from another; and even leaves of the various mandarins may not easily be distinguished from those of oranges in lush sprouts. Careless growers may end up pruning off the buds they inserted if they allow the stump sprouts to grow too large.

One serious problem in topworking is the possibility of injury to the bark and cambium of the remaining trunk and scaffold branches from sunshine when the tops have been cut off. Growers have learned by bitter experience that sunscald of the limbs of defoliated trees will result in partial or complete death to the system. Bark previously shaded by the canopy of foliage is not adapted to receiving the direct rays of the sun and must be shielded from direct sunlight when cutting back is done at any time other than just before the spring flush of growth. This is often done by whitewashing the trunk and limbs with a hydrated lime-water mixture with a "sticker" added at once after removal of the top of the tree, to reflect sunshine and thus prevent excessive heating of delicate tissues; or it may be accomplished by wrapping the exposed parts with burlap, Spanish moss, or kraft paper. Cement paints, such as are used to waterproof the outside of cement-block buildings, make excellent whitewashes that will generally remain effective a whole year from a single application. It is a good practice to topwork only one-third of a top each year, so that the foliage of the other two-thirds serves to continue the natural protection of the bark from the sun. In this way, the whole top is renewed in three years, there is never a period of no fruit production, and there should be no sunscalded trees to pull out. Great care must be taken in the second and third year of this program to avoid breaking off the young growth from the previous year's topworking when removing the rest of the top. However, if due care is taken (whitewash may need renewal before the new foliage shades the trunk) it is perfectly possible to do all the topworking at one time. In either case, a good job of topworking on a healthy trunk would produce a top with fruit production about equal to the original top in about five years from starting the work.

Another potentially serious problem exists for growers who wish to topwork trees. This is in the area of infection by viral disease. Introduction of a viral disease from infected budwood is always a possibility unless registered, certified propagation material is used. An equally troublesome problem can occur if existing plants are already infected, but may be symptomless carriers of a viral disease. Then, placing a susceptible scion on a tree by topworking may predispose the new plant to a disease-ridden future. Such problems can be minimized by understanding disease-plant relationships and the use of disease-free propagating material.

Inarching

Sometimes the root system of a tree is seriously injured or impaired by fungi or burrowing animals, so that loss of the tree is threatened. Usually it is best to remove such a tree and replace it with a healthy one, perhaps budded on a stock more suited to the soil conditions. However, in the case of trees with historic value it is often possible to replace the diseased or injured roots by inarching a vigorous seedling into the trunk. One or more seedlings of size suitable for budding or a little larger are planted as close as possible to the base of the ailing tree. As soon as they have become well established and have a stem at least two feet high, they may be grafted into the trunk of the tree. One common technique is to make an incision in the trunk as if for shield-budding and to insert the obliquely sharpened end of the seedling stem into this. Another is to cut a slot in the bark of the trunk of the same width as the seedling stem, and after cutting away a thin slice of bark and wood from the latter, press it tightly in place so that exposed cambium of seedling and trunk are in contact. In either case, the cuts must be made with care to assure matching of the two components to be joined, and the seedling stem must be held firmly in position by nailing a slender brad through it into the tree trunk until union takes place. Presently the new seedling roots will take over the functions formerly performed by the original root system, and the rejuvenated tree may have a long increase of life. This method is not at all recommended for commercial use, however, as it is too slow and expensive to be profitable. As with topworking, the viral disease status and susceptibility of plant materials should be thoroughly investigated before this sort of operation is undertaken.

4 /
Climate and Soil in Citrus Growing

Climatic Considerations

The term *climate* refers to the general or average conditions of a given area as regards the various atmospheric phenomena, while the term *weather* refers to the transient conditions of atmospheric environment for this area. In other words, weather is the climate of the moment, and climate is the average weather. Both the weather at any given time and the climate over many years are of importance to the grower. Their influence on citrus growing may be either obvious or obscure; they may make the growing of some or all kinds of citrus fruits entirely impossible in some areas, while in others they exercise an almost imperceptible restraint on commercial production. No major citrus-growing region of the world is without climatic problems of one sort or another. In spite of the fact that various citrus species flourish in some parts of Florida as though indigenous, a grower is forced to recognize limits set by climate; indeed, more time will probably be spent in worries concerning climate or weather than in administration of the production program.

Five phases of climate (or weather) are of interest because of their influence on tree growth and crop production: temperature, rainfall, relative humidity, wind, and sunshine.

Temperature

The temperatures found in the citrus-growing region of Florida are in general such as would be expected in a subtropical climate. During the period from April to October they are moderately high, but these summer temperatures, though long continued, do not reach values as high as those experienced in many more northerly areas. The highest summer and lowest winter temperatures occur in midcontinental regions, whereas the presence of either the Atlantic Ocean or the Gulf of Mexico within seventy-five miles of any point in Florida serves to moderate both summer maxima and winter minima. The highest daily temperature in summer is usually from 93° to 95°F, with higher temperatures at irregular intervals that rarely reach 100°F.

From October through March, lower temperatures prevail. Minima below 32°F are expected every winter and invariably occur in the northern part of the state, while they are not reached every winter in the southern part. Only the Florida Keys are completely free of frost, but the minimum temperatures are lower as one goes from south to north in the state. It usually follows also that the lower the minima in a given area, the longer will be the duration of low temperatures and the more often they will occur. Thus the northern part of Florida not only has lower minima in any winter than southern areas, but the cold spells last longer and come more frequently.

Injurious low temperatures may occur under two sets of conditions — those of a *frost* and those of a *freeze*. In both cases, the temperature of the air or of plant tissues goes below 32°F, but for different reasons; and the methods of preventing plant injury will be somewhat different under the two conditions.

Frosts are local occurrences, the cooling of the air and plants resulting from radiation of heat from soil and plants out into space. As the soil cools by radiation, the air above it gives up its heat to the soil and so is slowly cooled upward, with lowest air temperatures next to the ground. Rapid loss of heat by radiation occurs only on clear, cloudless nights, for clouds reflect back much of this heat. On a calm, still night the air forms a series of layers progressively warmer from the ground up—spoken of as a stratified condition (or temperature inversion)—but if there is a light breeze these strata become mixed. Then the warmer upper air mixes with the colder air next to the ground and prevents it from reaching as low temperatures. Thus frost damage is most likely to occur on still, cloudless nights, and frost may occur anywhere on the mainland of the state. Muck soils radiate heat faster than sandy soils, and for the same latitude danger of frost is greater on muck. Elevated areas are less subject to frost than adjacent low areas because of air drainage with the colder, heavier air flowing into the low areas from high ground.

Freezes are always general, not local, because they result from the advection of large masses of air at subfreezing temperatures. These masses of frigid air often follow certain channels for topographic reasons, somewhat as water flows in valleys. Because the air is near the same temperature from top to bottom of the moving mass, there is usually little difference between temperatures on high and low ground, at least on the first night of a freeze. Whereas a frost usually follows a warm, sunny afternoon, when soil and tree have stored considerable heat, the afternoon before a freeze is usu-

Fig. 4-1. Leaf freeze damage following a mild freeze.

ally cold and windy and may even be cloudy. A frost lasts only for a night, although it may recur the next night, but a freeze usually lasts for two or more days.

The first night is always cold and windy but rarely causes serious damage. A period of calm a little before sunrise may allow the air to stratify, which poses a possible danger. During the second day, there is usually little warming of the air or trees by the sun, and cold air continues to move south and chill things more. During the second night, the wind usually falls soon after sunset, and the stratifying air may reach a dangerous low temperature very soon in low areas, while adjacent high ground maintains higher temperatures. On the third day, there is usually a shift in the wind to start replacing the cold air with warmer air from over the ocean, and temperatures begin to rise from the south northward. Under the usual conditions of freezes in Florida, therefore, the second and/or third nights, after ground and trees have become cold and the wind has ceased, are most disastrous.

Freezes may occur in Florida anytime after 15 November until

Fig. 4-2. Dead trees. Aftermath of severe freezes thirteen months apart
(December 1983 and January 1985). After the first of these, the damaged
grove was pruned and cleaned of dead wood in an attempt to bring it
back into productivity.

15 March. Any condition which results in a lack of tree dormancy,
such as warm weather preceding a freeze, will usually exacerbate
the effect of the freeze. The most severe injury results when an
early winter freeze is followed by a period of warm weather sufficient to initiate new growth, and this in turn is followed by a
second freeze the same winter. Such was the pattern of the freeze
of 1894–95, still spoken of as the "big freeze." Trees were defoliated and fruit was frozen, but wood damage was not severe from
a freeze in early December of 1894. During January the weather
was mild, trees put out vigorous new shoots, and growers felt that
they had come through the experience in good shape. In this condition of tender growth, however, the trees were killed to the
ground by a second freeze in early February 1895. In January
1940 a freeze of several days' duration caused much loss of fruit
and considerable injury to the branches; yet, because there was no

later visitation of severe cold that winter, the new growth in February following the freeze developed normally and the trees were practically back to normal condition that summer. The freeze pattern of the winter of 1957–58 was again one of repeated cold waves interspersed with periods of sufficient warmth for renewal of growth, and again damage was severe in many areas. The "Big Freeze of December 1962" was the most damaging of this century until freezes in the 1980s broke all documented records. In the 1962 freeze, cold temperatures occurred from 11 to 16 December with hard freezes on 13 and 14 December. Other freezes have produced lower minimum temperatures in low ground locations; the convection (blowing) freeze of 1962, however, resulted in low temperatures and severe damages even on high ground locations. Less damage occurred in the Indian River area, and in southeastern Polk County and Highlands County.

Moderate freezes occurred in Florida in 1977, 1981, and 1982. However, back-to-back freezes in December 1983 and January 1985 exceeded all previous records and dealt northern citrus areas devastating blows. Nearly 20 percent of the state's acreage was lost due to the 1983–1985 freezes. Yet another seroius freeze occurred in December 1989. This freeze destroyed many of the replanted areas in the northern citrus region and brought extensive damage into all of Polk County and much of Highlands County as well. At this date, the full extent of the damage has not been determined.

Cold temperatures limit the northward expansion of the citrus belt and are the most adverse climatic factor with which the Florida citrus grower must contend, but high temperatures cause some trouble too. As just seen, relatively high temperatures (in the 1970s) during December and January may encourage growth and thus make trees more easily injured by later cold. In March and April, high temperatures, coupled with lack of soil moisture and hot, dry winds, increase transpiration until trees often go into permanent wilting. When such conditions are prolonged into May, even if not serious enough to cause such wilting, an excessively heavy "June drop" of fruit may be expected. Normal high summer temperatures in June and July, with high humidity and intermittent cloudiness, may accentuate sunscald and spray burns. Warm weather during October and November, particularly if nights are warm and rainfall is much above normal, usually results in delayed development of internal quality and external color, and in increased tendency for dropping of fruit, as well as in delaying maturity of tree tissues and thus increasing susceptibility to injury from winter cold.

Temperatures may vary significantly according to latitude and to proximity to the Atlantic Ocean or the Gulf of Mexico. Minimum temperatures are lower as one goes from southern to northern Florida, and as one goes from the coast inland if elevation does not change. Locally temperatures are influenced by such variable factors as: elevation, soil type, air channels, bodies of water, surrounding vegetation, extent of grove areas, presence of windbreaks, presence of hammock trees within a grove, and cultivation practices. Even though no way is known to prevent the occurrences of periodic freezes in Florida, the grower can minimize their effects by proper selection of site and varieties and by maintaining satisfactory cultural programs.

The temperature range for growth of most of the commonly cultivated kinds of citrus fruits is from 55° to 100°F. Within this range, the tree is able to develop and fruit, with best growth occurring around 85°, or from 80° to 90°F. The processes of fruit maturation, including production of sugars and development of rind color, reach their highest perfection in the lower portions of the growth range. Winter temperatures ranging from 35° to 50°F approach the ideal for dormant tree condition. Temperature ranges of 100° to 130°F and 32° to 55°F are considered, respectively, high and low endurance ranges. Very low metabolic activity occurs within the plant, no active growth is present, and no damages can be observed.

Injury from low atmospheric temperatures usually begins to be evident when the air temperature gets below 32°F, although under frost conditions the temperature of fruit or leaf may reach the point of injury before the air temperature is down this low, and cold, dry winds may injure tissues while the air is still above 32°. Only very tender foliage or flowers are injured by such temperatures. Fruit is damaged when its tissues reach the freezing point, which may be anywhere from 30° down to 26° depending on variety and maturity. How long it takes a given fruit to reach this temperature after the air temperature does depends on size, location on the tree, rind thickness, and initial warmth of the fruit. In commercial practice it is considered likely that fruit may show injury after exposure for two hours to air temperature of 28°, but individual fruits will vary widely in this respect, depending on the variable factors enumerated above.

Fully grown leaves may begin to show injury (evident as dead areas and/or as defoliation) after being exposed to from two to four hours of air temperature of 27° or lower, and because of the small volume of a leaf compared to its area, there will be little variation because of stored heat; however, location on the tree exercises an influence on foliage injury. Mature, dormant orange trees have been reported to survive ten hours below 25° with only 10 percent of the leaves lost from cold. Previous temperature conditions play an important role in the endurance of cold by trees.

Dormant twigs and limbs may be injured at temperatures ranging from 27° down to 16°, depending on size and maturity of wood and length of exposure to cold, as well as on previous temperatures. Even the most severe freeze known in the citrus-growing areas of Florida will not usually kill the older trees completely, if it occurs only once in a winter or if no warm weather intervenes between successive periods of cold. Because their tissues are less mature, their bark is thinner, and their heat capacity is lower, young trees may be killed outright by a single severe cold spell; older trees, even though not killed entirely, may have sufficient killing of limbs that they are no longer economically useful because new trees could be brought into production as soon as, and at less expense than, these frozen trees could be rejuvenated. Often serious damage to trees from cold temperatures is evidenced by "frost or cold cankers" on scaffold branches and trunk, particularly in the crotch area. Cambium, active at the time of freeze, is killed while the surrounding tissue is not harmed; the tree may be left in such a weakened condition that it is not capable of producing satisfactory crops of fruit. Large cankers, on the upper side of scaffold branches, may cause the branches to break under the weight of fruit. Even though the cankers do not become progressively larger, there is no way to eliminate them except by removing the affected branches.

The amount of injury caused by excessively low temperatures will vary, therefore, with the following factors: species and variety of scion and of stock; the condition of the tree with respect to vigor and degree of dormancy; the minimum air temperature reached; its duration; the exposure of the tree to heat loss by radiation; the conditions of soil cover; and the interrelations of temperature with other climatic factors prior to, during, and following the low temperature. Other things being equal, the vigor or health of the tree, resulting from previous cultural practices of the grower, plays a dominant role in minimizing injury from cold. Trees in good health, with no mineral deficiencies and free from serious insect infestations or disease infections, endure cold much better than weakened trees.

If trees are in well-matured or dormant condition, the trifoliate orange can endure the lowest temperature of any of the commercial citrus types, followed in descending order by kumquat, calamondin, sour orange, mandarin, sweet orange, grapefruit, shaddock, lemon, lime, and citron. The range is thus from the trifoliate orange of the temperate zone to the citron of the tropics. When trees are in active growth flush, however, there is little if any difference in ease of injury by cold between the various kinds of citrus. The big factor of difference is usually the readiness with which different citrus species tend to go into or come out of the dormant condition during the winter months.

The trifoliate orange, so hardy in most winters, may be seriously injured by early freezes of slight severity when the temperatures in the early fall have been unusually high. Apparently, lower temperatures are needed by trifoliate orange to induce dormancy than are needed by other kinds of citrus fruits, which may be much less injured by the same freeze. On the other hand, trifoliate orange requires higher temperatures to initiate growth than most other kinds of citrus and is therefore later than other kinds to start its buds in spring, thus escaping damage from spring frosts and late winter freezes that may injure the others.

The kumquats also are late in pushing out buds in spring, and so also tend to escape many cold injuries suffered in late winter and early spring by grapefruit, sweet orange, mandarins, and even sour orange, due to their tendency to start bud growth following a few days of warm weather. Within this group, the Cleopatra withstands cold better than other tangerines, but the satsumas are the outstanding example of cold hardiness among the mandarins. Lemons, limes, and citrons respond very readily to mild weather, and usually have flowers, new foliage, and young fruits at almost any time in the winter. This lack of dormancy renders them increasingly subject to winter injury.

Even when these species are used as stocks, cold susceptibility must be considered, not so much because of possible killing of the stock itself as because of its influence on the degree of dormancy of the scion. There is no exact correlation of cold hardiness of a species with the cold hardiness of a given scion worked on it as a stock, and there may be much variation in the effect of different varieties of the same species as stocks. However, rough lemon, a common stock of the Ridge area, is much less satisfactory on well-drained sandy soils of the northern citrus areas than sour orange. Still farther north the trifoliate orange gives the greatest cold hardiness, although attention has been called to its less satisfactory ability to make a hardy tree in areas where winters have alternating periods of cold and warmth.

Seedling sweet orange trees are considered to be able to endure more cold after they reach good bearing age than are budded trees of the same age. The same is probably true of grapefruit trees. It has also been noted that varieties within a species tend to be more cold hardy if the fruit is seedless and decrease somewhat in hardiness with increase in seediness. Probably this is a nutritional phenomenon, reflecting a translocation of mineral nutrients to the developing seeds, leaving the twigs somewhat deficient for a time.

The importance of the duration of subfreezing temperatures is often overlooked by growers, who simply observe the minimum reached. A recording thermometer will indicate better the true temperature situation, for a minimum temperature that causes no injury when it persists for only half an hour may do serious damage when it continues for four hours.

Two environmental factors that influence cold endurance by their effect on the temperatures actually reached by foliage or fruit are overhead and ground cover. Trees that are somewhat shaded by pines, palms, or other thin-foliaged trees are always less injured by low temperatures than trees fully exposed to the sky. Indeed, because this difference had been observed, slat shade was constructed during the freeze of 1886 over some orange groves. The shading reflects back much of the heat radiated by the citrus trees, which would otherwise be lost to space, and so prevents them from reaching temperatures as low as trees fully exposed to the sky. On the other hand, injury is usually greater when citrus trees have the ground under them covered by grass, weeds, or mulch than when the soil is cultivated. In this case, cultivated soil radiates heat more freely to the trees than soil covered with vegetation and thus prevents the trees from reaching an injurious temperature as soon.

Windbreaks may be helpful or detrimental in cold periods. A windbreak on the northwest side of a grove slows down the movement of cold air into the grove in a freeze. The stream of cold air flows up over the top of the windbreak and only slowly descends to ground level again, leaving a relatively quiet area in the lee of the windbreak. Heating the grove is more effective in this lee space since the warmed air is not carried away so rapidly as in a grove with no windbreak on the windward side. On the other hand, a windbreak down slope from the grove may prevent air drainage on a frosty night and thus cause more cold injury than if it were not there. If the windbreak is both on the northwest side and lower on the slope, occasional openings in it will permit slow drainage of cold air while still giving considerable protection in freezes.

The kind of weather during the weeks preceding a freeze has an important effect on the amount of injury done, through its effect on tissue maturity. If minimum temperatures during the preceding month have been down in the 40s continuously, especially if the weather has been dry, tree tissues will be well matured and will endure quite severe cold with little injury. The absolute minimum endured will vary, of course, with the particular scion and stock involved. However, a prolonged drought may put trees in a condition of water deficiency that renders them more subject to cold injury than trees with adequate moisture content. Attention has already been called to the undesirable effect on cold hardiness of a week or two of warm weather just before a freeze, or even a frost.

Rainfall

The amount of moisture made available by rainfall is an important consideration in the production of any horticultural crop, and citrus is no exception. The total amount of rainfall annually is not the only item of importance in determining adequacy; in addition, the distribution of the rainfall during the year, its seasonal fluctuations, and its intensity must be considered.

The average annual rainfall within the Florida citrus belt is approximately 52 inches. The larger portion of this precipitation falls during the rainy summer season, from May to September. During this period, the natural rainfall usually takes care of the needs of citrus trees for moisture and often provides an excess over what is needed. From October through April, and occasionally through May or early June, the rainfall is often insufficient for the needs of the trees.

The most critical period is usually in the spring, particularly during the months of March, April, and May, and especially if rainfall was deficient the preceding fall. The two periods in the annual growth cycle of a citrus tree when it is most sensitive to soil moisture deficiency are in early spring when the new flush of growth is tender and fruit is setting, and in late spring and early summer when fruit is rapidly increasing in size. Deficiency of available soil moisture during the period of fruit setting may cause abnormally heavy shedding of young fruit. Tender new shoots easily wilt if soil moisture is in short supply, and seem to have a prior claim on moisture within the tree over young fruit. Deficiency of soil moisture in May and June may prevent citrus fruits from reaching good size later. Shortage of rainfall during October and November is not likely to prove critical unless the fruit is desiccated at the time of picking or the trees experience an excessive wilting of foliage. Low temperatures during the winter months decrease transpiration rates of leaves, so that a given amount of rainfall goes further toward meeting tree needs than the same amount in summer.

While the average annual rainfall is about 52 inches, the amount that falls in any individual year may vary from 37 to 84 inches. In addition, the proportion of the annual precipitation that falls in any given month also varies from year to year. This annual and monthly variation gives a dynamic quality to the rainfall. There is also tremendous variability from site to site during any given rainfall occurence. Obviously it would be impossible for any one grower to operate for a sufficient time to profit by a short period of rainfall experiences. The static climatic picture gives the impression that predicting rainfall adequacy should be easy, but the dynamic weather pattern makes it very difficult to do so.

The intensity of rainfall, that is, the amount falling in any twenty-four-hour period, is also of importance. This amount may vary from a "trace" (less than 0.01 inch) to as much as 16 inches. A monthly rainfall of 6 inches may all have come in one heavy shower or it may represent a dozen rainy days with half an inch each. It makes a big difference to trees whether one or the other was the case. Rainfalls of one-tenth inch or less are of little use to citrus trees, except as they occur along with humid, cloudy days, which reduce transpirational losses. The precipitated moisture evaporates from the soil surface without ever affecting the soil moisture. A rainfall of one-half inch may wet a sandy soil to a depth of six inches, but its effect is temporary because soil moisture to this depth is readily lost by evaporation. Probably only 10 percent of such a rainfall is actually used by the trees. Rainfalls of from 1 to 3 inches are ideal for the Florida grower since they wet the soil deeply enough to supply moisture over a long period yet are unlikely to provide excess water, which percolates beyond root depth. Of course, several consecutive days of half-inch rainfall, with no sunny days for evaporation between them, may also provide satisfactory soil moisture conditions. The very heavy rainfalls accompanying hurricanes, which may run as high as 16 inches in one twenty-four-hour period, are very harmful because they

supply far more water than our sandy soils can hold and consequently they cause serious leaching of soluble nutrients.

Relative Humidity

The ratio of the amount of water vapor in the atmosphere at any
given time to the amount that the atmosphere would contain at
the same temperature if saturated is termed the *relative humidity*
and is always expressed as a percentage. It in no way indicates the
amount of water actually present in the air. Relative humidity exercises an important influence on tree growth and health, as well as
on the comfort of the grower.

The relative humidity of Florida varies normally from nearly 100
percent at night and early in the morning to an average low of 40
percent in midafternoon on clear, sunny days. Of course, it is also
100 percent whenever it is raining. There is little seasonal variation, so that daily average relative humidity of 72 percent is fairly
constant throughout the year.

This high relative humidity of Florida is advantageous for tree
growth, for it decreases the transpiration rate for any given temperature and thereby makes for greater economy of water use by citrus
trees in comparison with regions of low relative humidity. However,
it has some disadvantages, too, for it is chiefly responsible for the
proliferation of fungal diseases that cause much damage to fruit and
trees in Florida. Citrus scab, melanose, foot rot, and other diseases
are much more serious under humid than under arid conditions.

High relative humidity, especially in combination with abnormally high temperature, is the cause of much of the poor textural
quality, excessive "puffiness," and lack of bright color sometimes
noted as citrus fruits mature in Florida. The difficulty in curing
lemons in an area of high humidity was an important factor in the
decline of the early lemon industry here and would still be a
handicap to a revived production of lemons for the fresh market.

Wind

Three types of winds occur with some regularity in Florida and
may be detrimental to production of citrus fruits. Southeasterly
winds, which characterize the spring months (especially March
and April), increase the rate of water loss from trees by accel-
erating the transpiration rate and decrease the available soil
moisture by increasing the rate of surface evaporation. Soil moisture is usually not abundant at this time, and the new shoots

transpire faster than they will when they mature, so that the added stress due to these winds is often a problem at this time. If rainfall has been unusually low during the winter and spring, injury to tree or crop may result.

The hurricane season extends from 1 June to 1 November and is a period when very strong winds may be felt in the citrus area. Winds of hurricane velocity exceed seventy-five miles per hour, depending on how close the center of the storm passes by a given area, and are capable of causing severe physical damage to buildings and equipment as well as to the grove by uprooting trees and shaking fruit to the ground. Even if the trees and fruit remain in place, the fruit may be badly scarred by rubbing against branches so that its grade is seriously lowered. This may cause more loss to the citrus industry, on the average, than direct loss of fruit and trees, for it is rare that any one grove experiences the full intensity of hurricane winds, but a hurricane crossing the state anywhere will be felt as strong, fruit-bruising winds everywhere in the citrus belt.

Freezes always are brought to the state by cold, northwesterly winds, occurring any time between 15 November and 15 March.

Sunshine

Sunshine contains several components, notably heat, light, and ultraviolet rays. Light, all-important to green plants for photosynthesis, is never deficient for good plant growth in Florida. Heat has already been discussed. Ultraviolet rays are absorbed by the atmosphere to a much greater degree under the humid conditions of Florida than in more arid regions, resulting in less bright color development of oranges and mandarins. For this reason, artificial coloring of these fruits is practiced more in Florida than in other states.

Soil Considerations

Soils provide anchorage for plants and furnish the water and mineral nutrients required for plant growth. The native soils of Florida show wide variations in the way they serve these functions. These soils have been grouped by scientists into "series" on the basis of origin, color, structure, and other characters; and these are further subdivided into "classes" according to the texture (particle size) of the surface layer. *Astatula fine sand* (formerly classified as *Lakeland fine sand*) identifies the series *"Astatula"* and class "fine sand" of one of the important soils used for citrus production in central Florida. Such grouping makes possible the classification of soils as naturally occurring bodies and the study of soil characters with regard to their usefulness to horticultural industries.

Horticulturists have long recognized the extreme importance of certain soil characters and have selected planting sites with due regard for them, even when they knew nothing of the name by which the soil was classified—indeed, long before there was any such classification. Drainage of water is perhaps the most important of these characters, and in itself can be used for grouping soils. In the early years of the Florida citrus industry, great reliance was placed on the type of vegetation growing naturally on different soils as this provides the experienced grower with a good idea of the nature and properties of the soil.

Soils Classed by Native Cover

The early citrus grower noted that the native flora not only served as a rough index of soil drainage but also gave indications of the natural fertility of the soil and the relative degree of cold to be expected at that location. In the well-drained areas, the following types of land were distinguished, being listed in descending order of desirability for growth of citrus trees:

1. *High hammock land* maintained a heavy hammock growth of hardwoods such as live oak, magnolia, hickory, and dogwood. While "high" in comparison with low hammock, this type of soil was actually not elevated very greatly.

2. *High pineland* sustained good stands of longleaf pine, often with some scattered red oak and post oak and little underbrush.

3. *Blackjack oak land* supported turkey oak (sometimes called blackjack) and scattered pines. It represented a poor grade of high pineland.

4. *Scrub,* comprising areas of coarse sand with low organic matter, reflected its low soil fertility in its poor stand of sand pine, turkey oak, and other shrubby oaks.

High hammock and high pine lands proved very well suited to citrus culture, while blackjack oak land has never been found very satisfactory and is often treacherous because of cold pockets. The scrub will probably always remain in its native condition for it has little possible use in agriculture. Scattered through the high pine lands are limited areas of coarse white sand of the same character as scrub land. These small areas, called "sandsoaks," are quite as unsatisfactory for citrus production as large scrub areas.

On poorly drained soils the following types of land were recognized, again given in order of decreasing suitability for citrus planting:

1. *Low hammock land* bore a heavy growth of hardwoods, especially live oak, and of cabbage palmetto. Difficult to clear and to drain properly, it has produced some of the exceptionally good coastal groves of the state. The old, so-called hammock groves were established with the underbrush cleared out but many of the larger hardwoods and palmettos left in place, and were notable producers of fine crops of fruit. A few of these groves can still be seen along the upper east coast.

2. *Flatwoods land* is low and level, with scattered longleaf pine predominant in the northern part of the state and slash pine in the southern part. Frequently saw palmetto and wire grass cover the ground and a hardpan sometimes underlies the surface, making drainage very poor. In general these soils are very poorly adapted to growth of citrus trees, but properly modified by drainage and beds, can serve very well.

3. *Bayheads,* originally supporting stands of bald cypress and other trees that endure inundation, are areas of standing water, often associated with well-drained soils at the lower elevations. They are entirely unadapted to citrus culture.

The present-day horticulturist is usually no longer able to make use of natural vegetation as an index of suitability of soils for citrus planting. Most areas that originally supported tree growth have been cut over, especially on soil types reasonably well adapted for citrus culture. There are areas of cutover blackjack oak land, of flatwoods, and of scrub that have not changed greatly from their native condition, but these are the least desirable soils for planting citrus trees.

Soils Classed by Drainage Character

With the native flora no longer available as a guide, the grower must base his choice of land primarily on two characters: water drainage of the soil, with its effect on depth of rooting, and air drainage of the land for natural cold protection. Today the soils of many areas of the state have been well mapped, so that it is easily possible to ascertain the exact soil type or types in prospective locations within these areas. Knowledge of these soil types and their characteristics is important to the modern citrus grower. Based on drainage, they may be grouped as follows:

1. *The well-drained soils.*—Well-drained soils are found in the area extending north and south through the central part of the Florida peninsula as far south as Highlands County, with lateral extensions into Pasco, Hillsborough, and Pinellas counties. The main area from Clermont to Lake Placid is often spoken of as the Ridge. Isolated areas of well-drained soils are found along both coasts and even on some of the coastal islands.

These soils belong principally to the Astatula association and are the soils most extensively used for citrus culture as far north as winter temperatures permit.

Astatula fine sand is the predominant soil for citrus plantings throughout the greater portion of the central citrus area of the state. Its general characteristics are: usually sandy throughout the profile, although it may contain a small amount of clay at varying depth; surface three to four inches of brownish-gray, fine sand, with the subsoil of yellow fine sand; water table very low most of the time, although during the rainy season it may temporarily be high; soil reaction (acidity) under natural conditions ranging from pH 4.8 to 5.4, but under good cultural practices in citrus groves usually maintained at pH 5.5–6.5 or even slightly higher; and organic matter very low (1–2 percent), producing a low exchange capacity for mineral nutrient elements.

The main advantages possessed by the well-drained soils are good water drainage, good air drainage, and good depth for root development. Trouble is seldom encountered from waterlogging of these soils, although drainage may sometimes be slow because of compacted soil layers; usually drainage is only too good, resulting in deficient supplies of soil moisture. Although these soils are relatively frost-free because of their elevation, "frost pockets" frequently are present in the low areas between hills and must be avoided in planting. Soil uniformity, lack of hardpan, and generally low water table allow for deep, well-ramified root systems. Such an extensive rooting habit enables the tree to overcome to a considerable extent the handicaps of the low ability of these soils to hold water and nutrient elements. Deep, well-branched root systems enable trees to attain standard size and enjoy long life.

The disadvantages of these well-drained soils lie in their initial low level of mineral nutrients and organic matter and their small ability to hold water and the mineral elements applied as fertilizers. Excessive leaching through the centuries, together with the low base-exchange capacity, is responsible for the low nutrient level in the soil. Exchange capacity is based on the relative amounts of clay and organic matter in the soil, and both are low in these soils. The low content of the same substances reduces the ability of these soils to hold water, too. When clay occurs close to the surface, the groves respond far better to fertilizer applications than when it is present deep down or not at all. Any program of fertilization must take into account this low exchange capacity. As suggested above, development of a root system that occupies the soil very thoroughly to a good depth can overcome these disadvantages to a remarkable degree.

2. *The poorly drained soils of the coastal areas.*—The low hammock lands are found principally along the east and west coasts, although they also occur in isolated areas in the central portion of the state. They are represented by the Myakka, Oldsmar, Immokalee, Riviera, Winder, and other series. The first three soils are usually quite acidic and have an acidic hardpan. Riviera and Winder are similar, but they may occasionally have marl in the profile, making them somewhat less acidic. The organic matter content is high, ranging from 3 to 8 percent. Usually the water table is close to the surface, and in the natural state of these soils it may often be above the soil surface. They must be drained and bedded before they can be used for citrus planting.

The principal advantages of these soils are their high natural nutrient supply, their high base-exchange capacity, and their good water supply. The high exchange capacity permits better utilization by the trees of the nutrient elements present or added in fertilizer to the acid, surface layer. This is reflected in the great vigor of growth usually exhibited by trees in the early years of the grove life.

Many sites with some of these soils also have disadvantages for use in citrus groves, among them: poor air drainage, poor water drainage, shallow depth with small possible root volume, and occasional alkalinity of the subsoil. Although the soils of this type used for citrus planting are usually located geographically where frost hazard is relatively small, they are by no means free from frost and their low elevation does not allow for compensating air drainage. Ditching systems are absolutely necessary for these soils and will take care of normal problems of water drainage. In times of very heavy rainfall, however, such as may occur in the hurricane season, the ability of the ditching system to remove excess water rapidly may be exceeded. Pumping equipment may be needed to supplement the ditches, for excess water must not be allowed to stand long on the grove; and costs of removing this water add greatly to total production costs. Political subdivisions, set up as "drainage districts" supported by taxes, have long been established on the east coast to handle the area drainage into which water from individual groves is pumped. Stringent regulations now in place in most areas greatly restrict discharge rates. Therefore a holding pond or basin must be constructed so that water may be discharged in a controlled manner so as not to exceed the rates allowed.

Shallow depth to water table means that roots can only be formed to a shallow depth also, and thus only a small volume of soil is available for storing available water. In periods of drought, the moisture supply to root depth is quickly exhausted, so that these soils are "droughty" in spite of their high water table. Irrigation water must be applied in small amounts frequently, which makes its application more expensive than on the deep, well-drained soils.

The alkalinity of the subsoil in some sites renders unavailable to the tree many of the mineral elements of the micronutrient group. Copper, zinc, iron, manganese, and boron decrease in availability as the soil pH changes from acid to basic. Potassium and magnesium must be present in greater amounts before the tree can get an adequate supply because of the effect of the high calcium content of the subsoil. This situation has made it necessary for the grower to supply most of the above micronutrients as sprays—the nutritional spray program—because they are more readily absorbed through the leaves than through the roots in these soils.

As the result of the shallow root system and erratic soil moisture supply, sometimes accentuated by a hardpan layer, citrus trees tend to be somewhat stunted in size and short-lived on these soils and to produce low yields. Experimental work on the east coast has indicated that the root systems of citrus trees are often further restricted by temporarily high water tables. These prevent the efficient use of the maximum theoretical depth for rooting, which is already shallow. Practices that lower the water table and increase the depth available for root development on these soils will usually return more from the investment than any other practices that the grower may undertake.

3. *The flatwood and marsh soils of central and south Florida.*—The flatwood soils and associated swamp soils are found in any area of the citrus belt as soon as one leaves the elevated central Ridge. For years, these soils were used for open range of cattle and hogs; then, improved pastures were developed. They were considered quite unsuited for citrus plantings in general. Typical soil

types in the area include Myakka, Immokalee, Oldsmar, Pineda, and Wabasso, among others.

However, as urban and suburban populations have increased during the last two decades, a premium has been placed on the well-drained soil with expansion of existing communities and development of new population centers and urban sprawls. There appears to be no end in sight to the influx of new residents into the state. This has forced the new plantings of citrus onto a whole range of soil types, acid and alkaline in reaction and with varying degrees of drainage, for which there is no long-term commercial experience. With the establishment of drainage districts or large-scale area drainage by citrus corporations, and the installation of ditches, dikes, and low-pressure pumps of high volume, it is possible to provide artificially a drainage not present naturally.

Groves are planted on single- or multiple-row beds; spodic or hardpan layers are sometimes broken up by deep plowing or use of a dragline; limestone is incorporated in those soils with acid reaction. Water table wells, open-ended pipes seated on pervious gravel, are placed across the beds in various locations within the grove to determine the action of subsurface water. Aside from problems with high water levels, accumulation of sulfides due to aeration impairment has sometimes been serious.

4. *The oolitic limestone soils.*—One soil series in particular, Rockdale, occurs in Dade County and is extensively used for groves of various citrus fruits (especially limes) and for avocados and mangos. A very shallow layer of clay or sand overlies a very porous limestone formed by the cementing together of the shells of tiny marine organisms. To provide adequate depth for root development, this oolite must be broken up by heavy scarifying plows. Although the surface is not many feet above the water table in winter, the roots can penetrate a few feet at most and trees easily suffer from drought in the dry season. In summer, the water may be above the surface for some time in periods of very heavy rainfall, for while the soil is porous, drainage is slow because all of the land is near sea level.

In the early period of citrus growing in Florida, the grower could select land from observations on the native flora. Beginning about 1930 this was no longer feasible in most areas because the native vegetation had been cut off, and the grower has used soil types and natural drainage as guides in selecting grove sites. Since about 1950 there has not been enough land with naturally good drainage to take care of expanding demand, and the grower must now expect to incur greater expense for land preparation than formerly in developing new plantings. Utilization of artificially drained soil means greater initial capital outlay, greater operating expense to maintain good drainage, and greater vigilance on the part of the grower to guard against high water table and cold.

Factors of Importance in Choosing Soils for Citrus Planting

Several factors should be considered in appraising a given site for suitability for citrus planting. Two of them, water drainage and air drainage, are of major importance, and a third one, depth for rooting, may be closely related to the first two.

No single factor is more important than water drainage, for any accumulation of free water in the root zone results in poor aeration of the absorbing rootlets, causing impaired ability to absorb water and nutrients. If long continued, this condition will cause progressive injury and death of the roots, leading to decreased tree vigor. Such trees are short-lived. Water damage may be *chronic,* affecting the tree throughout its life, or *acute,* affecting the tree only for a brief period due to temporary lack of water drainage. Poor drainage also reduces the resistance of the roots to infection by foot rot and other soil-borne diseases.

Good air drainage is increasingly important as winter minima become lower, that is, as one goes northward up the peninsula or inward from the Atlantic seaboard. Low-lying soils are usually colder than elevated soils because there is no place for cold air to drain away to. Cold pockets—closed valleys in the hilly areas—are always hazardous planting sites because on frosty nights cold air flows down into them from the adjacent elevated areas, forcing the warm air up above tree height. After a severe cold wave there is usually visible a bench line around the sides of such a pocket, below which trees are damaged and above which they are undamaged.

Deep, well-drained soils with no impervious layers allow good depth for root development, which tends to produce trees of standard size, heavy fruit production, and long life. Conversely, shallow soils, whether shallow because of hardpan layers or high water tables, limit the size, bearing capacity, and life of citrus trees.

If a site satisfies the above three criteria, then attention may well be given to such factors of secondary importance as water-holding capacity, nutrient supply, and soil reaction. To the extent that a given soil ranks high in regard to favorable levels of these factors, it will permit lower costs of operation by the grower to achieve the same degree of vigor and productiveness.

Water-holding capacity is influenced by the texture (particle size) of the soil and especially by the content of colloidal material such as clay and organic matter. In addition, the volume (depth) of soil through which roots can ramify plays an important role. Each soil has a characteristic *field capacity* (the percentage of soil moisture remaining after saturation and free drainage) and *wilting percentage* (the amount of moisture remaining after plants have reduced the water content until they have become permanently wilted). The difference between these two percentages represents the *available water* that can readily be used by the plant. The higher the percentage of available water, the greater the supply in each foot of soil for tree use; and the greater the depth of the soil, the greater the total reservoir of water to sustain the tree in droughts. The amount of available water in a given depth of soil can be computed in inches of water, equivalent to inches of rainfall, and as such gives a valuable clue to whether or not there is need for irrigation during periods of extended drought.

The nutrient supply in most of the soils used for citrus groves in Florida does not vary greatly in the natural state because these sandy soils have been leached by high rainfall for millennia and all have a very low level. However, soils of relatively high organic content have a somewhat greater original supply of nutrients than those of very low organic content. More important is the fact that soils of high water-holding capacity—those with relatively high content of clay and organic colloids—also hold mineral nutrients applied as fertilizers against loss by leaching much more effectively than soils low in colloids.

Florida soils are classified as acid or alkaline in reaction, a condition customarily expressed on a scale of pH units where 7.0 represents the neutral reaction, values below 7 indicate increasing acidity, and values above 7 increasing alkalinity. The most favorable reaction for citrus trees on sandy soils is around pH 6.5, or slightly acid conditions. Most sandy soils are naturally more acid than this and require periodic applications of lime to maintain the desired reaction. Most alkaline soils of Florida cannot be acidified to reach this desired pH level, and require certain specialized management practices in compensation, notably in the application of microelements made unavailable by the alkaline reaction. In the case of moderately alkaline soils, regular application of acidic fertilizer materials will help to reduce soil pH over the long term.

Areas of Citrus Production in Florida

The first citrus plantings were made in the St. Augustine area
around 1565 at the time of the establishment of that settlement.
As the peninsula became populated, citrus seedlings were spread
throughout the state. Citrus growing expanded from home
orchards of seedlings and budlings to commercial acreages of
budded trees. The citrus industry of Florida, in 1890, comprised
approximately 114,800 acres with the ten leading counties in the
following order: Orange, Alachua, Volusia, Marion, Lake, Putnam,
Hillsborough, Pasco, Brevard, and Polk. Alachua County accounted for about one-third of the citrus production of 1889–90.
Production increased to an estimated 6,000,000 box production for
1894–95. Then, in December 1894, a freeze occurred that defoliated the trees; a second freeze, on 6 February 1895, killed most
of the trees. Acreage was reduced to 48,200 acres in 1895, of
which 97 percent was of nonbearing trees. Orange, Lake, and
Brevard counties accounted for over one-half of the acreage remaining after the freezes. Polk County, which later became the
leading county, was tenth in the county list; the growers had yet
to plant Polk County's large expanse of rolling, sandy soils. A cold
wave in February 1899 brought some of the lowest temperatures
experienced in the state and produced major damage to the industry. These freezes proved the necessity of moving the industry
southward to locations less vulnerable to low winter temperatures.

During the Florida land boom of 1922–28, large-scale plantings
were made in the central parts of the state and along the east
coast and west coast. These set the pattern of distribution of the
industry (as was discussed in the first edition) for many years.
Much of this boom-developed acreage received little attention, and
some was forced into a semiabandoned condition during the long
depression of the 1930s. However, this depressed period produced
leaders in research and production to whom credit must be given
for the continued health of the industry.

Further plantings were made, and abandoned acreages were
brought back to productive condition, with the resumption of
demand for citrus during the 1940s. By 1955 there were 522,000
acres of citrus; the leading counties were Polk, Lake, Orange,
Hillsborough, St. Lucie, Pasco, Indian River, Highlands, Brevard,
and Volusia.

However, the great influx of new residents from the north beginning in the 1950s has exerted a strong influence on the distribution and dominance of the industry. These new settlers began to occupy the best-drained areas along the coasts and in the central portions of the state; counties such as Orange and Pinellas began to lose many acres of citrus to the urbanites; land values and taxes began to increase to the economic detriment of citrus production. Citrus plantings were forced into less desirable locations. An attempt was made to expand citrus plantings along the upper west coast, but the winters of 1957–58 and 1962–63, with their severe freezes, aborted this move.

Therefore, the second great move was to the south onto soils that had earlier been avoided because of drainage problems. This move started in earnest following the 1962 freeze and reached a climax in 1969, at which time approximately half of the citrus acreage (and an even greater percentage of citrus trees due to closer planting schemes) was land of varying degrees of impeded drainage. These mineral soils of the flatwoods and marshes of central and south Florida presented to the growers and research workers many new problems quite distinct from those of the older areas, for which solutions had been found through years of research and commercial experience. By 1969 the better soils with drainage capability had been occupied, slowing the tempo of plantings. Furthermore, the federal income tax reforms of 1969 forced the capitalization of all expenditures during the first four years of a new planting, making such planting far less desirable to developers and speculators. Although new plantings will continue to be made, these were on a reduced scale until after the freezes of the early 1980s.

During the 1960s expansion of the industry, large acreages of citrus were planted in the flatwood areas of the Indian River counties of Brevard, Indian River, St. Lucie, Martin, and Palm Beach, and in the flatwood soils of counties in the southern part of the peninsula. By the late 1960s, the total acreage of citrus had reached almost 1,000,000. However, in the early 1970s, the new plantings did not keep pace with removals so that in 1971 there were approximately 877,000 acres with the principal counties being: Polk, Lake, St. Lucie, Orange, Indian River, Hardee, Hillsborough, Martin, Highlands, and Pasco. The freezes of December 1983, 1985, and 1989 devastated the northern citrus areas, and plantings increased tremendously, especially in southwest and southeast Florida.

The general citrus-growing portion of Florida lies within the limits bounded on the north by a line through McIntosh and Palatka with small extensions northward along the St. Johns River (although this area is sparsely planted after the freezes of the 1980s) and on the south by the Everglades with extensions on the east coast to Homestead and on the west coast to Naples. The principal area of lime production is along the lower east coast and southern part of the Ridge; that of lemons, the southern third of the peninsula and particularly Palm Beach, Martin, and Lee counties.

Approximately thirty of the sixty-seven counties grow and ship citrus fruits in commercial quantities and all of them lie within the area described above. To the north, winter temperatures limit commercial growing of citrus trees while counties at the southern limit frequently find either urban competition or extremely poor soil drainage disadvantageous. The citrus crop is of major economic importance in many of these thirty counties and, by far, the leading source of income in some. Polk, Lake, and Orange counties, in the center of the state, were for years the three leading producers. However, with increased plantings beginning in 1959 in the western portions of the counties, and the 1983–89 freezes, St. Lucie and Indian River have come into prominence. Tables 4-1 and 4-2 show how counties compare in acreage and production of citrus.

Environmental conditions, adaptation of stocks and scions, general cultural practices, and marketing opportunities vary considerably in different parts of the commercial citrus belt. The prospective investor in grove properties should study these factors in the area of interest. The investor may obtain help from established growers and production managers, IFAS faculty in extension and research centers, and representatives of allied industries and marketing agencies. Long experience has shown the value of consideration of land values and taxes, availability of production and market services, and general levels of production costs and returns. Studies of climatic, soil, and biotic conditions, stock and scion selections, and general conditions of grove properties with respect to tree size for age, uniformity of tree size, regularity of plantings, and incidences of inherent problems such as nematodes, viruses, frosts and freezes, soil drainage, etc., will be most valuable for the person who will be intimately involved in the industry and especially for the person in a managerial position. When soil drainage presents a problem, one must consider area drainage (through drainage district or otherwise) in order to

Table 4-1.
Citrus-producing counties of Florida
(acreage by county and type of fruit as of 1988)

County	Oranges	Grapefruit	Specialty fruit[a]	Total
Polk	88,036	14,639	5,871	108,546
St. Lucie	44,417	39,359	5,117	88,893
Indian River	29,645	33,522	1,995	65,162
Hendry	45,363	5,959	3,631	54,953
Highlands	42,902	3,564	3,103	48,569
Hardee	43,910	833	1,155	45,898
DeSoto	41,000	1,151	992	43,143
Martin	34,462	5,132	1,327	40,921
Lake	22,553	1,254	2,421	26,228
Hillsborough	23,503	989	1,015	25,507
Manatee	16,013	1,956	810	18,779
Orange	15,402	497	1,457	17,356
Collier	15,164	1,576	569	17,309
Palm Beach	9,693	3,018	2,176	14,887
Osceola	12,196	1,044	874	14,114
Brevard	8,916	2,190	535	11,641
Pasco	8,927	251	193	9,371
Charlotte	8,675	475	195	9,345
Okeechobee	7,016	854	254	8,124
Lee	7,076	520	651	8,247
Dade	0	0	6,308	6,308
Glades	6,001	148	86	6,235
Sarasota	1,633	225	71	1,929
Seminole	1,252	8	180	1,440
Volusia	1,185	159	35	1,379
Marion	1,053	42	114	1,209
Broward	593	131	40	764
Hernando	672	1	22	695
Pinellas	143	99	34	276
Citrus	182	2	7	191
Sumter	108	8	0	116
Putnam	46	0	0	46
Total	536,737	119,606	41,238	697,581

SOURCE: Florida Agricultural Statistics Service, *Citrus Summary, 1988–89.*

a. Includes limes and lemons.

Table 4-2.
Citrus crops in Florida by counties for 1988-89[a]
(in thousands of boxes)

County	Oranges	Grapefruit	Tangerines and hybrids[b]	Total
Polk	28,336	8,080	2,427	38,843
St. Lucie	10,389	15,883	1,427	27,699
Indian River	7,065	14,963	617	22,645
Highlands	13,068	2,210	1,207	16,485
Hardee	14,577	314	359	15,250
Hendry	10,727	3,272	540	14,539
DeSoto	12,587	437	368	13,392
Martin	9,234	2,554	355	12,143
Hillsborough	8,102	469	353	8,924
Manatee	4,757	868	357	5,982
Palm Beach	2,932	1,699	521	5,152
Osceola	3,805	481	324	4,610
Orange	3,862	210	523	4,595
Lake	2,915	341	729	3,985
Brevard	2,767	920	185	3,872
Collier	2,444	802	112	3,358
Charlotte	2,268	225	55	2,548
Okeechobee	1,452	391	51	1,894
Lee	1,628	213	45	1,886
Glades	1,678	89	23	1,790
Pasco	645	22	42	709
Sarasota	433	142	41	616
Seminole	310	4	68	382
Volusia	234	65	10	309
Broward	121	38	9	168
Pinellas	46	41	15	102
Other[b]	281	17	7	242
Total	146,600	54,750	10,770	212,120

SOURCE: Florida Agricultural Statistics, Citrus Summary, *1988–89.*
a. Excludes limes and lemons.
b. Citrus, Hernando, Marion, Putnam, and Sumter counties.

understand the drainage of a particular site or location. There are areas of better soils that could likely produce citrus successfully if provision for drainage and cold protection is considered.

In the first edition, six areas of production were discussed: the Indian River, the lower east coast, the lower west coast, the upper west coast, the north central, and the south central. These had developed from 1920 to 1960 through the community of interest of growers and the similarity of problems in each of the areas. The cohesiveness of these areas has changed considerably in the last few decades with the change in the distribution of acreage and the expansion of organizations with plantings in various parts of the state.

The Indian River Citrus Area is defined by state law (Acts of 1941), which specifies that the name may be used only for fruit grown on land adjacent to the Indian River, and lying totally within the area described by law, along the east coast. It includes all or part of Brevard, Indian River, St. Lucie, Martin, Volusia, and Palm Beach counties. Since fruit grown in this area, especially grapefruit, has a recognized superiority on the market, as evidenced by demand and prices, it is accorded separate regulations under the Marketing Agreement. Fruit grown in all other sections of the state is designated as "interior fruit" for purposes of marketing in the fresh-fruit channels of trade.

Figure 4-3 delineates five citrus-producing areas as defined by the Florida Agricultural Statistics Service for recording acreage and production of citrus each year: the Indian River District, Southern, Central, Western, and Northern areas. The freezes of the mid-1980s killed virtually all the citrus grown in Alachua, Putnam, Marion, Citrus, and Hernando counties, but there is some interest in limited replanting in the warmer locations of these areas.

County lines, as political boundaries, leave much to be desired in describing areas of similar climatic, soil, and biotic environments. One area grades almost imperceptibly into another, and within any area there will be islands of differences. Note that the East Coast Area includes all of the Indian River Citrus Area except for southeastern Volusia County. The East Coast, Upper Interior, and West Coast areas present few extreme differences within their boundaries, but the Lower Interior Area includes the well-drained counties of Polk and Highlands among counties that are generally poorly drained. Extensive planting has taken place during the late 1970s and 1980s in the southwest counties of

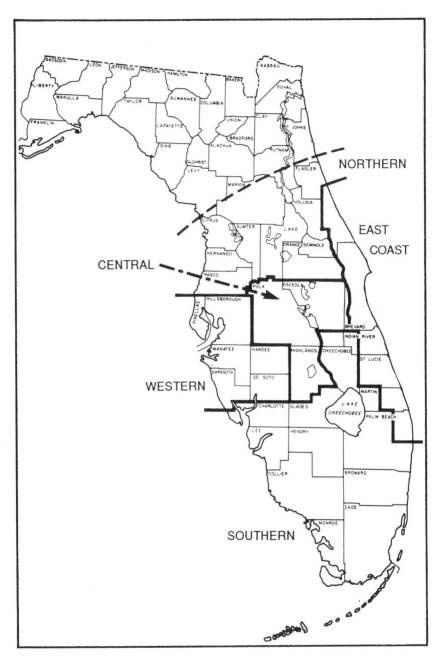

Figure 4-3. Five citrus-producing areas of Florida

Collier, Hendry, and others, which is reflected in the acreages shown in table 4-1. The actual citrus-producing belt of Florida, by legal designation, extends north and west to the Suwannee River.

The study of the area is a most valuable exercise. However, each particular site or location within an area presents its unique set of conditions, ranging from best to poorest of the area, which determine its value to the investor. Once satisfied with the general conditions of the area, the investor will seek the best of these items: natural cold protection; soil depth and drainage; land or grove costs (original, preparation, and continuing costs especially when concerned with soil drainage); and tax structure. Small differences with respect to conveniences may be considered as plus or minus factors but should never take precedence over the first four in the consideration of the site. Purchasers must have in mind their long-term objectives as an investment for citrus growing or for land speculation possibilities or both, which will greatly assist them in making a proper choice.

5 /
Planting Citrus Trees

Selection of the Grove Site

The first step toward planting a citrus grove is the selection of a suitable location. In view of the fact that satisfactory planting sites for citrus in Florida are becoming less available, the prospective citrus grower may often be concerned with the purchase of an existing grove. It should, therefore, be stressed that the following discussion applies, with similar effect, to the site already occupied by trees.

Two sets of factors are of dominant importance to the future economic well-being of the enterprise. The first of these relates to land values and the tax base. While investors are interested in the potential increase in land value in future years, they will restrict their search to areas that are still predominantly agricultural to avail themselves of the community of interests of other citrus growers. Urban expansion results in zoning changes and increased tax burdens for services that often render no advantage to the citrus enterprise. The matters of the total investment in view of increasing property values and taxation require the investor's keen judgment in order to realize optimum competitive economic returns.

The second set of factors are those of horticultural importance to the growing of the crop. Predominant are the need for natural protection against low winter temperatures and good soil drainage. Depth for rooting is essentially related to soil drainage in the Florida citrus belt. Other considerations are discussed below that will help to maintain the soundness of the enterprise.

Cold Protection

Natural protection from cold will vary from area to area, from section to section within an area, and from one location to another within a section. Each of the citrus areas of the state has its own

120

general range of climatic conditions. Within any area, slight differences in latitude or in proximity to the ocean or the gulf cause differences of several degrees in winter minimal temperatures. At the same latitude or distance from the coast, there will usually be found variations between general locations caused by differences in elevation, vegetation, bodies of water, and so forth. Older growers in any section of the state can point out areas that are, in general, colder than others, even though they appear to be similarly located.

The grove site itself is of particular concern to the prospective grower. Elevation is of prime importance because a site higher than nearby land will allow cold air to drain away on frosty nights. So far as possible a site should be avoided that is in one of the natural air channels followed by cold air masses bringing freezes to the state. Even areas that appear quite flat may have subtle elevation differences that make some parts of the area colder than others. The moderating influence of bodies of water on air temperatures has often been noted. These bodies must be large and deep to exert any marked effect. Usually the southeast side of a large lake is the warmest in a freeze because the coldest winds come from the northwest and are warmed somewhat in passing over the water. The Gulf of Mexico is able to influence temperatures appreciably, but Florida has few lakes large and deep enough to ameliorate the cold air blowing over them. Small lakes, especially if they are shallow, are of no value in warming masses of cold air, but they may still be an asset for cold protection in that they provide a fairly large, level area at low elevation for cold air to drain down to from any surrounding uplands. The compass direction of these lakes from the grove site is unimportant. Grove sites in an area where many groves already exist will receive some cold protection from these established plantings, which may function as windbreaks or may warm cold winds somewhat by artificial heating, to the benefit of any grove site to leeward. An isolated grove in thin, open pine woods is at the mercy of every freeze that descends into Florida.

Appraisal of the desirability of a site can be assisted by careful observations in old groves nearby. Regularity of stand, uniformity of tree size, and presence of frost cankers should be investigated. In areas of irregular topography, cold spots in old groves will be devoid of trees or will have trees showing poor condition. Even where there are not marked differences in topography, the presence of many vacant places in groves or of many replanted trees of different ages may indicate cold problems. Other possible causes for such irregularity should be carefully checked, to be sure whether or not cold is responsible. The grove with satisfactory site is one with uniform height and spread of the trees. Wide fluctuation in these dimensions from one tree to another indicates that some undesirable conditions exist. If low temperatures have influenced these conditions, further study will usually demonstrate a relationship to topographical features. It may sometimes seem that evidences of freeze damage are sufficiently slight to be discounted, but if they can be recognized at all they should be duly considered. The average size for their age of trees of any particular combination of scion and stock, for a given set of soil conditions, is an excellent guide to the possible future productiveness of the grove. If trees are even slightly below normal size because of cold injury, their yields will also be slightly below normal—and profits will be also.

Freezes often produce small areas of dead tissues, known as "frost cankers," on the bark of scaffold branches and trunks. The surrounding living tissues continue to grow and form an advancing front of callus around the edge of the canker. The dead tissues gradually slough off, leaving a depressed area in the bark that remains for some years as mute evidence of past cold damage. There is no way to get rid of them except by cutting off the whole limb, or, until after many years they may be obliterated by natural growth of bark.

The care exercised in the choice of a grove site for natural cold protection is reflected in the later cost of production of the grove. Even at best, "firing" operations add greatly to costs of production and to the administrative load of the operator. If grove heating is not practiced, then there are decreased yields from cold and these again increase the production cost per box of fruit. A site subject to cold injury, no matter in what degree, sets the range of costs per box within which the management can operate.

Proper selection of stock and scion varieties with respect to their cold hardiness can often render a cold site relatively more profitable, but cannot overcome entirely the basic handicap of a poorly chosen site. Likewise it is possible to develop operating programs that can reduce the hazard of cold, but these cannot be expected to compensate completely for the original lack of judgment in site selection. Careful selection of the grove site may provide long-term economic benefits over less satisfactory sites. The long-term nature of the investment must be carefully considered.

Soil Drainage

The greater the depth of soil for root development, the better the response of the trees to production practices: trees will be larger, yields will be greater, production costs per box will be lower, and productive life of the trees will be longer.

The soil series, as explained previously, will give considerable clue to drainage conditions and depth for rooting. The characteristics of the type should be understood as thoroughly as possible. Even if the name of the soil type is known—and usually the County Extension Agent can identify it—a careful appraisal of the particular site should be made. If the grower does not know the soil type, it is even more important that a thorough investigation be made of the nature of the drainage, the presence or absence of a hardpan layer, and any other textural or structural characters of the soil that will have an influence on either water drainage or root penetration.

No citrus tree can be grown successfully where much of the soil volume available for root development is occupied by water. Even if the water table is very close to the surface only for relatively brief periods each year, that location will usually have to be ruled out. Certainly the type of water relations characteristic of hard-pan (spodic layer) soils—wet in summer, dry in winter—will be reflected unfavorably in tree responses and production costs. However, roots will penetrate the pan layer if adequate drainage below the pan is provided. The pan can be broken up by deep plowing or dragline operations.

Most citrus investigators consider that the rooting depth of the soil, to be highly satisfactory, should be from four to six feet; a depth of two feet is considered as the minimum under most circumstances. If the depth of soil for root development is not satisfactory, then the site should be avoided unless it is evident that there are ways in which the depth can be increased. But it must be remembered that such ways of increasing rooting depth as ditching and bedding mean increased capital outlay, and interest on capital investment is part of production cost. Furthermore, there will annually be increased expense for current operations in water removal, including drainage district assessments, ditch cleaning and maintenance, etc., and these add to the total cost of grove operation. Cost of production per box will be increased also because of reduced response of trees to the production program—smaller trees with lower yields, and shorter tree life.

Grove operations may still be profitable, but the prospective grove owner should be aware of the negative factors involved in the use of a poorly drained site.

After satisfying conditions of cold protection and water drainage, the grower should investigate such secondary factors as soil characters other than drainage, facilities for marketing the crop, possibility of other operational problems, and availability of labor.

Soil characters other than drainage include the presence of clay in the soil, the level of natural nutrient supply, the content of organic matter, and the soil reaction. If two sites are equally well drained, then the choice may well depend on the extent to which one of them excels in these respects.

The site should be such that advantage can be taken of several different types of marketing. These include packinghouses, canning and concentrating plants, and gift-fruit stands. Transportation facilities are no longer a concern and paved roads are common in all parts of the citrus belt, yet the cost of hauling fruit to the packinghouse or concentrating plant is still based on the distance it is hauled. When the grove site is quite distant from the point where fruit enters the channels of trade, the grower is under an economic handicap. The type of market for which fruit is grown will determine to no small extent the choice of varieties planted.

Among other operational problems that affect production costs, besides soil characteristics, is control of pests. Most of the insects and diseases affecting citrus trees are present throughout the citrus-growing area of the state, but one or more of them may be a more serious problem in one section than in another. Tristeza virus and spreading-decline nematodes spread naturally from one grove to another. Other things being equal, a grove site adjacent to a grove in which either of these diseases is present would be much less desirable than a site fairly distant from any known infestation.

Labor costs have increased in recent years faster than most other costs of production, and at the same time competition for the labor pools has become more intense. Producers of vegetables, urban developments, the hotel and resort trade, and new factories all compete with the citrus grower and have constantly expanded their labor needs too. Even though the labor supply for grove work may be plentiful during some of the year, competition that interferes with this supply during certain critical periods may be a limiting factor. Such operations as firing during a freeze, irrigating in a spring drought, or applying sprays for critically timed pest control in summer cannot be delayed while additional labor is rounded up.

Much of the operation of a citrus grove calls for unskilled or semiskilled labor only, and in a high-priced market the citrus grower is at a disadvantage. Labor problems often make more demands on the time of the grove manager than any other. The solution of the problem for citrus growers, as for the industrial plant, is to mechanize their operations so far as possible so that fewer, more skilled laborers can be utilized. Marked advances have been made in recent years in mechanization of grove operations such as fertilizing, irrigation, spraying, and pruning, but there still remains the need for a small labor force of unskilled but dependable people. Further reduction is quite possible for grove heating, chemical control of weeds, and even for harvesting. So long as unskilled labor is a necessity, the grove operator in a community where competition has bid up the wage scale above that in other areas is at an economic disadvantage.

In summary, it must be remembered when selecting a grove site that citrus trees must occupy the same ground for many years to be profitable, and the crop must mature on the trees each year. Vegetable growers may lose a crop one year and recoup their loss the following year, but citrus growers must count on a regular crop every year. To the extent that they lose an occasional crop from cold or wind, they are losing profits permanently, and there is a limit to how many such losses they can take and still remain solvent. The level of crop production is determined at planting time by the site selected and the stocks and scion varieties chosen for that site. The small, short-lived tree on shallow, poorly drained soil is never an economically productive unit.

Preparing the Grove Site for Planting

Having selected with care a suitable grove site, in accordance with the considerations just set forth, this site must be cleared of all trees and shrubs. All large pieces of roots, and as much of small roots as possible, should be removed from the upper foot or two of soil, and the ground then plowed and harrowed until it presents a smooth, level surface. If the grove site itself is on a slope and it is considered desirable to plant on contoured benches, their preparation must await decision on planting distances to be used.

Drainage should be considered at this point for any site in a poorly drained area. Surveys will determine the slope of the land for proper runoff of surface water. Most groves requiring drainage are planted today on double-row beds with water furrows between beds at 50- to 55-foot intervals. The water furrows move accumulated water to ditches at the ends of the beds. Commonly, the beds are one quarter of a mile (1,320 feet) in length. The ditches carrying the water from the furrows then run to larger and larger channels until the water is moved off-site. Spoil removed from the ditches is usually built up along the side of the ditches to construct roadways which facilitate movement within the grove.

Drainage pipes are often used within the grove either as a substitute to water furrows or to further enhance drainage within the beds. Various types of perforated plastic pipes are buried beneath the soil surface sloping down to lateral ditches at the ends of the beds. Water enters the pipes through the holes throughout the length of the pipe, then runs down the slope to the ditches.

Means should be considered to allow rapid drainage during periods of heavy rains; at the same time, accessibility of water for irrigation during dry periods must be planned. Permits from all appropriate agencies must be obtained before grove construction commences. These are important considerations prior to the planting operation; consultations with extension personnel, engineers, and horticulturists may result in the necessity of slightly higher preparation costs but will greatly increase the future profitability of the enterprise. Such consultations are especially important in development of bedded groves since water control is the key to the success of the grove operation.

Choice of a Planting System

The planting system refers to the regular arrangement of trees on the land. Formerly several different systems were in vogue, each with its loyal advocates, such as rectangular, hexagonal, triangular, and quincunx. As with other orchard fruits, this former diversity has resolved itself into almost exclusive use of the rectangular system for citrus trees. Some of the other systems permitted planting of more trees per acre for a given spacing, but they required cultivation and spraying to be done along diagonals through the grove, which was troublesome and confusing when varieties were set in rows parallel to the boundaries of the grove.

The rectangular system has the trees at the intersections of lines that cross at right angles, and the rectangles may be square or oblong. The system is easy to lay out, to understand, and to use in grove operations. Such groves can be cultivated in two directions easily, and varieties in them can be planted in compact blocks of rows, making it easy to keep track of them in spraying or harvesting. Planting on the square was formerly by far the most common practice, but today it is desired to have trees closer in one direction than the other. In this case, care must be taken to have the wider middles the more easily accessible ones, for when the trees reach some size, they will have to be the middles used for nearly all work.

The hedgerow system of planting was adopted by some of the early growers of citrus in Florida. It permitted planting the largest number of permanent trees per acre in a satisfactory pattern for commercial grove operation; space between the rows allowed equipment movement, and space between the trees in the row was kept at a minimum. While trees were small and not crowded, higher yields were possible. This system required extremely good fertilizer and irrigation practices, especially on sandy soils low in organic matter, to effect satisfactory results; however, the problem of crowding in later years forced the general abandonment of the hedgerow system. Increased interest in early production, sophisticated pruning machinery, and more intense production management have brought about a revival of interest in hedgerows. Tree density has increased rapidly over the years from an average of around 70 trees per acre to 140 or more trees per acre. Some growers are planting 200 or even more trees to an acre.

In the contour system, the trees are planted in rows along lines of equal elevation or contours. Its use is limited to slopes steep enough for soil erosion to be a serious problem by conventional planting systems. If slopes are so steep that it is difficult to drive machinery along the contour lines, it may be necessary to make beds several feet wide for planting, so that machines can run on nearly level ground. Laying out contours requires surveying skill and takes much more time than laying out a rectangular system. A contour planting is harder to work and to understand, and the rows along contours will often not all have the same number of trees. The system is rarely seen in Florida and should never be attempted unless it seems absolutely necessary for erosion control. Other methods of controlling soil erosion should be given careful consideration before deciding to plant on contours.

Double planting of the various systems came into vogue in the

1940s to allow the best utilization of land while the trees were small during the early years of grove life. It was a means of setting twice as many trees as usual on one axis in a standard planting with the anticipation of removing the alternate trees as soon as they began to crowd. It did not constitute a distinct system but was simply a short-term expedient. In many cases, tree removal was delayed by first cutting back the alternate trees before finally removing them to allow room for the permanent ones. Quite fortunately, the hedging practices were developed in the 1950s; tree size was controlled to space, permitting many of these double-set groves to continue as viable plantings without tree removal.

Spacing of Trees

Regardless of the planting system used, it is necessary to decide how far apart trees are to be placed. Spacing was originally determined chiefly by the size to which the trees were expected to grow. Trees that are small by nature or that would remain small because of poor soil conditions would be spaced more closely than trees that naturally reach large size and are growing in favorable soil.

Under similar conditions, grapefruit trees grow much larger than orange trees, which in turn exceed the size of lime trees. In the early days of the citrus industry, average spacing in the row for the various kinds of citrus trees was: kumquats, ten to twelve feet; satsumas, limes, and lemons, fifteen to twenty feet; oranges and mandarins (except satsumas), twenty to twenty-five feet; and grapefruit, thirty to thirty-five feet. It was, however, desirable in commercial groves to have the work middles at least twenty-five feet in width in order to be able to use mechanized equipment such as sprayers, fertilizer distributors, and picking trucks.

These early plantings developed into canopied groves. The bottom branches died out as a result of shading and the fruit crop was borne by a canopy of branches overhead. Fruit was difficult to harvest, and yields were limited by the scant amount of fruiting wood.

A larger number of trees per acre does not necessarily produce a larger yield per acre (except during the early years of production), but planting too few trees to utilize soil and light efficiently is certainly uneconomical use of space. During the Florida boom of the 1920s, common spacings, on the square system, were twenty-five by twenty-five feet and thirty by thirty feet, giving, respectively, about seventy and forty-eight trees per acre. On deep, well-drained soils, twenty-five by twenty-five feet became too close eventually for ease of operations even for oranges; the same number of trees per acre was possible by use of twenty by thirty spacing to get a better work middle by crowding the trees slightly in the row. There was a suggestion in the early 1940s that the best spacing for grapefruit trees would be thirty-five by thirty-five feet, which would allow only thirty-five trees per acre.

The citrus grower, as well as the grower of other fruits, has long been troubled by this problem of how to use the grove space more fully while the trees are young without having them too crowded at maturity. The solution used during the 1940s was double planting (see above). In theory, this close initial planting and later removal of alternate trees after a few crops was a good solution. It was feasible to transplant the temporary trees to a new grove site if further plantings were being made. Growers, however, postponed as long as possible the removal of the nonpermanent trees because they were producing valuable crops; usually thinning operations were put off until the permanent trees had suffered considerable damage from crowding. A gradual thinning gave some promise. Alternate trees were pruned sufficiently to leave a two-foot clear space between them and their permanent neighbors. Each year these same alternates could be further headed back so that they never shaded the permanent trees. After twelve to fifteen years in a fifteen by twenty-five planting, they had been reduced to skeletons and could be removed entirely, leaving the unchecked permanent trees spaced thirty by twenty-five feet. Too often growers refused to cut into any good tree and resisted the efforts of production managers to do so. Therefore, it became apparent that it was better to sacrifice a little income during the early years of grove life, because trees were widely spaced, than to gain the extra return from close spacing at the expense of misshapen trees of poor bearing habit in the mature grove, because the interplanted trees were left too long in double plantings.

After much fumbling, the brilliant idea of hedging began as a practice in the 1950s. It began as a remedial operation simply for the safe operation of equipment through the groves. It proved, however, to be a means for controlling tree size to space with maximum production per acre for closely spaced groves, with many advantages and few disadvantages, as discussed in chapter 10. Today, hedging is considered to be a maintenance operation.

Staking the Tree Locations

After planting system and spacing have been determined, the tree locations may be marked by stakes. Boundary rows are first laid out, and then parallel rows established across the field. Once the tree locations are staked on two sides of a field by careful measurement, and perhaps a central row similarly measured and staked, the rest of the locations can be quickly sighted in and staked. Sometimes the tree positions are marked initially by cross-hatching the ground by means of an outrider on a tractor, with the trees set where the lines intersect. Other methods have been used, any one of which is satisfactory provided the tree locations are in ordered rows.

The Transplanting Operation

Selection of Trees in the Nursery

The question of the most desirable size and age of tree to plant still remains for consideration even though the decision as to stock and scion variety has long since been made. Trees formerly offered by Florida citrus nurseries were one-year buds on three-year stocks; i.e., the stock was a two-year-old seedling when budded, and the budling is a year old at digging. Such a tree is a one-year-old by nursery convention, which disregards age of the stock. A desirable one-year tree would "caliper" (i.e., have a diameter at a point a couple of inches above the bud union) at least one-half inch, and five-eighths inch is better. The pruning cut made in removing the stock above the bud should have healed over and be hardly noticeable, and the trunk should be straight. Such a one-year tree is probably the best one to buy since it shows good nursery care and gives evidence of having made vigorous growth as a budling. Trees such as these are still available, but are often much smaller than noted. This is due to less time in the field under more intense cultivation. Greenhouse-produced trees are also available and these are considerably smaller than the previously described field-grown trees. These greenhouse-produced trees are sold in a pot or plastic sleeve and may be only one year from seed, due to the fact that the plant was grown intensively under controlled climate conditions and given optimum care.

Price is a fairly good indication of tree value if one is dealing with a reliable nurseryman, and one often gets what one pays for. Nursery trees of unusual vigor, say three-fourths-inch caliper for one-year budlings, bring a higher price because they will grow faster in the grove than smaller trees. Trees that have been neglected in the nursery or have been improperly handled (especially if they have been dug with less than the minimum length taproot, twelve inches) are very costly trees in the long run though bought at bargain-counter prices. Greenhouse-produced trees should be vigorous with a good root system yet not held until the root system has been compromised by crowding. The cost of the trees is a rather small item in the total cost of bringing a grove into production, and this is a very poor place to economize. Current market prices for good nursery trees can easily be ascertained by reading the advertisements in citrus magazines, remembering that the price per tree in small lots will always be a little higher than it is in large quantities.

The only assurance that growers have as to variety and stocks, so that they are certain to get what they think they are buying, is in the integrity and care of the nurseryman. Florida has many citrus nurseries that have established and are careful to maintain a good reputation for nursery trees of good quality and assured name. The transient nurseryman may do as good a job, but the grower does well to investigate carefully before buying from an unknown source.

Trees propagated by nurseries with plant material registered by the Citrus Budwood Registration Bureau of the Florida Department of Agriculture and Consumer Services can be obtained free of psorosis, the most damaging virus of the early citrus plantings in Florida. Freedom from certain other viruses, propagable disorders, and abnormal genetic characteristics are possible in many varieties. Specific clones of most popular cultivars are now available and are designated by numbers assigned in the Budwood Registration Program. These are the "best of the best" as they have been selected over the years as being the best representatives of all the trees in the program. Information on the most desirable clones is available from the Budwood Registration Office or local County Extension Agents. The cost of such trees is higher than it is for trees from unregistered stock due to the extra efforts of the nurserymen, but this additional cost has proved to be an excellent investment. Repayment will come through longer periods of prime yield life of such high-quality trees.

Handling and Delivery of Nursery Trees

The handling of nursery trees will be quite different if one compares bare-root plants to those produced in containers. Each type will be examined separately, beginning with bare-root, in the text that follows.

The first step in preparing bare-root nursery trees for transplanting is to prune the top. Much of the root system will be lost in digging, and this decreased capacity for absorbing water requires a decrease in demand of water by the top.

The technique of digging nursery trees has already been given in chapter 3. Covering the tops with a moisture-retaining material is especially important if the trees are transported some distance by truck before planting. If it is necessary to delay planting after trees reach the grove site, they may be held for several days by "heeling them in," that is, by making a shallow trench and placing the roots in it while the trunk is inclined at an angle of 60 degrees or so from the vertical. The roots are covered with soil that must be kept moist. It is always better, however, to get trees into their permanent locations in the grove the day they are dug.

Trees produced under controlled environment (greenhouse) conditions are sold in a container (usually with a stake in place), and are simply collected and transported in a vehicle designed for that purpose to the grove site for the planting operation. Although these plants are smaller than a typical bare-root tree, the added pots and soil constitute considerable bulk, making transportation a little more difficult.

Some growers have been growing trees in bushel hampers for use in replacing nursery trees that fail to survive transplanting. The cost per tree is considerably greater than for the usual nursery trees, but there is no loss of roots or top when transplanting these hamper-grown trees. Such trees require less maintenance during the first year. Furthermore, resetting can be done later in the spring than with bare-rooted transplants. Fresh nursery trees would be many weeks behind the rest of the planting in getting started, whereas these container-grown trees are fully as advanced in growth as the earlier planted majority, and thus a more uniform grove is possible.

Season of Planting

Citrus trees in Florida are probably best planted during the winter months (December–February) while the trees are most fully

dormant. Roots are able to start regenerating an absorbing system before the buds push out into shoots because soil temperatures are higher at this season than air temperatures. By the time new leaves are present and demanding water, a new set of absorbing rootlets is ready to meet the demand. Such trees also have the longest possible growing season, but may face considerable risk from cold injury in some locations in some seasons. Spring plantings (March–April) are also made with considerable success especially now that irrigation is commonplace. Summer plantings are difficult, although possible. Leaf development tends to precede root development, and the growing season is very short for trees to mature their tissues properly before cold weather.

Fig 5-1. Young citrus tree with fiberglass wrap.

Methods of Planting

Bare-root and container-grown trees will necessarily be handled somewhat differently, but in general if the tree is set in the grove at the same depth at which it grew in the nursery, the roots are well spread out,* the soil is replaced without leaving any air pockets, and sufficient water is supplied to wet thoroughly the whole soil volume occupied by the roots, citrus trees respond well to many methods of planting. The hole may be dug with

---

    * Spreading out the roots of a container-grown tree may seem unusual, but research has shown that removing at least half the soil mix from such trees results in better tree growth. The soil removed exposes young roots to the new soil of the planting site and affords more rapid development of roots, and subsequently, the top of the tree. Soil that is removed is mixed with soil from the planting site. The significance of this operation is due to the great disparity between the highly organic soil mix the containerized tree grew in and the light sandy soil the new tree is set in. This difference in soil type causes interface problems that often results in less than adequate watering even if plants are flooded.

hoe, shovel, or machine; the tree may be set in place with or without use of a planting board; and water may be applied after each of several increments of backfilling or simultaneously with the soil in a "mudding-in" process.

Cost of planting will vary a little from one method to another, but low cost is not economical if the trees do not grow off well.

One method that has proven very satisfactory in commercial practice in the sandy types of soil chiefly found in Florida makes use of the marking stake (or a shortened hoe handle replacing the stake) to make a hole for the taproot, thus assuring that the tree is located accurately. Around this stake a basin is dug to a depth of six inches and a radius of a foot. The new tree is set in place with the taproot vertical in the stake hole and the fibrous roots well spread in the basin. A few shovels of soil are backfilled and soaked with water, then a few more shovels of soil are spread, and more water, and finally the hole is completely filled and a water-retaining ring formed above the ground level. The depth of planting is checked and the last buckets of water poured on. It is considered desirable to apply a total of around ten gallons per tree at planting. In making the backfill, it is desirable to use subsoil (if any was removed) for making the retaining ring. This method is slow, but speed should never substitute for care in planting trees.

Fig. 5-2. Young citrus tree with polystyrene insulating trunk wrap.

A method used on a large commercial scale greatly decreases hand labor in planting. The hole is dug by an auger operated as a tractor attachment, and the spoil dirt is formed at this time into a water ring by machine. Then the nursery tree is "jetted in." A stream of water under considerable pressure from a spray tank or from an auxiliary pump is directed at the location for the taproot by one man, while another places the tree in the proper position. Then the soil is filled in around the roots by washing it down from the sides by the jet of water, assuring freedom from air pockets. This operation is fast and economical.

No fertilizer need be applied at planting, although some growers apply it. There are few or no rootlets able to absorb fertilizer nutrients at this time and if the fertilizer is not very carefully distributed in the hole, tender new rootlets may be injured by

coming in contact with a high concentration of salts. Sometimes soluble fertilizers are dissolved in irrigation water and applied. Certain slow-release fertilizers are also sometimes used at planting time. The use of any chemical at planting time should be very judicious. Possible damage from fertilizer has already been mentioned. Applications of fungicides, nematicides, herbicides, and the like may also be made but are usually best applied after the tree has settled in after several waterings have been undertaken.

Fig. 5-3. Young citrus tree with patented wrap in place on the trunk.

Banking or Wrapping Newly Planted Trees

When winter plantings are made, as is common practice, it is necessary to protect the new trees from possible injury by cold—since they are more susceptible to such injury than they will ever be again—by banking soil or applying insulating wraps around them to a height of a foot or more, preferably up to the scaffold limbs. The important thing is to have the bud union well covered, so that new shoots can develop from the scion even though the top is partly killed back. If the union remains covered by a well-made bank of soil, it will survive any cold known to Florida. It is very desirable to make banks of soil free from decaying vegetation or particles of wood, as the former materials attract ants and the latter attract termites, and both insects may attack the tree under the bank if attracted thus to it. Wind and rain may carry away some of the banked soil, even to the point of exposing the union, so periodic inspection and replenishment of the banks is necessary. Normally the banks remain in place until the last danger from frost is past in spring, but in an extremely dry winter wilting leaves may indicate the necessity for applying water to the roots, and the banks must be torn down to permit this. Of course, they are at once replaced.

Insulating wraps may provide a satisfactory substitute for soil banks. While the degree of protection provided is not as great as a well-made soil bank, they do afford certain advantages. Most tree wraps, unlike soil banks, can be attached in the fall and left on the trees throughout the year or even for several years. Tree wraps also inhibit sprouts and protect trunks from herbicide and mechanical damage.

Selection of the proper tree wrap for a particular grove depends on a number of factors, including cost, ease of installation, and probability of freeze damage. For example, growers in northern regions of the state should choose wraps with good insulating qualities, while growers in warmer southern locations may opt for less costly, thinner wraps.

Should low temperature kill the exposed top of the tree, and there ensues a period of unseasonably warm weather, it is necessary to remove the banks or wraps because new shoots may start growth on the uninjured stem under the bank. If still covered under these conditions, the bark may become infected by soil fungi, become spongy, and slough off, with eventual death of the tree. A tree unbanked or unwrapped for this reason, with tender new growth starting, is exceptionally sensitive to cold and *must* be rebanked or rewrapped when further cold is forecast.

6 /
Bringing Citrus Trees into Production

During the first two or three years after planting a citrus tree, growers should not seek to obtain the earliest possible production of fruit but to develop a sturdy tree to good size so that it will bear productively over a long life. Apart from being topped at planting to assure development of low heads and being pruned of low-growing sprouts occasionally, citrus trees are given little or no formal training. They naturally form strong crotches, their wood is tough, and they easily obtain a sturdy framework of scaffold branches. Growers need to aid the growth of the trees only by supplying favorable conditions for their development. With no crop to consider, growers can devote all attention to promoting vegetative growth. Sometimes growers will give minimum attention to these young trees because they are not yet returning any income, but to neglect them is a mistake that will be regretted for a long time because of its adverse effect on the trees' future bearing.

By established custom in Florida, citrus trees are classed as nonbearing during the first four years after they are planted as yearling trees. Although they may bear a few fruits as early as the second or third year, all efforts are correctly directed toward tree growth, and any fruit production is incidental. The cultural program for these nonbearing trees is quite different from that for bearing trees.

In the following discussion, it is assumed that trees have been planted in the dormant season as one-year-old nursery budlings. The slight adjustments that are needed to fit this program to trees planted in spring or summer will be obvious and easily made.

Unbanking

When danger of frost is over (15 February in the southern area, 15 March in the northern), the young trees should have their cold-protection banks of soil removed. This is easily done with a large hoe or tractor attachment, removing the soil carefully so as not to injure the bark of the tree and spreading the soil around the tree to make a basin about a yard in diameter for holding water. (Where permanent irrigation systems that can deliver adequate water to the root zone of the young tree are in place, construction of basins will not be necessary.) The last remnants of soil adhering to the tree should be removed by hand to avoid scarring the trunk. Then the basin should be smoothed by hand and any exposed roots covered with soil. If wraps have been used for cold protection, they are usually checked and left in place, but may be removed if desired.

Watering

Watering young trees regularly during the spring dry season is far more important than fertilizing them, as many growers have learned the hard way. Trees lacking adequate mineral nutrients may be stunted in growth temporarily, but young trees suffering from insufficient water are likely to die.

Immediately after unbanking the trees and forming the water basins, each tree should be given about ten gallons of water. The purpose of the basin is to direct all this water down into the soil around the tree roots. Water must be poured into the basin slowly enough that it does not overflow the sides and run off into the middles. During the spring and until summer rains begin in earnest, water should be supplied to prevent the soil in the root zone from drying out. As a rule of thumb, if a week passes without at least an inch of rainfall, trees should again be given eight to ten gallons each, with more frequent applications during protracted dry periods. The basin is retained as long as watering is needed. Growers must be prepared to water all of their young trees within a two-week period, even if they have a large acreage, so that they are ready to water the first ones again within a fortnight of the previous watering. In some seasons, the spring rainfall may make any watering unnecessary, but this is unlikely; growers must be prepared to deal with the worst situation that may arise so far as drought is concerned.

Watering in the fall is not as critical because by that time tree roots should have penetrated the soil for some distance so that they have access to a much larger reserve of water than they had in spring and decreasing temperatures reduce the rate of water loss from the tree. Except in extreme drought, it is better to encourage early winter dormancy by allowing the soil moisture content to become a little low in the fall, particularly in colder locations. Even though summer is the rainy season, there are sometimes periods of two or three weeks without rain. Young trees in their first season of growth may not have root systems able to carry them through such dry periods and may need watering almost as much as they do in spring.

Where low-volume irrigation such as microsprinklers or drippers are used, the irrigation scheme obviously requires some modification. With young trees during the months from November through February, if no rainfall occurs, two to four drip irrigation applications or one to two microsprinkler applications per week may be necessary. During the warmer months of March to October, three to seven drip irrigations or two to three microsprinkler applications may be necessary during weeks with no rain. The recommended intervals assume that drippers are run three to six hours and microsprinklers two to three hours per application. The length of time actually required varies with emitter output.

It is in the first year of grove life that watering is most urgently needed; by the second growing season, the young tree is more nearly able to take care of its needs for water, but it is still not self-sufficient. All through the three to four years of its non-bearing stage—indeed, even after it comes into full bearing —regular inspection should be made during periods of prolonged drought to see if leaves are wilting and water is needed. When it is evident that watering is necessary, enough water should be applied to soak the soil thoroughly—ten, twelve, or fifteen gallons per tree in successive years—and not just a bucketful to wet the surface soil. Such an application will be lost in a day or two by evaporation, and the tree will hardly have the benefit of it longer than that. Such frugality is poor economy.

Where irrigation systems supply water, the same guidelines will apply. The ease with which water is applied, however, will often result in superior growth since trees will not have to suffer the stresses of their hand-watered counterparts. Care must be taken to ensure that overirrigation does not occur. Besides obviously leaching away nutrients and encouraging weed growth, overirrigation can actually damage citrus roots by flooding of the root zone.

Fertilization

Citrus trees differ little from other evergreen trees or shrubs in their need for mineral nutrients, and the fertilizer mixtures generally used for garden ornamentals give satisfactory results with young citrus trees. Such a general garden analysis as 6-6-6, 8-4-8, or 8-8-8 may be used. High analysis mixtures can be used with low poundage per tree and proper care to assure distribution. Small amounts applied at rather frequent intervals may be more effective than the same total amount applied at intervals of several months. Fertilizer should be spread evenly over the ground in a circle whose diameter is twice that of the spread of the tree top. For nonbearing trees, especially in the first year or two, the fertilizer is usually spread by hand, although some operators with large acreages of young trees use machine distribution. Uneven distribution of fertilizer may result in a relatively high concentration of soluble salts in some places, causing injury to roots under those locations. Large applications are wasteful and may cause the same type of injury even more widely.

A satisfactory schedule of applications during the first three years is to apply fertilizer five to six times yearly. The first application is made as soon as the banks have been removed and the trees watered in the spring—15 February in south central Florida. The other four applications follow at intervals of about six weeks—1 April, 15 May, 1 July, 15 August. In the northern part of the citrus area, the first application will be a few weeks later, and the succeeding applications will be at intervals of about five weeks. It is often considered risky to apply fertilizer after 1 September in areas north of the Orlando-Tampa line or after 1 October south of this, lest the young trees be encouraged to continue vegetative growth too long, resulting in tenderness at the time of first frost.

The quantity of fertilizer to apply at each application will increase each year. In the following schedule, it is assumed that fertilizer with the 8 percent nitrogen content commonly employed for young citrus trees is being used. It is equally satisfactory to use fertilizer with 6 percent or even 10 percent of nitrogen, but the rates should be adjusted to reflect the increase or decrease of nutrients in the fertilizer (see table 6-1).

It is advisable to use a fertilizer that contains not only nitrogen, phosphorus, and potash (whose percentages are given by the first three numbers of a fertilizer analysis), but secondary and microelements as well. The fertilizer mix recommended by research contains magnesium, manganese, copper, and boron and would have an analysis of 8-8-8-1.6-0.4-0.2-.025. The amount of phosphorus could be reduced to 4 percent for trees grown in previously planted areas such as resets.

As the quantity per application is increased, the area covered by the fertilizer should increase proportionally so that the amount of fertilizer per square foot of soil surface remains fairly constant. Thus with twice the quantity applied in August the second year, the diameter of the circles of application should be half again as large the second year, and in the third year twice as large as in the first year.

Table 6-1.
Schedule of fertilizer applications
for young trees

Year since planting	Number of fertilizer applications per year[a]	Pounds per tree per application
First	5–6	0.75–1.25
Second	4–5	1.75–2.25
Third	3–4	3.0 –4.0
Fourth	3–4	3.5 –4.5
Fifth	3–4	4.0 –5.0
Sixth	3–4	4.5 –5.5
Seventh	3–4	5.0 –6.0

SOURCE: "Recommended fertilizers and nutritional sprays for citrus," edited by R.C.J. Koo. IFAS Bulletin no. 536D.
a. Use 8-8-8-1.6-0.4-0.2-0.025 mixture or equivalent.

Trees planted in spring can follow this schedule the first year except that each application is made six weeks later than indicated. The second year they can be fertilized exactly according to schedule. Trees planted in summer will receive only the first two or three applications. In the spring of the next year, they will start with one pound and gradually be given larger amounts until by the end of summer they are receiving almost as much as the dormant-planted trees.

It is not worthwhile trying to adjust the amount applied to each tree to take account of small differences observed in the size of the trees of a single variety. Uniformity in size is desirable and will most nearly be attained by applying to all what is considered satisfactory for the average tree. Some varieties, however, grow more rapidly than others, and on some soils a given variety grows faster than on others. Such differences between varieties and locations may well warrant a small variation in the amounts applied, increasing them when average growth of a particular block is above normal, decreasing them for markedly slow growth.

The third or fourth year is a season of transition from the vegetative to the fruiting condition. Growers often wonder whether to begin the distribution of fertilizer by mechanical spreaders, which are commonly used in fertilizing bearing groves of uniform tree size. As a rough guide, it may be considered that distribution by mechanical spreaders will prove satisfactory when the radius of the crown—the distance from tree trunk to the circle formed by the outermost drip of rain from the canopy—is at least one-fourth the width of the work middle in which the spreader operates.

After this fourth year, the trees are considered to be of bearing age. The culture of bearing trees is described in the next chapter.

Spraying

The extensive spraying programs needed in bearing groves are not required during the first three to four years since little or no fruit is produced and these programs are chiefly concerned with keeping fruit free of pests. There are, however, some insects and mites that may attack the young trees and cause considerable injury by their feeding if they are not controlled. Serious defoliation may take place from such infestations, resulting in shortage of food for plant growth and tissue maturity since leaves are the organs of the plant chiefly responsible for food making. The trees should be regularly inspected several times a year so that infestations may be detected before pest populations have become seriously large. These same pests also seriously threaten bearing groves, and methods of controlling them are discussed in more detail in chapter 9.

Fungus diseases are not much of a problem in young groves except for citrus scab. This disease causes distortion and malformation of foliage, tender shoots, and fruits of grapefruit, Temples, satsumas, lemons, and certain tangerine hybrids, but it does not attack oranges or tangerines. While rarely as injurious to the trees as scales and mites, scab does cut down on the machinery for food making and therefore retards growth. Again, control methods are given in chapter 9.

Minor fertilizer elements, especially zinc and copper, may not be available in the soil in sufficient quantity to meet the needs of the young trees and may be more readily assimilated by them through the leaves if applied as a spray. Certainly spray applications of the minor elements should be made whenever deficiency symptoms appear, but in many areas it is well known that young groves are likely to suffer from these nutrient deficiencies. It is better never to let serious deficiency symptoms appear than to correct them after they have retarded growth. Transient deficiency symptoms, however, are usually no cause for concern in a rapidly growing young tree. Persistence of deficiency symptoms is cause for concern and corrective action, which often takes the form of correctional sprays of microelements applied in the spring. Details of these sprays can be found in chapter 8.

Pruning

Undesired sprouts frequently appear on the trunks of young citrus trees. These should be checked several times during the growing season so that they may be removed before they have become large enough to offer much competition to the desired shoots. Various types of trunk wraps have been used to reduce sprout formation. While the food made by sprouts may have some value to the trunk and roots, the nutrients and water that they divert from the permanent branches more than offset any benefit they bestow, and the earlier they are removed the better. Sprouts develop chiefly either from the stock below the union or from the first six to eight inches of the scion above the union, and any sprout arising less than twelve inches from the ground should be removed. While sprouts are still only a few inches long, they are easily pushed off with the thumb. If they are allowed to grow larger and to form woody tissue, pruning shears will be needed. During the first year, the young grove should be gone over every two months from March to November for sprout removal. In succeeding years, the interval between inspection may be lengthened until in the fourth year a single inspection in summer will suffice.

Pruning of the permanent branches is not usually required during the first three years. Citrus growers are free from the necessity to train carefully the young tree that is required of the growers of apples or peaches. In the fourth year, however, just prior to the bearing period, it is well to examine the trees for weak limbs, branches that are parallel to and just above stronger branches, and limbs that lie across and rub against others. Such branches should be pruned out to strengthen the bearing framework. The objective is a well-shaped head with evenly spaced scaffold limbs and space for branches to develop properly without excessive competition from other branches for light. Only a light thinning should be made and not a heavy pruning-out of branches, for while it is always easy to cut out, it is very difficult for the tree to replace branches unadvisedly removed. This shaping and thinning operation should be entrusted to an experienced person and not to a novice as a means of supplying experience.

Painting pruning wounds is unnecessary. It is, however, just as important with small limbs as with large ones to make pruning cuts flush with the surface of the parent limb or trunk and not to leave any projecting stub that will heal over only slowly or not at all, thus leaving a site for wood-rotting fungi to enter the trunk of the tree.

Cultivation

Competition from weeds is a much more serious problem for young trees than for old ones because of their shallower rooting and smaller volume of absorbing area. Weed control is important, therefore, for rapid and vigorous tree growth in the young grove. Weeds used to be controlled by hoeing, but now chemicals are used almost exclusively. All weeds should be removed in an area extending from the trunk to at least a foot beyond the spread of the branches.

Chemical weed control has been the subject of much research. A number of herbicides are now available for use in the young, nonbearing grove (and in other situations as discussed in chapter 10). These can be used along the tree rows to reduce to a minimum the necessity for hand labor and mechanical cultivation. Their proper use reduces mechanical root injuries and incidences of foot rot, improves the health and growth of the tree, and reduces slightly the need for water during periods of drought. The single-grain structure of Florida soils does not require cultivation to maintain root development. No specific recommendations for chemical control of weeds are suggested here due to the rapid development of materials and techniques. Growers should seek the advice of IFAS extension personnel or industry representatives regarding available chemical agents and their proper usage.

Probably the best weed control management technique for young citrus would be a herbicide-treated strip down the tree row extending out from the trunks to just beyond the branches. Weeds in the middles between the rows can then be controlled by mechanical means, usually by mowing during the summer months.

Instead of permitting the natural growth of weeds in the middles, the grower may wish to plant a leguminous cover crop such as hairy indigo or beggarweed, which will produce more beneficial organic matter in the soil later. In September this cover crop—whether natural or planted—should be disked down. If the growth is so heavy that a plow must be used, disk after plowing to level the ground and to mix the cover crop better with the soil. Plowing is likely to cut many citrus roots and should be avoided if possible. A standing cover crop is a fire hazard, and it increases cold injury to young trees by preventing free air drainage. On the other hand, wind erosion is much more severe in hilly ground when the soil is not held together by a mass of plant roots. For this reason, the middles should be cultivated in autumn only enough to assure freedom from risks of fire or frost, leaving the cover crop roots at a depth of a couple of inches undisturbed. In bedded groves, cultivation is usually avoided completely to prevent bed deterioration. For these situations, a close mowing of the cover crop is recommended.

Ant Control

Several kinds of ants make their nests in grove soils and feed upon the leaves or even the bark of young citrus trees. These pests may injure trees so seriously that they die, and in any case the trees are weakened and delayed in development. In making inspections for other pests, a watch should be kept for lines of ants moving up and down the trees. Approved materials for ant control are now under the regulation of the U.S. Environmental Protection Agency (EPA). Current recommendations can be obtained from IFAS extension or industry personnel. Ant control is important not only for tree health but for worker safety as well since the imported fire ant is one of the most common, and most serious, ant pests.

Cold Protection

Young citrus trees will require banking or wrapping for the first three or four years, at least in the colder areas, or until the trunk reaches a diameter of two inches. As trees get larger, the thicker bark and the denser canopy decrease the chance of cold injury to the trunk.

After the tree has been banked or wrapped, it should be inspected at monthly intervals to ensure there are no problems. It is very important after unusually low temperatures to assess the extent of any cold damage. Previous discussion has dealt with correction of any of these situations if they are found.

Beginning with the fourth or fifth year, when the trees are considered of bearing age, practices in grove management differ somewhat from those outlined above. The following chapters are devoted to the care of bearing trees.

7 /
The Bearing Grove and Efficient Performance

During the early, nonbearing years of the life of a citrus grove, the cultural practices described in the previous chapter are aimed primarily at producing healthy trees having good structural framework and the capability of bearing satisfactory crops for many years. For trees of bearing age, the primary objective of cultural practices is to produce large crops of fruit of satisfactory quality at commercially competitive costs.

Basic Factors in Production

Every commercial grower of citrus fruits expects to make a profit and certainly should make one. Some growers devote their entire time to the business of citrus production; some grow citrus as one of two or more business activities, not always the major one; and still others have a very minor, even avocational, interest in grove operation. These last include many people who entrust the operation of a relatively small citrus acreage to a production organization, although the owner may spend many pleasant hours in observing his grove and in following the program carried out in it. Still other growers are corporations for whom citrus production is often only one of several corporate enterprises. While such operations may be quite impersonal, the professional manager employed to run the grove is often seen as the grower. All growers have a real financial interest in the production program and therefore may be expected to have an interest in obtaining sound knowledge of the basic cultural principles involved.

Climate, soil, stocks, and scions, taken together, define any particular citrus grove. No citrus enterprise can be profitable if these factors are not suitable, and they are permanent factors inasmuch as they usually remain the same throughout the life of the grove. Sometimes a grower can, at some cost, vary soil or scion factors to make production more profitable. Two other factors also enter the situation—the biotic environment and market demand. The biotic factor includes all of the living organisms that come into the grove and affect the productive capacity of the trees. A lack of market demand may render even the most efficient production unprofitable.

These factors are taken into consideration when choosing a production program. In the bearing grove, the way the grower utilizes the permanent factors of grove potential and overcomes the handicaps of the biotic and market limitations determines the profitability of operations. The successful grower maintains a grove at maximum efficiency. This includes keeping a full complement of fundamentally healthy trees in the grove, fertilizing the trees for vigorous growth and heavy crops, spraying to prevent pests from limiting production or lowering fruit grade or quality, and helping trees to respond properly to fertilizers and sprays by cultural practices such as cultivation, drainage and irrigation, pruning, and frost protection.

These seven programs of the production schedule may not all be necessary in every grove, but each of them must be thoroughly understood by the grower if only to determine intelligently what is not needed. The first three operations—maintaining full tree strength, fertilizing, and spraying—are soundly based on scientific research, which influences the way they are carried out. The last three operations listed above do not rest upon such a firm research base, yet each of them has received much careful study. All citrus-production practices presently being used have been influenced not only by professional scientists but also by the many intelligent citrus growers who have developed logical and satisfactory programs through years of trial and error. These thoughtful, far-sighted people have had a large share in making the Florida citrus industry strong and progressive.

The extensive accumulation of scientific knowledge about citrus production is of little value unless the grove operator is familiar with it and knows how to apply it. For this reason, many growers with small acreages of citrus trees have preferred to entrust the operation of their groves to a professional grove management service, either a cooperative organization or a private one, so that a trained and experienced manager can bring this knowledge to bear on grove operation. The work of this manager will be easier, and a more satisfactory business relationship can be enjoyed, if the owner has some understanding of the problems involved.

Grove Rehabilitation

For maximum efficiency of a production unit, or grove, it is essential that every tree location be occupied by a tree and that every tree be healthy. Only then can the grower utilize proven fertilizer and spray practices with maximum benefit. If a grove is laid out so as to have seventy trees per acre but by actual count has an average of only sixty-five because the other five have died, then the grove can never reach more than 93 percent of its theoretically possible production. A similar loss of productive efficiency occurs at any planting density. In cases where trees were too closely spaced originally, some may be removed without decreasing the grove's permanent capacity to produce. Prompt replacement of dead trees means higher average returns from the grove.

In many cases, however, the situation involves not only vacancies in the grove but also trees that are unthrifty or declining. If these trees remain in the grove, growing steadily weaker and yielding less fruit each year, the potential production capacity for the grove declines annually even though costs of production remain the same. In short, potential profits decline slowly but steadily. It is not sufficient, either, simply to remove and replace such trees once it is clear that they are declining. Unless the reason for the decline can be found and the condition corrected, the replacement tree may suffer the same fate. Extensive treatment may be needed before a new tree can safely be set, or a change of stock may be necessary to fit the soil conditions. Furthermore, a tree may be healthy but producing small crops, or it may be producing large crops of undesirable fruit, as when an unfavorable mutation has been propagated as a strain. Such a tree also should be removed and replaced.

It may be possible to rehabilitate the unsatisfactory tree if it is diseased or by topworking if the strain is poor. Growers should consider carefully the cost of such remedial work to decide whether it will be economically profitable. Often they will decide that restoration will be more expensive in the long run than replacement.

Only replacement can be effective if the stock is poorly chosen or the tree is affected by an incurable disease. Since the grove is the unit of production and each unproductive tree in the grove must be restored to productivity, it is better to think not of tree rehabilitation but of *grove rehabilitation,* meaning by this term the practices necessary to maintain the full complement of trees of full theoretical productive capacity in the grove. This program should be conducted regularly rather than being deferred until serious losses in production have been suffered.

Programs of grove rehabilitation are usually much less important in the early life of the grove than in later years, although problems sometimes arise even in the first or second year that may affect susequent production. Climatic factors may be more harmful to young trees than to older ones, and an unwise choice of site may be reflected in retarded early tree growth. Before the trees have borne their first crop, topworking is sometimes resorted to when the grower decides that marketing opportunities are greater with a variety other than the one originally planted. Debilitating disease complexes have sometimes made necessary the entire removal of the first trees planted and their replacement with a different combination of stock and scion.

Because a few trees are likely to be lost during the first few years due to various causes, it is a wise precaution at planting to set out a few "spares" (1 to 2 percent of the total) in some convenient location within the grove for use in replacement as needed. This assures having trees of the same type and age as the original trees for resetting.

Administration of the grove rehabilitation program involves *identification* of what is wrong with a tree, *appraisal* of the extent of current damage and the likelihood of additional future damage, *selection* of an appropriate treatment or remedy, and *action* to remedy the situation. Citrus trees may become unproductive or may decline in vegetative vigor or even die from many diverse causes, among them climatic factors such as freezes, droughts, hurricanes, floods, lightning; soil conditions, especially improper drainage or excessive salt concentrations; nutritional disorders resulting from deficiency or toxicity of mineral elements; pathogenic diseases of various types, such as bacterial, fungal, or viral; insects, mites, and nematodes; pests such as rabbits, gophers, or other animals; and even injuries caused by grove machinery. Any or all of these may have an unfavorable effect on the tree and result in lowered vitality and production.

In some cases, identification of the problem is a very simple matter, while in others it may prove very difficult. A tree may respond to several quite different causes by exhibiting a condition of "decline" or "dieback" or "gummosis." Such general symptoms are of little or no diagnostic value since they indicate only that in some serious way the normal functioning of the tree has been disturbed.

When the whole tree seems to be affected, the grower is likely to consider the problem systemic even though the cause may be a localized infection, as with foot rot, or an injury that is both local and very limited, as when rabbits have girdled a tree. To make a correct identification, the grower or production manager often needs the assistance of trained personnel of IFAS extension or research or state regulatory agencies. Even with such expert help, there are sometimes cases when it is not possible to be sure of the fundamental cause of decline.

Once the cause has been identified, it becomes possible to appraise current damage and its effect on the productive capacity of the grove as well as to determine with some degree of accuracy the expectation of future damage to tree and yield. Such appraisals are necessary as a basis for deciding what corrective measures will be economically worthwhile. Furthermore, in the course of appraisal, additional information may be brought out, such as the interrelationship of certain factors, that may indicate the problem is more or less severe than it first appeared. Appraisal of water damage, for example, must include not only mapping of the trees to record their relative degree of injury but also investigating the water table and the possibility of reducing future damage. If the study shows that it will not be possible to change the height of the water table, then it may be wise to abandon the site. A site that is subject to frequently recurring freeze damage may have to be abandoned if no way can be found to alleviate the damage. The appraisal may suggest that a change in the stock and/or scion variety is desirable to prevent immediate recurrence in new plants of the same problem, especially if the cause is one of the viral diseases.

Appraisal requires study of the problem itself, of contributing environmental conditions, and of current and future damages and economic losses. In making these studies, too, specialists may be of great help in determining what measures should be taken.

Selection of an appropriate remedy must include consideration of how much that remedy will interfere with production, which, in addition to its direct costs, is an important element in its economic feasibility.

The final step in the rehabilitation program consists of remedial treatment, if feasible, or the removal of declined or dead trees and resetting of new trees after any underlying causes have been corrected. Declined trees should be taken out just as soon as they fail to return costs of production and appraisal shows that they cannot be restored to health.

Tree removal is often done in fall but might be delayed until winter in the case of an early bearing variety so that a last small crop could be gathered. Trees are usually removed by a front-end loader designed for the task, then the area is carefully raked to remove roots. The hole is then refilled to its previous level. If any corrective measures are needed, they should be taken at this point. Soil fumigation or fallowing before replanting should be considered. Several fumigants are on the market; they should be used as directed on the label with a proper interval before replanting.

Replacements should be made in winter or early spring, preferably with the same cultivar already in the block unless a change of the whole block is being made to another, more profitable variety. Groves can be found in the state in which the grower has used no consistent plan in making replacements, having used for resetting whatever was in demand in the given year. As a result, one finds replacements of various ages of different types within the same grove. Many of these trees will never be picked because it is not economically feasible to send pickers into such a grove for the small number of boxes there of each of the different varieties. Under such conditions, it is hardly possible to operate a logical production program. If the cultivar already in the block is an undesirable one, then the grower should use the best means—topworking or replanting—to change the whole grove to another variety, an operation that certainly can be fitted into the concept of grove rehabilitation.

Replacements planted in an old grove should be given the same attention as young trees planted in a new grove. Sometimes growers tend to leave the replants to fend for themselves, assuming that the operations employed for the old trees will be adequate for the new. Resets need much more attention, however, because of competition with the older, well-established trees. The program for young trees as set forth in the previous chapter should be followed for replacements during their first four years in the grove. They should be cared for quite independently of the program followed for the older trees. Broadcast fertilizer applications adequate for the established trees may leave the replants in an impoverished condition, and they may even decline for lack of sufficient nutrients unless they are fertilized individually by hand. Although soil moisture may be adequate for the older trees, watering may also be needed by these reset trees because of their much shallower root systems.

Growers and managers derive benefits from a well-conducted program of grove rehabilitation, even beyond having a grove maintained at efficient producing condition. Additional benefits result

from the fact that continued, intelligent observations in the grove
will allow more intimate knowledge of the grove and the ability to
meet its needs more certainly in all phases of the production program.

Diseases Often Make Grove Rehabilitation Necessary

There are many causes for a decline in tree growth. Previous
chapters have discussed the roles of cold and soil moisture in citrus tree growth, and the following chapters will cover nutritional
requirements and the diseases controlled by a spray program.
There are some serious diseases, however, that are not so controlled and that are often the reason for a progressive decline in
tree health and productivity. Among the most important of these
are root and foot rots, viral infections, and nematode infestations.
And although the cause, or even the type, of the malady is unknown, a discussion of citrus blight is presented here.

Citrus Blight

In 1964 the first symptoms of a new and unknown malady appeared in flatwood and marsh areas of Florida. Affecting trees
from approximately five years of age, the symptoms were sparse
foliage and premature leaf drop, zinc and manganese chlorotic
patterns, and small, misshapen fruits; the name "young tree decline" was given to this condition. Unlike the tree losses of 1 to 2
percent per year, which had been considered "normal," much
larger random losses and clustered losses rapidly became a
serious threat to the industry. At the beginning it seemed to be a
problem of rough lemon stock when budded to sweet oranges, but
other stocks with other scion varieties appear not to be immune.
Similar symptoms showed up in groves in well-drained areas, and
there the name "sand hill decline" came into vogue. Overall, the
name "lemon root decline" suggests the high incidence on rough
lemon stock. No definite cause of the condition has as yet been
identified; active research is being vigorously pursued. We now
recognize these to be symptoms of a disease that apparently attacks citrus trees of all types on all stocks. The problem seems
most acute, however, on sweet oranges on the more vigorous
stocks. The name "citrus blight" is now used to identify this problem.

"Scion-rooting," whereby a mound of soil is placed around the
tree trunk, usually by mechanical means, to eliminate the under-

stock as roots developed from the scion, has been a practice in some affected groves. Even this therapy is worthless, however, after the trees have become weakened. Total replacement is the best treatment. Loath to continue to use rough lemon stock, growers are left with choices of sour orange, Carrizo citrange, Swingle citrumelo, trifoliate orange, Cleopatra mandarin, Macrophylla (*Citrus macrophylla*), or other stocks even though these show varying degrees of susceptibility to the malady. As with the Milam, a rough lemon variant that resists the effects of the burrowing nematode, perhaps a variant type may be found. Hopefully the efforts of numerous scientists and managers will determine the causative agent and its correction; in the meantime, the grove manager must be aware of the problem and plan accordingly.

Foot and Root Rots

Foot rot was one of the first diseases to attract attention in Florida. As early as 1876 it was observed to attack sweet orange seedling trees, most of which were grown on relatively low ground. Resistance to this disease shown by sour orange trees under the same conditions was an important factor in the change from sweet seedling trees for grove planting to sweet orange budded on sour stocks. The disease is caused by the fungus *Phytophthora,* which is present in the soil and attacks susceptible kinds of citrus trees under certain conditions. High soil moisture, mostly found in low, fine-textured soils, is the most common of these conditions. Citrus species vary greatly in susceptibility, the order of decreasing resistance usually being reported as trifoliate orange, sour orange, Cleopatra mandarin, rough lemon, grapefruit, and sweet orange. So far as foot rot is concerned, the species more resistant than rough lemon can usually be satisfactorily used on moist soils as stocks for more susceptible species.

Foot rot is a disease of the base of the trunk or of the crown, when stocks are susceptible, and can develop when the tissues of susceptible species are near enough to the ground for fungus spores to be splashed by raindrops onto stem tissues. Budding very low on resistant stock may still permit infection to occur. Trees budded high but set low in the ground may be diseased. Conversely, trees that are budded high on resistant stock, planted in wet soils set at proper height, and given good air circulation are less likely to be infected. Weeds or low-hanging canopies that prevent free circulation of air are conducive to infection.

When foot rot has developed sufficiently to girdle one-quarter or more of the trunk's circumference, decline becomes quite visible, although it is often seen only on one side of the tree if girdling is partial. The foliage becomes progressively more yellow due to the cutting off of mineral nutrients from the roots, and finally twigs and branches die back extensively.

Before chemical treatment alternatives were available, if inspection showed decline due to decay of the bark at the base of the trunk, growers might cut away all diseased bark back into healthy bark. The exposed wood was then painted with a safe disinfectant and covered with pruning paint. If the crown and main roots were diseased, the soil was pulled away to expose all diseased members freely to the air. Then the diseased bark was treated as above. In sandy soils, it is well to leave the crown exposed indefinitely unless there is danger of injury by freezing. If grove trees are regularly examined once a year for the first signs of foot rot and remedial measures undertaken, decline symptoms can be forestalled. The value of satisfactory aeration cannot be overemphasized.

Chemical treatments are now available to help deal with the problem. While cleanliness and good aeration remain extremely important, treatment with appropriate fungicidal materials can actually cure infections or be used preventively. Local extension agents and chemical sales representatives can provide current information and details.

Root rot caused by the fungus *Clitocybe* often produces a decline similar to that of foot rot. The roots are attacked first and the infection may spread to the base of the trunk. Small mushrooms appearing from the trunk make identification of the infection certain, but they do not always develop. The fungus is usually present in pieces of oak or hickory roots, and the disease is largely prevented if all such roots are thoroughly removed from the soil in preparation for planting citrus trees. This is a disease of high, sandy soils, not of low, heavy soils as foot rot is, and it is not related to the stock used. Infected trees should be removed as soon as productive capacity is lost. Clean area of root debris prior to resetting. As of 1989, there are no known chemical controls.

A root rot caused by *Diplodia* fungus may also occur in citrus groves and is often the cause of decline of trees in heavy, wet soil after flooding by very heavy rains or excessive irrigation. The bark of the roots may be seriously decayed before the tree suddenly goes into a marked wilting and decline follows rapidly. By this time, the trunk has usually been girdled also. A characteristic feature is the blackening of wood beneath diseased bark. Wilting is likely to occur during a drought because even the badly diseased roots may still supply sufficient water while it is abundant. No cure is known for the disease, but it may largely be prevented by care in irrigation and by improvement in drainage conditions. After diseased trees are removed, it is desirable to fumigate the soil before replanting.

Virus Diseases

Viruses are very small parasitic agents consisting of nucleic acid and a protein coat and capable of reproduction only within a living host. Viroids are similar but lack the protein coat. They are responsible for many serious ailments of plants and animals. Citrus trees can suffer from several viral and viroid infections. Some cause a very rapid decline, while others cause a slow decline or merely a permanent dwarfing. The principal viral diseases of citrus trees are psorosis, tristeza, exocortis, and xyloporosis.

Psorosis, also called "scaly bark" in California, was the first recognized viral disease of citrus. Since 1896 a disease characterized by severe scaling of the bark of trunks and large branches had been known; for many years it was supposed to be due to a fungus, though none could be shown present. As the scaly patches become larger, the underlying wood and bark turn brown because of gums and resins produced by diseased cells, and eventually the top begins to die back. Usually trees do not show the scaly bark symptoms until they are mature, and they may decline slowly for many years. This disease, now called "psorosis A," was shown by Fawcett in 1934 to be virally caused. It is most serious on sweet orange and tangerine, but it attacks all types of citrus worldwide, and incidence of the disease is not unique to any particular rootstock or scion. Any combination is susceptible if infected budwood is used.

Several other forms of psorosis—psorosis B, blind-pocket psorosis, concave gum psorosis—are known. Caused by strains of the same virus, they are much less common than psorosis A. Not all kinds of citrus trees show scaling of bark or exudation of gum as symptoms of infection, but all do show a characteristic chlorotic pattern in the partially grown leaves. This pattern is a symmetrical one of light yellow areas, either small flecks or large blotches, which are translucent when the leaves are held up to the light.

There is no known cure for trees infected with psorosis. The virus is apparently transmitted almost entirely by budwood, not by insects or pruning tools, so there is no hazard to other trees from leaving the diseased trees in place. They should be removed and replaced when declining yield makes them unprofitable. This disease is easily prevented with careful selection of budwood.

In 1952, at the request of progressive growers, a citrus budwood registration program was inaugurated to prevent the extreme losses that often were caused by using psorosis-infected budwood. Now the Citrus Budwood Registration Bureau of the Division of Plant Industry of the Florida Department of Agriculture and Consumer Services, the program has been expanded to include other viral problems and other types of problems of a propagable nature. This program now assures the industry seed and budwood sources free of many of these disorders. It has added vastly to our knowledge concerning such disorders.

Tristeza first came to serious attention in Florida when it wiped out the citrus industry of Brazil almost completely in the 1940s. It had appeared first in Argentine citrus groves between 1925 and 1930, where it rapidly killed trees on sour orange stock, and had spread to Brazil in 1937. At first the cause was unknown, but eventually it was shown to be a viral infection. The quick decline disease of California was soon found to be due to the same virus. In 1951 the virus was found to be present in Florida also, but in a very mild form that has not caused major damage. In various areas of the state, tristeza has since been found in apparently more virulent form and has now become a source of concern. It is transmitted by budding and grafting and by the three prominent aphids of citrus in Florida (the green citrus aphid, the cotton aphid, and the black citrus aphid). *Toxoptera citricidus,* the brown citrus aphid, which vectored the disease in Brazil, wiping out millions of citrus trees on sour orange stock, does not occur in Florida. The low incidence of tristeza among grapefruit on sour orange rootstock offers some justification for continued use of sour orange stock for grapefruit varieties, but the current popular use of sour orange as a rootstock for sweet oranges and mandarins is discouraged.

This virus causes trouble only when certain stock/scion combinations are involved. Sweet orange and other species used as scions are able to carry viral infections without any injury or evidence of infection unless they are budded on sour orange or other susceptible rootstock. Susceptible rootstocks, other than sour orange, include *Citrus macrophylla,* sweet lime, citremon, grapefruit, some tangelos, and shaddocks. Citranges and trifoliate orange have been reported as susceptible in some areas. The virus creates a barrier where the stock and scion tissues join, preventing movement of food from the top to the roots. Before long the stock dies, then the scion. There is no easy way for the grower to identify decline due to tristeza in the field; indicator plants are used in the budwood registration program. However, since rootstocks other than sour orange used in the commercial citrus belt do not generally manifest the symptoms, a decline limited to sour orange stock may be suspected of being caused by tristeza if no other cause is obvious. The decline progresses through yellowing and various chlorotic patterns of foliage to heavy shedding of leaves and dieback of twigs. Usually a piece of the inner bark of sour orange stock, taken just below the bud union, will show a "honeycomb" pattern of fine holes, readily visible under a hand lens.

No practical cure is known for tristeza, and affected trees should be taken out as soon as identification is positive because the virus may be carried by aphids to other trees. Use of tolerant stocks will avoid injury from this virus in new plantings.

Exocortis is a viroid that affects trifoliate orange and some of its hybrids (citranges), Rangpur lime, sweet lime, and citron. Like tristeza, this viroid is present in the twigs of many kinds of citrus all over the state. Injury occurs when it is transmitted to a susceptible stock by use of infected budwood or when exocortis-contaminated pruning tools carry the virus to a susceptible combination. Susceptible and nonsusceptible stocks should not be mixed in a commercial grove in order to avoid the latter type of transmission. Exocortis-free budwood should be used regardless of the type of rootstock. The disease has been of minor importance in the Florida citrus belt only because the stocks of susceptible nature were used to such a limited extent. However, several of the newer stocks and many in experimental plantings are exocortis-susceptible.

The symptoms of exocortis are scaling of the bark of the stock below the union and/or a stunting of scion growth. Stunting may be the only symptom and is often extremely severe; when scaling of bark occurs, stunting is also present. Soon after 1900 there were reports of dwarfing of some varieties of sweet orange on trifoliate stock while other varieties made normal growth. It is now recognized that this virus was absent from the budwood of the normally growing group. No cure for infected trees is known. With an understanding of the hazards, the disease should be avoided at planting time by proper selection of stocks and scions.

Xyloporosis is a viral disease apparently transmitted only by budwood. The virus occurs without symptoms in tolerant combinations of stock and scion, but symptoms develop when xyloporosis-infected budwood is propagated on *Citrus macrophylla,* Rangpur lime, or Palestine sweet lime. Furthermore, Orlando and Minneola tangelos, Murcott, satsuma, Robinson, Osceola, and Lee (and probably Page and Nova) are susceptible, as scion varieties, regardless of the rootstock type used. The characteristic symptom of infection, found on the trunk of sweet lime stock or tangelo scion, is the development of small pits in the outer surface of the wood into which little projections from the inner side of the bark fit. This is easily seen when a flap of bark is cut and lifted just below the bud union (sweet lime) or just above it (tangelo).

Decline occurs in infected trees. Symptoms include bark scaling, gum infiltration, diminution in leaf size, chlorotic patterns of mineral deficiency, leaf fall, and stunting, often with flattened tops, small fruit, and poor yields. Infected trees are an economic loss in a few years and must be replaced. To avoid this disaster, xyloporosis-free budwood (which must as a nursery requirement also be free from psorosis), now available for every citrus variety propagated in Florida, should be used. Sweet lime, once eliminated in Florida because of this virus, along with other susceptible stocks can be used with this budwood. The industry continues to desire the total elimination of xyloporosis.

Nematode Infestations

For many years, Florida citrus growers, like other horticulturists, thought only of the nematode species causing root knot (to which citrus trees are immune) when nematodes were mentioned. This outlook radically changed in 1946 when the citrus nematode was reported widely spread in Florida groves and was strongly suspected of causing "spreading decline," a mysterious disease that had baffled researchers for years. In 1953, however, it was definitely shown to be another species, the burrowing nematode, that was the cause of spreading decline. As the name implies, spreading decline is characterized by a condition of decline that slowly but steadily spreads through a grove, at an average rate of fifty feet a year from the point or points of its first appearance. The symptoms shown by the aboveground portion of the tree are very general and common to decline from many other causes —steady decrease in vigor, size of fruit, yield, and amount of foliage—but the infestation of the roots by the nematode and the progressive spread from tree to adjacent tree are distinctive. Nematode infection potential is greatest in the subsoil immediately below the topsoil, several inches below the surface. Therefore, greatest damage can occur at any depth, usually below ten inches.

The burrowing nematode, *Radopholus citrophilus,* widely distributed in tropical areas of Asia and the Americas, attacks a large number of plant species. Only in Florida is a strain of the nematode known to attack citrus trees. The nematode moves through the soil in search of new roots after the one it has been feeding on becomes diseased and damaged. Since citrus roots extend out into the soil, the pest can move from the roots of one tree to those of another. If any of its numerous other hosts, particularly among the weeds, are in the intervening area, they can also become infected and result in further spread. The nematode is widely distributed in the soil throughout the citrus area of Florida but it is only in the deep, well-drained sands, such as on the Ridge, that heaviest damage occurs and the typical symptoms of spreading decline are found.

Control involves preventing introduction to new groves and elimination from infested ones. Citrus nursery stock can be obtained that is certified to be free of infestation. Commercial nursery sites must be determined to be free from nematodes by the Division of Plant Industry to be approved by the division. In home plantings of citrus there is danger of planting ornamental shrubs or herbaceous perennials that may be infested with this parasite too near the citrus trees, thus providing a source of infestation.

Citrus stocks that show resistance to the nematode have actively been sought with some success. Milam, a citrus hybrid of unknown parentage, was discovered in 1954 in a Polk County grove that had become infested with burrowing nematodes. The individual tree from which this variety originated showed no symptoms of spreading decline. It has been used as a rootstock for over twenty years with a small number of nursery propagations. It is particularly recommended as a "biological barrier" to prevent spread of the nematode. Two other discoveries in infested groves have not had widespread acceptance. The Estes, a tolerant rough lemon type, has never become popular, while the Ridge Pineapple, though resistant, has, like other sweet seedlings, been unpopular because of foot rot and drought susceptibilities. Carrizo citrange owes some of its current popularity to the fact that it is tolerant, although not resistant, to the burrowing nematode.

Buffer zones have been established to prevent the spread of the burrowing nematode from one area to another in a grove. Buffers are maintained around the known infested areas, treated with fumigants, and kept free of grass and weeds by use of herbicides. This program seeks to limit the advance of the nematode through the grove.

The citrus nematode, *Tylenchulus semipenetrans*, occurs throughout the world wherever citrus has been grown for any length of time. It was considered a minor problem after its discovery in California in 1912 and in Florida about 1913. Its widespread distribution in Florida in 1946 caused much alarm, but because citrus trees can endure quite heavy infestations without showing symptoms so long as growing conditions are good, it maintained its status as only a minor pest. There is reliable evidence, however, that the citrus nematode is causing considerably more damage than was thought earlier, even though the symptoms are not as bizarre and devastating as those of burrowing nematode infestations. All types of stocks have shown damage with the exception of the trifoliate orange, which appears to exhibit a resistance to this pest. Badly infested trees appear undernourished, with small, slightly yellow leaves, small and often unmarketable fruit, and general stunting and deterioration. Unlike current methods for dealing with burrowing nematodes, citrus nematodes can be reduced while the trees are in place by using certain chemicals. Furthermore, for planting new groves or resetting trees in old groves, nursery trees free of infestation should be used. Also, soil fumigation of reset areas prior to replanting is advised.

The root-lesion or meadow nematode, *Pratylenchus coffeae*, has caused damage to citrus in a few cases. This pest is very limited in distribution in Florida citrus and should not become a serious problem if nurseries are kept free from infestation and resets are treated prior to replanting, as is now required for the burrowing nematode.

8 /
Fertilizing Bearing Citrus Trees

The soils on which citrus trees are grown in Florida are low in both native fertility and in ability to retain nutrient elements applied to them in fertilizer. Consequently the trees can obtain an adequate supply of nutrients for satisfactory growth and production only if they are periodically provided with fertilizers in proper amount and kind. The costs of fertilizers and their application constitute nearly a fourth of total production costs, and all other cultural practices are in vain if fertilization is not done properly. To a large extent the vigor of the tree and the quantity and quality of its crop are dependent on the fertilizer it receives. Understanding citrus grove fertilization is, therefore, of greatest importance to the grower. In passing it may be noted, however, that the soil conditions that make the annual fertilizer bill so large are clouds that have a silver lining. The soil's low capacity to hold nutrient elements and Florida's heavy rainfall assure the grower that soluble salts will not accumulate in the grove soils to the toxic level—a condition seriously troubling to citrus growers in some parts of the world.

The Essential Nutrient Elements

Fifteen chemical elements have been found essential to satisfactory growth and functioning of citrus trees and to most other green plants. Three of them are adequately provided in any environment suited to tree growth and are largely beyond the control of the grower so far as their nutrient functions are concerned. The other twelve are elements supplied in fertilizer.

The three elements provided by nature are carbon, hydrogen, and oxygen, which together make up about 95 percent of the dry weight of a tree. Carbon and oxygen are taken into the leaves as carbon dioxide from the air, and there they combine with hydrogen, taken up as water by the roots, to produce carbohydrates. This process, called "photosynthesis," can take place only in green cells (those containing chlorophyll) in the presence of light, whose energy is stored in the carbohydrates. These carbohydrates, together with proteins, fats, and other organic compounds derived from them, are the true foods of the plant; they are used by the plant to make new tissues and provide energy for growth.

The twelve fertilizer elements, often miscalled "plant foods," are rarely present in adequate supply in Florida soils and must be provided by the grower. Some of them are used by the tree in making proteins and other compounds while others seem to have some regulatory function. When any of them is not present in sufficient amount, the tree function is restricted. The severe shortage of an element usually produces a characteristic deficiency symptom exhibited by the leaves (or other organs), and this symptom usually persists until the deficiency is corrected. Often, however, two or three elements are deficient in varying degrees simultaneously, and the resulting symptoms do not permit the specific deficiencies to be so easily recognized. Conversely, excessive amounts of some elements may be present in the soil and may prevent the tree from functioning properly. It is important that the fertilizer elements be present in proper balance as well as in certain minimal quantities.

These fertilizer elements are divided into two groups, often termed major and minor but probably better known as *macronutrient* and *micronutrient* elements. The adjectives "major" and "minor" convey the implication that one group is of greater importance than the other, whereas the elements in both groups are equally essential for plant growth and fruit production; and with both groups the amount of any element needed is affected by the amount of the other elements present. The macronutrient elements are those needed by the plant in rather large amounts, while the micronutrient elements are needed only in very small amounts. These latter are sometimes called "trace elements" (a label to which no objection can be taken but for which there is no convenient contrasting label for the other group).

The macronutrient elements in turn are usually divided into two groups, the primary elements (nitrogen, phosphorus, and potassium) and the secondary elements (calcium, magnesium, and sulfur). The distinction between primary and secondary has historic roots, reflecting the opinion of plant scientists of the nineteenth century that the elements of first and greatest importance for plant growth were nitrogen, phosphorus, and potassium. These were the elements that produced large increases in plant yield, whereas the other three elements seemed to exert a subordinate effect and therefore were deemed secondary. We recognize now that these responses merely reflected the degree of deficiency commonly encountered. Today the labels have no significance as to the relative importance of these six elements, although for most crops the fertilizer mixture is likely to contain the intended amounts only of the primary elements. In Florida, magnesium is sometimes added as a supplement, but calcium and sulfur are hardly given any thought in nutrient planning, although they are important in connection with control of soil reaction.

The micronutrient elements of interest to the citrus grower are iron, copper, manganese, zinc, boron, and molybdenum. In general they are needed by plants in amounts equal to about one one-hundredth or less of the amounts of the macronutrient elements needed. Until about 1920 none of these elements except iron was known to be needed by plants (it was difficult to purify sources of the macronutrients sufficiently so that they did not contain the micronutrient elements as impurities in amounts adequate for the modest requirements of plants). Today all of the above micronutrient elements must sometimes be applied to citrus trees in Florida for satisfactory growth and fruiting. They are not always needed as fertilizer components since they are present in some soils in sufficient and available supply or present in organic matter added to the soil or in certain sources used to supply macronutrient elements.

In general the micronutrient elements are needed by the plant to form organic catalysts, or enzymes, in combination with a protein. Only minute amounts of them are needed because very small amounts of enzymes control chemical reactions within plant cells between large amounts of plant foods or other compounds and are not themselves used up in the process. Whereas the macronutrient elements (except potassium) enter into the composition of living plant substance, cell walls, and stored food, the micronutrients do not become part of these products but are used over and over again in their formation or degradation.

Deficiencies of micronutrients usually result in rather distinctive patterns of leaf chlorosis, the intensity of the chlorosis being proportional to the severity of the deficiency. Sometimes twigs and fruits may also exhibit characteristic symptoms of deficiency. On the other hand, deficiencies of the macronutrient elements do not usually produce characteristic symptoms in leaves, twigs, or fruits of comparable distinctiveness unless the deficiency is quite acute. Excessive amounts of the macronutrient elements are often merely tolerated by the plant, result in lowered quality of fruit, or, in the case of nitrogen, reduced yields. An excess of the micronutrient elements often results in toxicity and will interfere with absorption of the other elements, which may cause lower yields and reduction in fruit quality.

As a final important contrast, it should be noted that there is usually a relationship between the amount of the macronutrient elements available (up to an optimum) and the amount of tree growth and fruit production. For citrus trees, the levels of nitrogen and potassium availability are especially related to yields. There is no such relationship with the micronutrient elements. A certain level is necessary to avoid deficiency symptoms, but amounts in excess of this have no effect on tree performance until they reach toxic levels.

Soil Reaction and Nutrient Availability

The term *soil reaction* refers to the acidity or alkalinity of the soil and is expressed in units of *p*H. In Florida these values range from *p*H 3.0 (an exceedingly acid condition) to about *p*H 8.5 (a moderately alkaline condition). The neutral point on the scale, where neither acidity nor alkalinity exists, is *p*H 7, and each scale unit represents a tenfold change. Thus *p*H 5.0 is ten times as acid as *p*H 6.0. Two general situations are found in the state as regards soil reaction. Groves on alkaline soils are found in some sections, almost all in coastal areas, but the great majority of groves are planted on acid sands.

The alkaline soils of Florida are all calcareous, and contain large quantities of calcium carbonate. They have been leached of all bases other than calcium, and the very high content of this element in the soil solution makes magnesium and potassium added in fertilizers less available so that those elements must be supplied in larger amounts than will suffice on acid soils. All the micronutrient elements except molybdenum are only very slightly available at the high *p*H values of these calcareous soils; they are usually not made available by soil applications but must be applied as sprays for the trees to benefit. Molybdenum is more available in alkaline than in acidic soils, and iron is not satisfactorily absorbed from sprays by citrus trees. Sulfur may be used to change the soil reaction of calcareous soils, as it can be in acid soils, but very large quanities are required, making the job very difficult and of a long-term nature. Regular use of acidic fertilizers will also help.

Some citrus groves are on soils in which the topsoil is acid but the subsoil is calcareous. Most of the absorbing roots are in the topsoil, and such groves usually need the same treatment as groves

without alkaline subsoil, except that the treatment will be modified
to take into account the depth of the acid layer.

The well-drained, sandy soils are naturally acidic—sometimes
too acidic for citrus trees to grow on them—and they may increase
in acidity under grove culture. Partly this is due to the loss of basic
elements of fertilizers from the soil through absorption by roots and
through leaching by heavy rainfall, but the greatest cause of increasing acidity is the accumulation of sulfur used for control of rust
mites. (The use of sulfur for rust mite control is on the wane due to
its adverse effects on soil and other insect populations.) As soils become more acid, the micronutrient elements leach out more readily,
increasing deficiencies, and the basic phosphates that keep magnesium and calcium available are also leached. The nitrification process, by which ammonia is changed to the more readily available
nitrate form, is inhibited in sandy soils when the pH gets below 5.5.
Within the range of pH 5.5–6.5 there is maximum availability of
mineral nutrients to citrus trees, as well as active nitrification, and
it is very desirable that the grove soil be kept within this range of
soil reaction. At pH values above 6.5, magnesium, potassium, and
the micronutrient elements are increasingly unavailable to the
trees, so the soil reaction should not be allowed to exceed pH 7.0
except where the pH of the soil in its natural state is that high.
When high copper or manganese content makes iron unavailable,
however, it is advisable to keep the soil reaction between pH 6.5 and
7.0. Control of soil reaction is normally accomplished by use of finely
divided limestone.

The Nutrient Elements in Fertilizer Practice

Nitrogen—This element may be considered as the "balance wheel"
of citrus production, for it is the one whose level of availability will,
in general, determine the yield throughout the normal range of tree
response. This is because nitrogen (N) is used in large amounts for
production of new plant cells and tissues, and when it is in short
supply all new growth is limited. When nitrogen is supplied in
slightly subnormal amounts over a long period of time (chronic mild
deficiency), the tree responds by reduced growth and fruit production not accompanied by any specific foliar symptoms of the deficiency. If the nitrogen supply is cut off or greatly reduced for trees
that have previously enjoyed an adequate supply, the tree responds
rather soon (depending on residual supplies of organic nitrogen)
with a marked chlorosis. The older leaves become yellowed and drop

early, and later the new leaves also are unable to develop a good green color, followed in cases of persistent severe nitrogen shortage by defoliation, fruit drop, and shoot death. Above the levels of visible deficiency, shoot growth and yield increase steadily with nitrogen supply up to a maximum value unless some other element is so limiting that the tree cannot utilize the increased nitrogen efficiently. Since nitrogen level is more closely correlated with growth and fruiting than that of any other element, it usually determines the need for other elements. In fertilizer formulas or analysis ratios, the nitrogen percentage is always listed first.

The amount of nitrogen needed for a bearing citrus tree is best based on potential yield. While this amount varies somewhat with differences in the type of soil on which the trees are growing, in general it averages about 0.4 pound of nitrogen per box of fruit for oranges and 0.3 pound for grapefruit.

A high level of available nitrogen increases vegetative growth, flowering, fruit yield, and percentage of acidity in the juice; it causes a slight increase in percentage of soluble solids in the juice even though fruit production may decrease at excessive rates. Level of nitrogen has no effect on rind thickness, although a high level may delay coloring of the rind somewhat. A high nitrogen level may also decrease tree uptake of phosphorus, potassium, copper, and boron, making it necessary to provide higher levels of these elements. Excess levels of nitrogen are of no value and should be avoided. In fact, research has shown that yields are actually reduced with excessive nitrogen levels.

It used to be considered that the most important items in choosing a source of nitrogen were the rates of availability and leaching, but it is now evident that there are other factors involved of perhaps greater significance. Natural organic forms seem less satisfactory, even apart from their much greater cost, than inorganic forms because of lower quantity and quality of crop. Only if micronutrient elements are not supplied deliberately in fertilizing would organic nitrogen sources have any advantage. The availability of organic forms of nitrogen over a longer period of time, as compared with the readily leached inorganic forms, is often cited as an advantage, but research has shown that this characteristic is of little practical value, perhaps because of the unexpected ability of citrus trees to take in and store up nitrogen during rather short periods of absorption.

Choice of the two principal inorganic forms—nitrate and ammoniacal—is largely a matter of cost. Citrus trees do not distinguish between the various sources, so the cheapest per-unit cost may be the best. Exclusive use of ammoniacal forms, however, requires more frequent checking of soil reaction and subsequent correction since trees decline markedly as the soil reaction becomes more acidic. A mixture of nitrate and ammoniacal forms is a very satisfactory compromise in every way; synthetic ammonium nitrate, half nitrate and half ammonium nitrogen, is a regular and low-cost source material. The differences in tree response are rather slight, however, if pH is controlled. Nitrogen in either form is readily leached from sandy soil, so that it is not possible to build up a supply in the soil for future use except for rather short periods by use of green manures.

Nitrogen is applied in traditional dry formulations or as a liquid. Where liquid forms are used, they may be applied directly to the soil, usually as a 21–32 percent nitrogen solution or mixed with irrigation water. This mixture of water and fertilizer is known as fertigation.

Nitrogen is absorbed by citrus trees in Florida at all times of year. The rate of intake in winter is about half of the intake rate in summer, but as leaching is also much less in winter, nitrogen applications are about as effective at one season of the year as at another.

Phosphorus—This element is analyzed by the chemist and guaranteed on the fertilizer tag as equivalent P_2O_5, usually spoken of as available phosphoric acid. In spite of a fairly low natural level in many of Florida's sandy soils, it has not been possible to demonstrate symptoms of phosphorus deficiency in citrus trees grown without added phosphate on the well-drained soils of central Florida. Some of the soils used for new citrus plantings in poorly drained areas have very low native phosphate content and may require phosphates regularly in the fertilizer. Phosphorus is recommended in all areas for young trees up to seven years of age. However, applied phosphorus does not leach readily where soil pH is 6.0 or higher and the fruit crop removes very little phosphorus. Therefore, regular phosphate applications are usually not necessary. In former years, phosphorus was applied very liberally, half of each ton of fertilizer often being superphosphate. The cost of phosphorus was much lower than any other element, the superphosphate enabled cheaper forms of liquid nitrogen sources to be used in preparing fertilizer mixtures by its reaction with them, and no evidences of toxicity from the large residues of phosphate fixed in the soil have ever been found in the general citrus belt of Florida. It is clear, however, that much of the money spent in supplying these large amounts of phosphorus through many years has been wasted. A high phosphorus level actually decreases the percentages of solids and acidity in juice and delays coloring of Valencias. Approximately 0.05 pound of available phosphoric acid is required per box of fruit. Groves that have been bearing for a dozen years and have been supplied with phosphorus regularly will show no benefit from further applications, and even young groves will really benefit only from a small fraction of the amounts that have been customary. A soil test can be used to determine if phosphorus is needed.

Potassium—This is calculated and guaranteed on the fertilizer tag as the equivalent K_2O, or potash, although it is never present in this form in fertilizers. Until 1945 it was standard fertilizer practice to include more than twice as much potash as nitrogen in the mixtures applied to citrus trees. The high potash level was believed to produce fruit of better external quality as well as to cause early maturity of stem tissues in autumn. Now it is known that in oranges such high levels of potash actually produce large size, coarse skin texture, and slow loss of green color as fruit matures —conditions long supposed to result from excess of nitrogen. Ratios of nitrogen to potash today are usually 1:1, although ratios of 1:1.25 may be needed on calcareous soils. Since growers have always used some potash in citrus fertilizers and have almost invariably used excessive amounts, it is not surprising that potassium deficiency is little known in commercial citrus practice. Potassium deficiencies are now seen from time to time and are usually the result of high nitrogen rates and high production of fruit, resulting in rapid potassium depletion.

Approximately 0.4 pound of potash per box is recommended annually for oranges and 0.3 pound for grapefruit, just as for nitrogen. All of the usual source materials seem to supply available potash about equally well. There is practically no absorption of potassium by citrus trees during cold weather, but the element is readily stored for future use by trees.

Magnesium—Only since 1930 has this element assumed an important place in fertilization of citrus trees in Florida. After the discovery that bronzing of grapefruit leaves—a chlorotic pattern in which green was gradually replaced by a dark yellow color—was due to magnesium deficiency, it was recognized that deficiency of this element often was limiting yields and made trees very subject to cold injury. Today, magnesium compounds are regularly supplied to augment the very low natural amounts in the soils of Florida.

Dolomitic limestone, a naturally occurring mixture of calcium and magnesium carbonates, serves as well as ordinary calcic limestone to correct acidity and at the same time puts large amounts of slowly available magnesium into the soil. Magnesium is needed at about 30 percent of the rate of nitrogen for seeded varieties, and 15 percent of the rate of nitrogen for seedless types. In general, most of this will be provided when dolomite is used as an amendment to control soil reaction. The balance of the needed magnesium, or all of it when calcic limestone is used, is supplied by a readily available form in the fertilizer mixture. With regular use of dolomite to maintain the soil pH between 6.0 and 7.0, magnesium may be eliminated from ground applications of fertilizer. Where native soil pH is naturally high, calcium is usually abundant and is an antagonist to magnesium. In such situations, foliar applications of magnesium nitrate are effective. Seedy varieties respond to magnesium applications to a greater extent than seedless ones because seeds store large amount of magnesium and remove it from the leaves, where it is needed to produce the green coloring pigment, chlorophyll. So long as magnesium is provided in amounts that prevent deficiency symptoms, there is no increase in growth or yield as magnesium levels increase. Absorption of magnesium, like that of potassium, slows dramatically in winter.

Calcium—While this element is needed in large amounts by green plants, the citrus grower need not be concerned about it for its nutrient role because the supply is rarely inadequate. This is true because of the regular need of large amounts of calcium carbonate for controlling soil acidity as well as the further large amounts of calcium supplied in superphosphate. Alkaline soils usually have an abundance of calcium.

Sulfur—As with calcium, sulfur deficiency has never been found in citrus plantings in Florida and probably never will be. There are two good reasons for this. Large quantities of combined sulfur in available form are regularly supplied in the materials used primarily to provide other elements, especially in superphosphate but also as sulfates of the heavy metals and ammonia. Sulfur is sometimes used for control of rust mite, eventually being washed down to the ground by rain and undergoing changes in the soil that make it available as a nutrient. The problem of sulfur for the citrus grower is not one of its possible deficiency or excess as a nutrient element but of the effect of pesticidal sulfur on soil reaction, as will be discussed later.

Iron—Chlorotic patterns due to iron deficiency have been recognized far longer than any others and always appear first on the young shoots. A striking feature is that the soil may have a high content of iron, yet plants may either not be able to absorb it or be unable to utilize it after absorption. Iron deficiency occurs often in plants growing in high pH, in waterlogged soils, or in soils very low in organic matter—the so-called sand-soaks. Other iron deficiency problems have occurred where high levels of copper are present. The copper residues, sometimes as much as a thousand pounds per acre, had resulted from the combination of copper fungicidal sprays and copper added in fertilizer mixtures. Accumulations of either manganese or zinc also have a depressing effect on iron availability, but neither of these metals has yet reached the level in citrus groves where its effects are as serious as those of copper have been. For some reason, application of iron by spraying has not proven satisfactory on citrus trees, and soil applications merely increase the already large amount of unavailable iron in the soil. The solution to the problem has been the use of chelated forms of iron, which puts iron into the soil in an organic combination immune to the effects of copper but available to plant roots. On acid sandy soils a 5 percent chelated iron, applied at a rate of fourteen ounces per trees, gives prompt recovery. On calcareous soils it is more difficult to overcome the factors making iron unavailable. Another type of iron chelate (hydroxy-chelates) is usually effective when applied at the rate of five to twelve ounces of 6 percent chelate per tree. The higher rates are for larger trees.

Copper—The conditions known variously as red rust, exanthema, dieback, or ammoniation were noted in Florida citrus trees as early as 1875 and were attributed to various causes, especially the use of ammonia or manure. About 1912 it was discovered that application of copper sulfate ("bluestone") to the ground under citrus trees cured this disease, although no one then thought copper could be essential to plants, but it was not until the late 1930s that regular use of copper eliminated dieback as a serious problem. Growers and research workers alike tended to overlook the fact that when copper sprays were regularly used for fungus control, no other measures were needed to prevent dieback. In planning fertilizer mixtures to avoid mineral deficiencies, copper was included without regard to spray residues, and after some ten to fifteen years of double dosage, the excessive accumulations of copper in grove soil brought about the iron deficiencies. Today, it is recognized that no copper should be included in fertilizers if copper sprays are regularly applied or if a grove soil test shows over fifty pounds of copper

per acre in the top six inches. In young groves not yet bearing or in groves where copper sprays are not employed, about one-fortieth as much copper should be included in the fertilizer mixture as the amount of nitrogen. Soil applications should cease as soon as the accumulated copper in the top half foot reaches fifty pounds. Where soil tests show copper levels in excess of a hundred pounds per acre, the pH should be maintained above 6.5 to prevent toxicities.

Zinc—The effects of zinc deficiency are most often expressed in citrus trees as frenching of foliage, a severe chlorosis in which leaf tissue becomes nearly or quite white except for green veins. At the same time, leaf size grows progressively smaller as the deficiency becomes more severe, and shoot internodes become shorter, giving a rosette effect. Recognition of this condition about 1934 as due to zinc deficiency led to realization that other metallic elements might also be deficient. Since frenching severely decreases the leaf area for food making, zinc-deficient trees make very restricted growth and bear little fruit. Citrus trees are not readily able to obtain adequate supplies of zinc from soil applications, but the metal is readily absorbed from sprays. After visible symptoms of deficiency have been corrected, smaller quantities of zinc are applied in an annual spraying to prevent recurrence of the deficiency. If these preventive sprays are used from the start of the grove, there need never be any deficiency. The standard dosage of zinc sprays is calculated as five pounds metallic zinc equivalent per five hundred gallons of spray.

Manganese—A mild form of chlorosis has since about 1932 been associated with deficiency of manganese on acid, sandy soils. The marl chlorosis or marl frenching found on calcareous soils is the result of combined deficiencies of manganese and zinc, and also sometimes of iron. In the 1930s serious cases of manganese deficiency were found in many groves on acid soils because the pH had been allowed to drop well below 5.0 and manganese had been leached out. With maintenance of the soil reaction above pH 5.5, manganese accumulates in the soil. Because of the widespread manganese deficiencies, this element was commonly added in fertilizers from 1934 on, but by 1950 excessive accumulations of it were becoming apparent. A temporary mild deficiency pattern on new shoots is not detrimental to the growth or fruiting of citrus trees. Only in the case of persistent deficiency symptoms should corrective measures be taken. On sandy soils, manganese sulfate, at seven to ten pounds per acre, is usually effective from ground application, but on calcareous soils this is not true. On such soils, manganese sulfate may be applied as a spray, but the effect is only noted for one season. If sprays are used, three to five pounds of manganese equivalent per five hundred gallons is the recommended dosage.

Boron—Florida growers first became aware of this element because of the toxic effect of boron impurities in certain potash salts. Occasionally, also, boron toxicity occurred in trees around which borax-dipped field boxes from packinghouses had been stacked. Once the source of the injury was identified and further additions were stopped, boron could be eliminated from the soil by liming and irrigation or, more slowly, by the leaching action of normal rainfall. Deficiency of boron is not often found in Florida, but it does occur sometimes when growers use only high-analysis fertilizers or following a prolonged drought. Boron is easily available to citrus trees from applications of a soluble borate either on the ground or as spray, the latter method giving quicker response. The difference between amounts of boron that are beneficial and those that are toxic is very small, so unusual care is needed in applying this element. It should never be applied in the fertilizer mixture and as a spray in the same year, and it should not be applied at all unless there is some evidence of need. Trees on rough lemon show deficiency more slowly than those on sour orange stock. Where one desires to avoid any possibility of deficiency arising, boron may be included in the fertilizer or in a spray application at about one three-hundredth the amount of boron as of nitrogen.

Molybdenum—Ever since the turn of the century, a peculiar chlorosis of citrus leaves had been noted, later called "yellow spot," that did not respond to any of the treatments that corrected other chlorotic symptoms. Only since 1950 has it been realized that yellow spot is a symptom of molybdenum deficiency. This element is less available in acid than in slightly alkaline soils, unlike all other heavy metals, and since deficiency occurs usually on soils that have been allowed to become undesirably acid, soil applications of molybdenum compounds do not relieve the deficiency. However, molybdenum sprays, using ten ounces of sodium molybdate per five hundred gallons in severe cases and five ounces for milder deficiencies, give prompt correction. Groves in which the soil pH is maintained above 6.0 are not likely to exhibit molybdenum deficiency.

The Citrus Fertilizer Program

A fertilizer program has as its objective making available for plant growth nutrient elements that are not obtainable under natural conditions. Some of these elements may be present in concentrations too low for plants to survive, some may be present and available in quantities that severely limit growth and yield, and some may be present in ample supply if only they were available to the plant. The fertilizer program must either augment the existing supply until it reaches adequate levels or increase the availability of present but unavailable elements. The citrus fertilizer program accomplishes both of these. It is designed not only to meet present needs of the trees, to enable them to produce a current crop of desired size and quality, but also to maintain a satisfactory state of health and vigor for future crop production. The effectiveness of a fertilizer program, therefore, should never be judged by the results it produces for a single year, for these are largely influenced by previous programs. It is only by following a program for three or four years that a grower is in a position to assess its worth with confidence.

The citrus fertilizer program may be considered broadly as having three divisions: (1) the application of soil amendments, primarily for control of soil reaction; (2) the application of nutrient elements on the ground, or conventional fertilizing; and (3) the application of nutritional elements as foliar or nutritional sprays.

Soil Amendments and Soil Reaction

The term *soil amendments* covers materials that are incorporated into the soil for the purpose of improving soil characteristics and making them more favorable for plant growth. It properly includes organic matter mixed with the soil to improve the ability of sandy soils to hold water and nutrients and to increase aeration and tilth of clay soils. Organic sources of nitrogen, such as castor pomace and tankage, have some effect as amendments in addition to their primary function of supplying nitrogen, but the amounts added by their use in commercial fertilizers are so small that they can have only a negligible effect. Some growers have hauled into the grove such bulky and low-nutrient materials as water-hyacinths and meadow hay, but the cost of such practices usually far exceeds their value to the grove. Soil organic matter is usually increased best by growing and disking-in green manure crops.

The soil amendments of chief significance for Florida citrus groves are those that influence soil reaction, namely dolomitic and calcium limestones. Annually up to two thousand pounds of one of these materials may be required per acre to maintain the desired pH range on acid sands. Since each pound of sulfur applied in some pest control programs requires slightly over three pounds of limestone to neutralize its effect on soil reaction, it is obvious that as little sulfur should be used as is consistent with good control of pests. The present trend toward control of rust mites by materials other than sulfur has changed the need for liming groves and is making it possible to avoid fluctuations in soil acidity during the year. The widespread use of irrigation has also resulted in a reduction in the need for lime since irrigation water contains substantial quantities of calcium and magnesium carbonates.

Soil reaction should be checked annually, taking a number of samples in each grove to a depth of six inches from locations under the outer edge of the foliage canopy. Samples taken nearer the trunk are likely to give very low pH readings because of the drip of sulfur from leaves to ground, while samples taken in the row middles will be high because of no sulfur involved to lower previous corrections of soil reaction. A composite sample combining individual samples from twenty trees is very desirable.

The amount of lime needed will depend not only on the pH reading but also on the texture and organic matter content of the soil. The lower the pH value, the more lime is needed, and the finer the texture and the higher the organic matter content, the more lime is needed for a given pH. Under average conditions in sandy Florida soils, about two hundred pounds of limestone are required per acre to raise the pH value by 0.1 point, that is, from 5.0 to 5.1. If the very satisfactory practice is adopted of raising the pH by liming to 6.5 whenever it reaches 5.5, then 10×200, or 2,000 pounds (one ton) of limestone, will be needed to make this correction. Applications of lime may be made with equal satisfaction at any time of year; usually it is planned for a time when other grove work is slack. As indicated previously, dolomitic limestone is usually preferred because it supplies magnesium at the same time as it corrects acidity.

Application of Nutrient Elements on the Ground

Research has shown that the number and timing of fertilizer applications are of little importance provided a sufficient amount of needed nutrients in satisfactory balance with one another is applied each year, preferably during the months from October to June when heavy rains are less likely to leach away nutrients before the trees can take them in. The traditional practice has been to make three fertilizer applications a year: one in the autumn (October-November), one in the late winter (January-February), and one in early summer (May-June). The first of these assures

Fig. 8-1. Bulk fertilizer spreader in operation.

the tree of a store of nutrients to replenish what is lost in fruit harvested and leaching by summer rains; the second is immediately important for fruit set and new vegetative growth; and the third provides for rapidly developing fruit and for the summer growth flush. This practice is eminently safe and satisfactory, but there is expense for labor as well as for fertilizer at each application, and fewer applications would save money if the trees thrived as well. Many growers have found that they can get along satisfactorily by making only two applications per year, in October-November and in April-May, supplying the same total amount of nutrients as would usually be supplied in three applications. There is good research basis to consider it probable that a single annual application in April or May would be equally satisfactory, for citrus trees have shown an unexpected ability to absorb and store nutrients for future use; but this is not firmly enough established to be recommended as a safe practice yet. Young trees need more frequent applications, and trees growing in impoverished sites may also benefit from more frequent applications.

Fig. 8-2. Bulk fertilizer trailer used to transport fertilizer to groves for application.

The needed nutrient elements may be provided from many source materials and in various types of mixtures. Regardless of the sources and combinations, the amounts and ratios of the elements are the factors of real importance for a successful program. The commercial grower must vary this program to take account of variations in stock-scion combinations, in environmental conditions, in cost of fertilizer materials, and in market demands and prices. Fertilizer recommendations for commercial groves of bearing trees are based on the expected yield per tree, as estimated from the known yields of the past few years. The basis of fertilizer application currently favored by research is to supply 0.4 lb of nitrogen for each expected box of oranges, mandarins, lemons, limes, or tangelos, while 0.3 lb per box is sufficient for grapefruit. Murcotts, tangelos, lemons, and limes should receive 0.5 lb per box. Other elements are added in a fixed ratio to nitrogen. Potash is usually supplied in equal quantity with nitrogen, magnesium at about one-fifth this rate (if a need is indicated), phosphoric acid is included at one-fourth the nitrogen amount (again, if needed), manganese at one-twentieth, copper at one-fortieth, and boron at one-three-hundredth this amount. On groves over ten but under twenty years old, the three micronutrient elements are eliminated unless deficiency symptoms indicate their need. Iron in the chelate form is applied either mixed in fertilizer or as a separate application when deficiency symptoms show it is needed.

Usually fertilizer mixtures containing all of the needed elements are used, and by convention the successive numbers represent the percent of available nutrients in the order N, P_2O_5, K_2O, Mn, Cu. Formerly mixtures with 4 percent nitrogen were common, but currently the minimum percentage of nitrogen is usually 6, and the mixture may contain 8, 10, or even 15 percent or more because of decreased cost of applying smaller quantities of higher analysis.

Up to the age of ten years, a citrus tree is rapidly increasing in size, and fertilizer applications must take account of the vegetative growth as well as of crop. For the young bearing tree, therefore, fertilizer recommendations are better based on age than on yield. By the time the tree is ten years old, vegetative growth has usually slowed down to a more steady pace and there are several years of fruit production on which to base yield expectations.

Recommendations for nonbearing and young bearing trees have already been presented in chapter 6. Bearing trees may require between one hundred and three hundred pounds of nitrogen and amounts of other elements are based on the quantity of nitrogen applied. Florida citrus in unlikely to benefit from nitrogen in excess of two hundred fifty pounds per acre no matter how large the yield, and groves grown in shallow soils may actually require substantially less. A typical orange grove might require fertilizer in the following amounts (assume a yield of five hundred boxes per acre):

Nitrogen needed = 0.4 lbs. N/box × 500 boxes = 200 lbs.

Potash needed = 0.4 lbs. K_2O/box × 500 boxes = 200 lbs.

Other nutrients applied on basis of need.

Therefore, this grove would need two hundred pounds each of N and K_2O per year based on yield. This could be supplied by a fertilizer mixture of 10-0-10 applied at a rate of two thousand pounds per acre per year. This could be split into two applications of a thousand pounds each or three applications of 666 pounds.

Table 8-1 gives general recommendations for oranges and grapefruit based on nitrogen needs.

Application of Nutrient Elements in Sprays

Usually when spraying citrus trees is mentioned, it is pest control that is in mind, but spraying to provide certain micronutrient elements is standard practice in citrus culture. These elements may be applied separately but are usually incorporated into pest control sprays to reduce the costs of applying them. Nutritional sprays for Florida citrus trees date from around 1934, when zinc was found to be required and to be poorly available from ground applications but readily so in sprays. Other micronutrient elements are occasionally applied as sprays.

Nutritional sprays are costly to apply by themselves, and the residues they leave on the foliage contribute to increase the populations of insects and mites. While these sprays are often beneficial to the tree, or even necessary to its well-being, undesirable or harmful plant reactions may result from their indiscriminate use. They should be used only when benefits can definitely be expected. The two situations that always warrant their use to correct observed deficiencies are (1) when applications to the soil are not effective, and (2) when a more immediate response is considered desirable than can be obtained by soil applications. Nutritional sprays are satisfactory only for supplying elements needed in very small amounts—the micronutrient elements, or for supplying magnesium (as magnesium nitrate) to trees on alkaline soils. They may be corrective sprays, aimed at correction of an observed deficiency condition, or maintenance sprays, intended to hold the nutrient level above the point of observable deficiency by regular application of smaller amounts than were needed to correct the deficiency.

Zinc compounds are absorbed to only a very small extent by citrus trees from soil applications, and because this element is often deficient in Florida soils, it is sometimes applied as a nutritional spray. For such maintenance spraying, 2.5 pounds of metallic zinc per five hundred gallons of water satisfies the annual requirement. This amount of zinc may also be provided by five pounds of neutral zinc compound (55 percent Zn). The spray application may be made either during the dormant period or shortly after blooming, and it needs to reach only the outside of the foliage canopy. If zinc deficiency symptoms have developed in the

Table 8-1.
Pounds of nitrogen fertilizer to be applied to furnish nitrogen requirement of orange and grapefruit trees under normal conditions

Fruit production (boxes/acre)	Pounds of nitrogen (N)[a] needed per acre per year		Pounds of nitrogen fertilizer needed per acre per year[b]					
			15.5% N		33.5% N		45.0% N	
	Orange	Grapefruit	Orange	Grapefruit	Orange	Grapefruit	Orange	Grapefruit
<200	100	60	645	485	300	225	220	165
300	120	90	775	580	360	270	265	200
400	160	120	1030	775	480	360	355	265
500	200	150	1290	965	600	450	445	335
600	240	180	1580	1160	715	538	535	400
700	280	210	1805	1355	835	620	620	465
>800	300	240	1935	1450	895	670	665	500

SOURCE: Taken from "Recommended fertilizers and nutritional sprays for citrus," edited by R.C.J. Koo, IFAS Bulletin no. 536D.

a. Nitrogen needed is based on 0.4 pound per box of fruit for oranges and 0.3 pound per box for grapefruits. In most cases, do not use less than 100 pounds or more than 300 pounds of nitrogen for orange trees and not less than 60 pounds or more than 240 pounds for grapefruit trees per acre per year.

b. The figures given should be divided by the number of applications per year to obtain pounds per application.

grove before any nutritional spray has been used, a corrective spray will be needed. This should contain twice as much zinc as the maintenance spray and usually need be used only one season.

Yellow spot, due to molybdenum deficiency, is quite uncommon, and is noted first in summer as small, water-soaked areas on the leaves. Mild symptoms can be corrected by spray containing five ounces of sodium molybdate per five hundred gallons of water, while severe symptoms require double this amount. Only the outside of the canopy needs to be covered. Spraying is done only when deficiencies are seen.

Manganese and boron are often poorly available from ground applications on alkaline soils, and their deficiencies must then be corrected by sprays. The same is true of copper if no fungicidal copper sprays are employed. Manganese and copper are used at the rate of 3.75 pounds of metallic copper per five hundred gallons of water. Boron sprays regularly contain 1.25 pounds of soluble borate in five hundred gallons of water. In all cases of nutritional sprays, avoid excess applications.

In summary, the complete nutritional program for commercial citrus production must include (1) soil amendments of liming materials to adjust the soil reaction to the pH range of 6.0 to 6.5 for acid soils; (2) application on the ground of sufficient amounts in proper proportions of the elements not naturally present or available in the soil, through a two- to three-application fertilizer program; and (3) nutritional sprays as needed to supply elements that cannot be furnished by soil applications.

Soil and Leaf Analyses

Testing the soil and evaluating the nutritional status of leaf tissues may provide growers an opportunity to refine the fertilizer program. These tests are diagnostic and may help in solving nutritional problems as well. As mentioned previously, soil tests are used to determine soil pH and whether or not liming is needed. This is the principal value of soil tests, but they may also be used to assess phosphorus levels and to detect toxic levels of soil copper. Testing for other elements is of little value due to inherent sampling errors that arise from taking comparatively few and small samples to represent a large volume of soil that is not at all uniform.

The analysis of leaf tissue provides a very accurate method of determining the actual mineral content of the plant. Proper sampling is extremely important and, therefore, both sampling and analysis are most often left in the hands of the analytical laboratory staff.

A standard leaf sample consists of 100 or more spring flush leaves, usually collected in late summer. The leaves should be taken from nonfruiting twigs of at least twenty trees to assure a representative sample. The leaves must not have been sprayed with nutritional sprays since this will cause a contamination that cannot be resolved.

After chemical analyses have been run, the values obtained can be compared against leaf analysis standards such as those found in table 8-2.

Table 8-2.
Leaf analysis standards for citrus based on
4- to 6-month-old spring-cycle leaves
from nonfruiting terminals

Element	Deficient	Low	Optimum	High	Excess
N (%)	<2.2	2.2–2.4	2.5–2.7	2.8–3.0	>3.0
P (%)	<.09	.09–.11	.12–.16	.17–.29	>.30
K (%)	<.7	.7–1.1	1.2–1.7	1.8–2.3	>2.4
Ca (%)	<1.5	1.5–2.9	3.0–4.9	5.0–6.9	>7.0
Mg (%)	<.20	.20–.29	.30–.49	.50–.70	>.80
Cl (%)	?	?	.05–.10	.11–.20	>.20
Mn (ppm)	<17	18–24	25–100	101–300	>500
Zn (ppm)	<17	18–24	25–100	101–300	>300
Cu (ppm)	<3	3–4	5–16	17–20	>20
Fe (ppm)	<35	36–59	60–120	121–200	>200
B (ppm)	<20	21–35	36–100	101–200	>250
Mo (ppm)	<.05	.06–.09	.10–1.0	2.0–5.0	>5.0

SOURCE: Taken from "Recommended fertilizers and nutritional sprays for citrus," edited by R.C.J. Koo, IFAS Bulletin no. 536D.

9 /
The Citrus Pest Management Program

In the earlier editions of this book, pest control was discussed in a chapter entitled "The Citrus Spray Program." As scientists have gained a more comprehensive understanding of pest biology and have developed alternative methods for the control of pests and diseases, growers have adopted strategies dramatically different from wholesale chemical spraying. Therefore, we now refer to this phase of the production program as pest management.

The climate in Florida encourages pest problems greater than those in many other citrus-producing areas. While a subtropical or tropical climate is required to grow citrus, few other areas have the long periods of high humidity and heavy rainfall that Florida enjoys. There are areas in the tropics, of course, where the climate is even more favorable for pest development, but in most cases citrus is not a commercial crop in those areas.

Pest Management Strategies

While there are many approaches to citrus pest management in Florida, there are three that emerge as most important. Often, the easiest way to deal with some pest problems is to do nothing at all. Nature has provided ecological systems of checks and balances that maintain some degree of order in the world around us. In citrus management, we would call this program of nonspraying and encouraging nature to help us with our problems a biological control program. Citrus was originally grown in Florida under this program and, in some areas, such programs are still reasonably successful. Biological control programs do best in isolated areas away from the influence of pesticides used by other growers. Pesticides can upset the delicate ecological balance in the grove where you are trying to effect biological pest management. Fruit produced in groves under a biological pest control system are rarely blemish-free since such a system usually operates with a low pest population at all times. Where top exterior quality and maximum productivity are not essential, such a program may be satisfactory for some growers.

A second approach to pest control is represented by the extreme at the other end of the spectrum from biological control. This, of course, would be total control of all pests by chemical sprays. Intensive pest control could keep fruit and trees in the best possible condition (assuming no slip-ups), but such a program would be costly and inefficient and would contribute to pollution of our environment. Further complications would also arise because sprays to control one pest often will destroy biological control agents that could help control other pests. The scenario becomes very complicated and is certainly less than ideal.

The third approach is really a combination of the first two and is usually referred to as *integrated pest management*. This program uses biological control where possible, supplementing it with pesticides and mechanical control only when biological agents are unable to do the job alone. Another important aspect of this integrated pest management approach is the judicious selection of pesticides with specificity for the target organism and without adverse effects on "friendly" biological control agents. Most Florida citrus is grown under the integrated pest management program for reasons that should be obvious.

Philosophy

Pest management strategies should be developed with several factors in mind, but the overriding consideration must be the intended destination of the fruit in the marketplace. Fruit destined for processing simply does not have to have the external quality of fruit going into fresh market channels, and the pest management program will differ substantially between groves producing fruit for different types of markets. Some groves producing the highest quality fruit for the gift-fruit market may receive four to five (or even more) sprayings per year to achieve the highest external quality possible. Other groves that routinely produce fruit destined for processing may receive only one spraying each year, or in some cases none.

Not only the intended market determines pest management strategies, even though this is a dominant consideration. Current and historical levels of both insect and disease populations must also be considered. Careful inspection and record keeping are very important in all pest management operations. Some pest problems may be debilitating and require attention lest tree condition and subsequent fruit production suffer.

Spray Application

Spray application may be made in several ways when it is required. The most frequent method of application is through the use of air carrier sprayers, where a solution of water and appropriate chemicals is injected into a large volume of high-velocity air, which carries the material into the tree canopy. Hydraulic spraying is another method of application and is accomplished by spraying a water/chemical mixture directly on the tree through a spray gun thereby washing the tree down with the spray solution. While very effective when properly done, this method is very slow and not economically suitable to large-scale operations.

Aircraft provide other methods for the application of chemicals for pest management. Both fixed-wing aircraft and helicopters are sometimes used, especially when rapid application is important. Although aircraft application is the quickest way to spray, it can be one of the most superficial. Because the volume of material applied is quite small and aircraft speed is quite high, most of the spray is applied only to the outer tree canopy areas.

The mechanics of spray application is a science and technology in its own right. A great deal of information is available on the subject from a variety of sources. Since comprehensive details would be beyond the scope of this book, this chapter will offer only a brief discussion of the application of sprays. The best information available is probably found in "Florida Citrus Spray Guide," a publication that is revised and published annually by the University of Florida IFAS Cooperative Extension Service. Copies are available from most county extension offices in Florida where citrus is produced.

Fungal Disease Control

Pest management for Florida citrus necessarily revolves around disease control. This is because the three major fungal diseases affecting citrus must be controlled by prophylaxis, or prevention. After the organism has infected the plant material, the damage is done and is usually irreversible. Therefore, timing of the disease control sprays is of paramount importance. Since each disease has a prime (and slightly different) time of maximum infection on

citrus, the diseases are best discussed individually, as that is how
they will have to be handled in the spray program.

Scab

The fungal disease called "scab" causes problems on only a few different types of citrus. It is often most serious on Temple, Murcott,
and many types of lemons. It also affects certain types of the tangelos and may be troublesome on grapefruit, especially in southern and coastal areas of Florida.

Since only young tissues (fruit, leaves, and twigs) are susceptible and peak spore release occurs in the early spring months,
control is essential during the spring flush period. Sprays may be
needed to protect the young fruit when about two-thirds of the
flower petals have fallen and again in late April to early May
when disease pressure is heavy. Proper timing and thorough
coverage is essential to success.

Melanose

The fungus associated with melanose spends part of its life cycle
in dead citrus wood. Therefore, regular pruning of deadwood will
assist in control. In fact, groves on a regular hedging and topping
program have less trouble with this disease than their unpruned
counterparts.

Unlike scab, melanose affects all citrus cultivars and is often
most troublesome on grapefruit. The disease, which can blemish
leaves, fruit, and twigs, is usually not severe enough to require
control on trees where fruit is destined for processing. On fruit
grown for fresh fruit, however, blemishes on fruit peel can make
them unusable and must be controlled for maximum pack-out.

Infection from melanose spores is most prevalent with warm
temperatures (75–80°F) and abundant moisture (nine to twelve
hours continuous wetness). Such conditions often occur in the
spring and happen to coincide with the period of susceptibility for
both fruit and leaves. Where melanose is to be controlled, spray
application should be made in late April–early May. Sprays applied earlier to control scab, even though the same materials may
be used, will be of little benefit in controlling melanose, especially
if disease pressures are heavy.

Greasy Spot

This fungal disease affects leaves and occasionally fruit and can
attack all types of citrus although it is historically worst on grape-

fruit. Rind blemishes on the fruit can reduce fresh fruit grade but most problems from greasy spot result from leaf damage, subsequent leaf drop, and reduced yields.

Warm temperatures and long periods of wetness or very high relative humidity are essential for spore germination. Such conditions occur in late May and June most years in Florida, and this is also a period when summer flush leaves are expanding and are vulnerable to attack. Since spore germination and infection proceed rather slowly with greasy spot, sprays are best delayed until the month of July for maximum effectiveness.

Insect and Mite Control

As stated earlier, timing for disease control is usually more critical than for insects and mites. We have already discussed three spray periods (delayed dormant and/or two-thirds petal fall, spring or postbloom spray, and a summer spray usually applied in July), and only one other major period of possible concern is the fall.

This is not to say that other pest problems can't occur at odd times. Flare-ups of certain insects and mites often occur when least expected and must be controlled. Therefore, the value of regular inspection and monitoring of all pest levels becomes increasingly obvious.

Major Spray Periods

For purposes of convenience, we'll discuss the major spraying periods, what insects and mites we might need to control at these times, and assume we can take care of any other problems on an as-needed basis.

Bloom Spray

This spray period is principally for control of scab, but inspection may show other problems are present. If so, they may be controlled by including another chemical in the scab spray. A troublesome pest sometimes occurring at this time is the citrus rust mite. Since scab is primarily a disease affecting only fresh fruit varieties, rust mite control should be considered as well.

Many pesticides are effective against the rust mite and one may be included with the regular scab spray if it is needed. Tank-mixing of two or more pesticides may result in some incompatibility problems, so be sure to read specific label instructions carefully.

Spider mites are rarely a spring problem, but some scales, whiteflies and aphids may be present and require control. The postbloom or spring spray may be a better time to control these pests.

Postbloom or Spring Spray

This is the time period for effective melanose control. If disease pressures have not been heavy, and especially if the fruit is to be processed, the melanose spray may not be necessary. Other pests such as rust mites, scales, whiteflies, aphids and mealy bugs may be troublesome and require control. Careful monitoring of all pest levels will help make this judgment more effective.

Summer Spray

If a spray is needed for maximum production of citrus in Florida, this is the one. This is because greasy spot may have a serious adverse effect on tree vitality and production. This spray is best timed for July to maximize greasy spot control. Populations of other pests are also peaking at this time of year, so additional chemicals other than those used for greasy spot may be necessary. As always, careful inspection should dictate the choice of chemicals based upon population pressures. Careful consideration should also be given to adverse effects of sprays on nontarget friendly organisms that could assist with biological control.

Fall Spray

The fall months are inactive times for control of diseases, but often are busy ones for growers to control mites. Both rust and spider mites often build up in the cool, dry fall months. Rust mites cause fruit blemishes of special concern to growers of fresh fruit, while high populations of spider mites can cause damage to leaves that, if left unchecked, may defoliate the trees.

The foregoing text is a rather brief discussion of a very complex subject. Many factors should be considered before any spray is applied. Local Extension Agents and fertilizer and pesticide representatives can help with your questions and should be consulted. Local extension offices have many publications on the complex subject of pest management. The remainder of this chapter is devoted to a more detailed discussion of some of the major pests of citrus and other factors to consider in a spray program.

Major Citrus Pests

Scales, Whiteflies, and Mealybugs

This group of closely related insects comprises a larger number of active pests of citrus trees than any other in the state. Although individual species sometimes may require particular control measures, usually control for one member of this group will control other members also. Therefore, a single application of spray may be effective for several different pests.

Purple Scale—This armored scale was for many years the most destructive insect pest of citrus in Florida and used to require regular spraying for its control. This situation has changed greatly since the introduction in 1958 of a new parasite, the larva of the wasp *Aphytis lepidosaphes* Compere. With its establishment throughout the citrus belt during 1958, purple scale populations have been reduced to such low levels that little or no spraying is necessary. Weather conditions appear to have little relation to the effectiveness of this parasite. If sulfur is used repeatedly, its harmful effect on the *Aphytis* will probably make it necessary to include a scalicide in the spray program to control purple scale.

The slender, dark purple, male scale is usually found on the upper surface of leaves, while the much larger female scale, a little over 1 mm long, club-shaped, and brownish, mostly prefers the lower sides of leaves. These scales often congregate in groups and by their sucking of cell sap cause yellow-brown spots on the leaves. Where they have fed on fruits, green spots persist even after the rind develops its mature color. They also attack twigs and even limbs. The long scale, very similar to purple scale but longer, is often found mixed in these colonies.

Florida Red Scale—Although not distributed as generally over the citrus belt as purple scale, Florida red scale formerly required equal effort for control; sometimes, especially in the southern part of the state, it superseded purple scale as the major insect pest in some groves. After mild winters it was apt to occur in unusually heavy infestations. The armor of this scale is circular with a prominent central nipple, is up to 1.5 mm across, and varies in color from reddish-brown to reddish-purple. Control measures are exactly the same as for purple scale. However, due to the activity of parasites (principally the larvae of another *Aphytis* wasp species), the early scourges of this pest are no longer experienced.

Citrus Snow Scale—The name is derived from the fact that the clustered white male scales look like driven snow on the trunks or limbs, where they are mostly found. Since 1969, it has spread over the state and by 1971 had become a serious pest, considered today to be the most serious of the armored scale insects. Feeding on the trunks and limbs, chiefly, heavy populations (another *Aphytis* wasp species) spread onto the leaves and fruit. In some cases, parasite populations have been established that help keep this pest in check.

Glover Scale—This relative of purple scale, often referred to as long scale, does the same damage and is controlled similarly. This scale has been in the state since the introduction of citrus, but it occurred in only small numbers. It was thought to be held in check by parasitic activity. Surprisingly enough, as purple scale became less important, Glover scale populations increased. It can be distinguished from purple scale by its longer, narrower armor, particularly of the female.

Yellow Scale—This pest has a round armor much like that of the Florida red scale but lighter in color. No eggs will be found under the armor since the females give birth to living young. Like the Florida red scale, it attacks only leaves and fruit. In recent years, this scale has spread throughout the state and at times had demanded control.

Chaff Scale—The scales are brownish-gray, nearly circular, often clustered densely, especially on branches, like overlapping pieces of wheat chaff. The most distinguishing feature of this scale is the purple color of the female, the eggs, and the crawlers. With heavy infestations the leaves and fruit develop considerable populations of this scale, and the persistent green spots left on the fruit by its feeding are particularly serious on tangerines. The chaff scale appears to hold its own as a pest in various groves throughout the state.

Other Scale Insects—While the above-mentioned six scales belong to the armored scale group whose representatives are major pests in all parts of the citrus world, there are other scale pests that may, at times, be injurious.

The cottony-cushion scale belongs to an entirely different family. The adult female is conspicuous because of its greatly expanded, fluted, white cottony abdomen filled with red eggs. It is rarely a serious problem in bearing groves because the Vedalia ladybeetle, introduced to Florida from Australia via California in 1899, keeps the populations low. Control of this scale by the Vedalia is the classic example of biological control. In the nursery, however, it may require control measures at times.

Another family, the soft scales, whose apparent armor is part of the actual insect body, includes the black scale, brown soft scale, and green scale. These rarely appear in damaging numbers, unless parasite activity is retarded, although black scale does require control measures at times. Ridges on the upper part of the body of the female black scale portray the letter "H."

Citrus Mealybug—Usually not a pest requiring control, this insect may at times become numerous enough to cause serious injury. It is most readily recognized by its white masses, enveloped in cottony frass, which are seen on tree trunks in very early spring. In heavy infestations, this mealybug causes dropping of fruit and lowering of grade, especially with grapefruit, because of the hard lumps on the fruit rind, which become yellow prematurely. Any control measure is best applied before blooming or immediately thereafter, before the crawlers have become established under the calyx (button) of the fruit.

Whiteflies—The common citrus whitefly, which lays yellow eggs, and the cloudy-wing whitefly, whose eggs are black, are both serious pests at times. Often they occur together, but the former is more abundant in the northern area and the latter in the central and southern areas. The woolly whitefly is widely distributed but rarely troublesome. The name whitefly comes from the adult form, which is a small, two-winged, flying, white insect and is harmless in itself. The damage is done by the feeding of the larval stages (nymphs), which are much like scale crawlers and suck food similarly from tender leaves, especially those of vigorous sprouts. They are found mostly on the lower surface of leaves, rarely attacking the fruit. These whitefly larvae, along with aphids, mealybugs, and soft scales, produce a sweet secretion, called "honeydew," which serves as food for the sooty mold fungus, often seen as a black film coating leaves or fruit. Besides making fruit unattractive, this coating delays the natural loss of green color as the fruit matures and serves as a protection for various other pests.

Natural enemies, especially the friendly fungi, and the sprays for control of scale insects have long since reduced populations to a low level. Control is easily obtained with the same materials used for scales, and usually sprays applied for scales take care of whiteflies too, so they rarely require special control.

Other Insect Pests

Aphids—Aphids feed upon succulent growth, especially very young developing shoots. Several species of aphids are found generally throughout the citrus belt. Although winged forms may occasionally be seen, aphids are usually observed as colonies of wingless forms densely clustered on tender shoots. The young leaves from which they suck food become curled inward toward the feeding area, and remain permanently dwarfed and twisted. The green citrus aphid is perhaps the most destructive species, but the melon and black citrus aphids do very similar injury to new growth. All these species are able to transmit the tristeza virus disease.

Control of aphids is usually not necessary in mature citrus groves. Trees that produce a succession of succulent growth flushes, trees that have unusually vigorous and succulent growth because of heavy pruning, or trees whose foliage is valued highly may warrant spray applications. Young trees, whose foliage is worth so much to future crops, often require control measures for aphids.

Aphids multiply rapidly and do their damage quickly. Any control measures must be anticipated in order to kill the pests before deformation of leaves has occurred and, for ideal control, repeat applications are often required. As vectors of tristeza, all three species must be considered in areas of active spread of this virus where susceptible rootstocks are used.

Plant Bugs—The true bugs found as pests in citrus groves include the citron bug, which feeds on the seeds of the wild citron (related to watermelon) found on the sand hills of central Florida, and the leaf-footed plant bug and the stinkbugs, which feed on the immature pods of crotalarias and other legumes. After their usual food supplies have dwindled in the fall, these bugs often fly to nearby trees and feed on mature citrus fruits, causing them to drop. Since they puncture the rind with their piercing-sucking mouth parts, it is almost impossible to see where this feeding was done unless the rind color is slightly changed at that point. These pests have declined in importance in the last decade.

The best control measure is to cut down the cover crop in the grove in September, before citrus fruits have become attractive to these bugs or while they are still in an immature, wingless stage.

Grasshoppers—These pests breed in outlying fields, or even in citrus groves at times, and may develop to such numbers as to become very harmful when the grasses on which they usually feed are eliminated by cultivation or are killed by drought or frost in late autumn. Then they feed on citrus leaves and may destroy practically all the foliage in a grove in a short time. Two species are common in Florida, the large American or bird grasshopper, which is sometimes a very serious pest, and the even larger but less active lubber grasshopper, which is only of minor importance. If they are developing in fields adjacent to a grove, chemical control may be necessary after the grove cover crop has been chopped or disked. When the infestation develops within the grove, however, proper management of the cover crop is very helpful in control. Clean cultivation during the early spring (February to May) and after the middle of August will reduce grasshopper infestations by preventing laying of eggs in the grove soil.

Root Weevils—Several species of weevils (often referred to as beetles) cause serious damage to citrus trees, particularly in the larval stage, which feeds upon the roots. The adult stage feeds upon the leaves but damage is not serious; feeding is often so slight that the insect would hardly ingest sufficient material to kill the leaf if an insecticide were applied to the aerial parts of the tree.

The grayish-brown Fuller rose beetle has been known for many years in Florida. In 1952 its white, legless larvae were first found feeding destructively on the roots of citrus trees in the Indian River area; since then it has been reported from other citrus-growing areas of the state. The adult causes some injury by feeding on the leaves, making characteristic notches in the margins.

The citrus root weevil, known as the blue-green beetle in the Indian River area, is a serious problem there and may be found in other citrus regions. The sugarcane rootstalk borer weevil was inadvertently introduced into Florida and found near Apopka (Orange County) in 1964. This weevil has a wide range of host plants and constitutes a serious threat to the citrus industry.

Mites

Mites are related to spiders, often spinning webs, and several kinds of them make trouble for the citrus grower. They differ from insects most obviously in having eight legs normally, whereas insects have six, but they are so small that the grower is not likely to try leg counting. By far the most important is the rust mite.

Rust Mite—This was one of the first pests to be noticed by early citrus growers in Florida because of its causing oranges to be "russeted" or grapefruit, lemons, and limes to show the silvering of rind called "sharkskin." The presence of rust mites is difficult to detect until they have demonstrated it by their characteristic injuries because they are exceedingly small—hardly one two-hundredth-inch long. The yellow, conical, segmented body, broadened at the front end, has only four legs (the other four having been lost) and can be detected only with the aid of a good hand lens. Rust mites feed on leaves, fruit, and green twigs, and are capable of causing serious injury. The population peak is usually reached in midsummer, and fruit russetting occurs in the period from postbloom to September.

Citrus Red Mite—Although citrus red mite is the approved name for this pest, the name "purple mite" is unfortunately firmly established in Florida. It is one of a group of mites often called "red spiders"; it is about one-seventieth inch long, rose-red to purple in color, with the typical eight legs except in the first stage, when it has only six. The tiny, round, red eggs can be seen with a hand lens along the midrib near the base of leaves. This mite attacks leaves, fruits, and green twigs, but the principal feeding is done on the upper leaf surface.

The citrus red mite has been in Florida for many years, sometimes producing damages that were ascribed to other causes. The damage it was known to cause began to increase in severity in about 1935 until it became one of the major citrus pests. In recent years, its importance has declined. The feeding causes leaves to become grayish and produces mesophyll collapse, characterized by translucent, or necrotic, areas of the leaf due to death of mesophyll cells. Firing, drying, and browning of leaves while still attached to the twigs and defoliation often occur in the winter and spring as a result of heavy infestations. The mite also feeds on the green wood and fruit; it causes a scratched appearance on the green rind of the fruit but the final grade is not impaired.

Texas Citrus Mite—This mite was found for the first time in Florida in 1951 in Brevard County and had become generally distributed over the state and a major pest by 1966. Under a good lens, it can be seen to be tan to brownish-green in color, with greenish spots along the sides. Like the citrus red mite, it is found chiefly on the upper side of leaves, and its tiny, flat, discoid eggs, light tan in color, are laid along the midrib. It causes the same sort of injury as the citrus red mite and is controlled by the same materials.

Six-Spotted Mite—This long-time pest in Florida is a heavy-bodied, yellow mite with six dark spots on its back; it lives in colonies only on the lower surface of leaves and is very widely distributed throughout the citrus area. Its appearance in individual groves is sporadic, requiring vigilance on the part of the grower. During the summer period, it cannot be found in the groves. Like the citrus red mite, this pest increases in numbers rapidly during the winter and spring months if not controlled. It prefers grapefruit varieties as hosts but may also be found on other kinds of citrus trees. It seems to prefer areas in the grove of low humidity and is often most abundant in trees next to a road. Damage consists chiefly in the greatly decreased ability of leaves to make food because of its feeding, but leaves may drop in severe cases. Heavily infested leaves are characteristically crinkled, with large yellowed areas. Dropping of fruit may be an indirect result of impaired leaf activity.

Other Mites—The leprosis mite, which causes leprosis of branches (Florida scaly bark) and fruit (nailhead rust) of citrus trees, was considered a serious pest in the first quarter of this century.

The broad mite feeds on young fruit and immature leaves. While it is sometimes observed, particularly along the east coast, by its causing "sharkskin" blemish on fruit and rolling of leaf margins, it rarely causes much damage. It has, however, become a serious problem of limes in south Florida.

The citrus bud mite was first recorded in Florida in 1959 from Dade County. How serious this pest, which distorts tender new shoots, will become still remains to be seen.

Predacious mites, discussed later, are sometimes mistaken by growers for mite pests, resulting in unnecessary spraying. They cause no plant injury.

Diseases

Diseases may be caused by bacteria, fungi, algae, viruses, or nematodes. The latter two groups cannot be controlled by sprays or dusts and so are not included in this discussion of pest management. The first three diseases mentioned here are also discussed in the early portion of this chapter but are also discussed here so that all important insects and diseases are covered.

Melanose—The fungus causing this disease produces its spores only on dead twigs but attacks only young leaves, fruit, and twigs. The chief damage of melanose is the lowered grade of infected fruit. It appears as brownish, raised lesions on affected parts, but the same fungus also causes a stem-end rot of mature fruit after harvesting. Melanose costs more to control than any other production disease, for fruit of good grade can only be assured by frequent and regular spraying. Pruning of dead wood is an important aid to control, but by itself is not adequate.

Scab—Temples, satsumas, lemons, sour oranges, certain varieties of grapefruit and tangelos, and young Murcott trees are often attacked by scab, a disease caused by a fungus that grows in green tissues and causes unsightly warts on fruits and distorted leaves and twigs. On fruits, early scab lesions differ from those of melanose, being much lighter in color, larger in size, and more elevated. Fruits and leaves are often much deformed by early infection with scab, whereas fruits are not so deformed by melanose. Except for injury to nursery stock of sour orange and rough lemon, the principal damage by scab is lowered fruit grade, as it is with melanose.

Greasy Spot—This fungus-caused disease, which is seen as dark, grease-like spots scattered irregularly over the leaf surface, may be observed at any time of year, but is often more prominent on summer flush leaves. Greasy spot is usually controlled by spraying with fungicide during the month of July.

Brown Rot—In coastal areas especially, but also in other areas in years of high rainfall, early and midseason citrus varieties are apt to show rotting of fruits on the tree in early autumn due to infection by the same fungus that causes foot rot. Cultural practices such as pruning low-hanging branches and mowing or disking the cover crop will be helpful in control by permitting better circulation of air and lowering humidity.

Citrus Canker—Citrus canker is the only bacterial disease of citrus trees that has been found in Florida. It was first found in 1913 following its accidental introduction in 1910. An intensive program of eradication was instituted at once, resulting in complete eradication over several years. This eradication program was the primary factor in establishing the need for the services of a Division of Plant Industry (formerly called the "State Plant Board"). Citrus canker had not been found in the state since 1926 until it was rediscovered in 1984. A weak pathogenic strain was discovered in a central Florida citrus nursery and subsequently in other nurseries and groves. An eradication program was immediately begun, resulting in the destruction of millions of trees in nurseries and groves. A more virulent strain was discovered in the west-central Florida area about a year later, resulting in strict quarantines and additional tree destruction. The drastic actions of quarantine, destruction, and spraying of nearby trees has resulted in slow but steady reduction of this disease as a problem. It is hoped this will again result in elimination of citrus canker disease from the state, as was accomplished after earlier infestations were detected.

Other Diseases—Many other diseases attack citrus trees, from their nursery years, when damping-off of young seedlings is a hazard, to their advanced age in the grove, when dieback or root rots afflict them. Red-alga spot is the only algal disease menace to citrus. It affects seriously only limes and lemons. Control of these other citrus diseases is not accomplished by spraying or dusting but by cultural and harvesting techniques or by pruning. Some diseases attack only trees that are already weak; others attack trees on stocks unsuited to the soil. In controlling diseases in general, good sanitary practices and maintenance of tree vigor by proper nutrition and soil moisture are factors of great importance.

Biological Control of Pests

By no means are all of the living organisms found on citrus trees harmful; indeed, some of them play an important part in holding pests in check—a role spoken of as biological control of pests. Often they greatly decrease the need for applying sprays or dusts, and sometimes the choice of a material for pest control should be made with due consideration for its possible effect on these helpful organisms.

Beneficial Insects—Predatory insects that feed on other insects contribute greatly to the control of some insect pests, sometimes giving a very high degree of control, sometimes being only partially effective. The Vedalia ladybeetle is so effective in keeping down the population of cottony-cushion scale that spraying is almost never needed in bearing groves. The Chinese and blood-red ladybeetles feeding on aphids and the Australian (Crypt) mealybug ladybeetle feeding on mealybugs do not obviate all need for spraying although they decrease that need. These ladybeetles are rather specific in their choice of prey, but several other ladybeetles, and various lacewings, mealywings, and thrips, feed on a variety of insect and mite pests.

Parasitic insects, whose larvae devour the host from the inside after hatching from eggs laid in it, also help greatly in control of certain insects. There are several wasps that parasitize Florida red scale and small flies that parasitize aphids, but the outstanding examples are the *Aphytis* wasp that controls purple scale and two related species that attack the Florida red scale and citrus snow scale. Certain insecticides have proved undesirable for use in spraying citrus trees because they kill these natural predators and parasites so effectively that insect pests increase following their use more than if no spray had been applied.

The beneficial insects are today receiving increased attention, especially in areas where a regular spray program is not required. They may be a major factor in controlling insect pests. Furthermore, their activity often reduces or eliminates the use of chemicals that may have detrimental side effects on plants, animals, or humans.

Beneficial Mites—A few species of mites that are to some extent predators of pests are often found on citrus foliage. To a large extent, they live on the remains of dead insects and mites, but some species are known to consume scale eggs and crawlers, and others feed on six-spotted mites. The extent of their effective control is not well understood at present, but they certainly do not harm the tree and they are predacious to some extent.

Beneficial Fungi—Many kinds of fungi have long been known to hold in check various insect and mite pests, especially purple scale, mealybugs, whiteflies, aphids, and rust mites. Although some of the most conspicuous of these "friendly fungi," once thought to be of great value in pest control, have been found only to attack insects already dead, as is true of the redheaded scale fungus, others are of genuine effectiveness. The outstanding example is the very considerable degree of control of whiteflies by the red and yellow Aschersonias, which make spraying for this pest rarely necessary so long as spraying for scales is done. The high rainfall of Florida and the resultant high humidity that are so conducive to development of diseases are also very favorable for growth of beneficial fungi.

Nonpest Sprays

Sprays are sometimes applied to citrus trees, not for control of pests but for affecting more or less directly the vegetative growth process or the rate of development of chemical compounds in the fruit. These are called "physiological sprays" since they have an influence on physiological functions of the tree and its fruit.

Nutritional Sprays—Sprays to supply mineral elements to the tree have been discussed fully in the chapter on fertilizers since they really are just an alternative method of fertilizing. They could equally well have been discussed here because very often the mineral salts are applied in the same spray mixture as insecticidal or fungicidal materials. Thus zinc is usually added to the postbloom spray made for control of melanose, and this same spray may also contain materials to control mites and scales if needed.

Growth Regulators—Spray applications of gibberellic acid (GA) applied between full bloom and petal fall have materially increased fruit set and yields of fruits of Orlando, Minneola, Robinson, and Osceola tangelos.

10 /
Other Grove Maintenance Practices

The programs of grove rehabilitation, fertilizing, and pest management, with their scientific foundations, have been discussed in the previous chapters. Four other programs are included in the total production schedule for citrus: (1) cultivation and cover crop management, (2) pruning, (3) drainage and irrigation, and (4) cold protection. Cultivation and cover crop management, and pruning, should become standard practices according to their respective requirements. Drainage and irrigation, and cold protection, which are related to the soil and climatic conditions of the grove location, may involve considerable costs and require extensive study. Expenditures for grove road maintenance, upkeep and repair of buildings and fences, etc., which do not fit into any one of the seven standard programs, should be itemized as miscellaneous to obtain the total operational costs.

Weed Control, Cultivation, and Cover Crop Management

Soil management practices for the various tree-fruit crops have been developed primarily as means of creating or maintaining the soil conditions most favorable for tree growth, especially those related to moisture and nutrient supplies. Soil management may also have a more direct influence on tree health by reducing injury by pests or by cold. Soil management systems used in different parts of the country vary greatly with differences in soil type, climate, topography, and the particular tree-fruit involved. In Florida, as in many other areas, the systems in use have evolved chiefly by growers' trials and errors, and, because they are largely independent of organized research, they often include practices that can be justified only because they have become customary.

Three soil management systems have been used in Florida citrus groves—clean cultivation, continuous cover crops, and a combination of these two. The term *cover crop* properly refers to plants grown as a soil covering to prevent erosion by wind or rain. Various herbaceous crops called "green manures" are also grown in

199

Fig. 10-1. Large "bat wing" rotary mower in young bedded grove.

orchards and fields for the organic matter they add to the soil when turned under before they reach maturity. In most of central Florida, cover crops are grown for the sake of their additions to soil organic matter rather than for erosion control; they would more correctly be spoken of as green manures in most instances.

The sandy soils of Florida are very low naturally in organic matter and benefit greatly from regular additions of it so far as their ability to support good tree growth is concerned. Groves planted on raised beds (usually located in coastal and flatwood areas) are usually kept under a permanent sod cover to ensure that the beds are not eroded. The only cultivation exercised in such groves is mowing of the middles and weeding, usually by chemical means, of the tree rows.

At one time, clean cultivation throughout the year was advocated by some growers, whose ideal was that no living plants should ever exist in citrus groves except the trees. This resulted in the disappearance of practically all organic matter from the soil, severely reducing its ability to hold water and nutrients. Constant cultivation was expensive, and the trees decreased rather than increased in vigor; consequently this system was abandoned. A new application of the concept of clean cultivation has now emerged in

Fig. 10-2. Sophisticated herbicide applicator.

which chemical control methods are utilized, in most cases completely eliminating mechanical cultivation and mowing. Tree growth has been very good under this system, probably because the nonmechanical techniques used do not damage the tree roots as constant cultivation did. This system of clean cultivation using herbicides is often referred to as a "trunk-to-trunk" weed control management system.

The system most commonly used in Florida citrus groves is to grow cover crops during the summer rainy season and to practice clean cultivation during the dry period from early fall to late spring. Where this system is used in bedded groves, the cultivation employed is usually limited to mowing. The heavy stand of cover crop that is encouraged to grow in the summer months does not compete with the trees since the rainfall normally is ample for both, and it does provide large amounts of organic matter (and of extra nitrogen, in the case of legumes) for improving the soil. As soon as the rainy season is past, the cover crop is turned under to conserve soil moisture for the trees, to eliminate fire hazard from dry plant material, and to prevent the additional possible cold injury due to interference by cover crop plants with radiation of heat from the ground and with flow of cold air. Bedded groves are usually mowed as close to the ground as possible.

Two general types of cover crops are used—leguminous and nonleguminous. Many growers favor legumes, usually planted in April, because of the additional nitrogen that they are able to take from the air and add to the soil through the agency of certain bacteria living in nodules on their roots. Beggarweed and cowpeas were popular at one time, then Alyce clover and the crotalarias were in favor, and more recently hairy indigo has been much planted. While it is quite true that legumes do increase soil nitrogen, the amount is negligibly small, so that no distinction is made in calculating fertilizer needs of groves with leguminous cover crops from those with nonleguminous cover crops. Legumes are more expensive for seed and seeding, or they require special timing of the autumn cultivation to assure that mature seed is disked in for next year's crop. And some of them, especially the crotalarias, create a problem in connection with plant bugs, as described in chapter 9. Because the disadvantages of using legumes as a cover crop often outweigh the small advantages, many growers prefer to make no special planting of a cover crop and simply allow the native or naturalized weeds to cover the ground. They calculate that the amount of organic matter produced for a given expenditure is the more important measure of a cover crop's worth. The cover will consist of various grasses, especially the pink-plumed Natal grass but even including sandspurs, the Spanish needle, and other broad-leaved weeds. Because a considerable amount of organic matter is thus grown at no cost, this system is probably most to be recommended.

As has been suggested, the cover crop may directly affect tree health while it is standing, quite apart from its contribution to the soil after it is turned under. It may increase the chance of cold injury on frost nights, as stated just above, or encourage certain insect pests, or fuel a fire set by a carelessly tossed match or cigarette. Prevention of frost injury and fires has already been discussed, but pest control by cultivation requires accurate timing and an understanding of how the insects develop.

Chemical Weed Control

It is always necessary to eliminate weeds around buildings and young trees (see chapter 6) and along fence rows. These operations formerly entailed the exhausting and expensive manual labor of hoeing. It is now possible to use recommended herbicides with considerable savings in cash and human energy. Using herbicides may also be easier than hoeing in particular situations within the grove or nursery such as in and along ditches, in burrowing nematode buffer zones, and in spot eradication of serious weed encroachments that threaten to compete with the tree. The contemporary citrus grower now uses a combination of chemical and mechanical methods in a weed control program. With bedded groves, tree rows are usually cleaned year-round with appropriate chemicals, and middles and ditches are mowed as needed. Nonbedded groves, especially those in colder locations, are maintained in a similar manner but are usually clean-cultivated during the winter months to provide cold protection and reduce fire hazard.

Research has developed many new herbicides that act systemically or by contact or by soil sterilization. These will gradually supersede mechanical weed control by reducing the growers' costs and labor requirements. All require approval by the Environmental Protection Agency prior to their commercial use. Care must be taken to see that undue amounts on citrus foliage or excess amounts in the soil do not bring on toxicity symptoms in the trees. Because of the diversity of their uses (in ditches, nurseries, young groves, bearing groves, spot treatments, and barriers), their varying dosages for different soil types, their timing and soil treatment requirements, and, especially, the rapid development of new products and techniques, growers should familiarize themselves with the latest information from IFAS extension and commercial personnel in the field.

Irrigation

Irrigation is not a necessary operation in Florida citrus groves on deep, well-drained soils; many groves have survived productively relying only on rainfall even though periods of water stress within the trees have occurred. Nevertheless, with sound management, the irrigation program has been profitable. In groves on shallow soil, in which drainage facilities are required during rainy months, irrigation becomes obligatory during droughts. To understand why this is so and what factors determine the desirability of irrigation, we shall have to consider the needs of plants for water and how those needs are satisfied.

Fig. 10-3. Microsprinkler irrigation emitter (ball point pen placed for scale).

Water Needs

Protoplasm, the living substance in plant (and animal) cells, is able to carry out its functions only when it contains a good deal of water. In a dry seed, the protoplasm is alive but almost completely inactive. The first step in germination is absorption of water until the liquefied protoplasm is able to carry on metabolic activities, divide, and grow. Most plant tissues die long before the protoplasm of their cells ever reaches the low moisture content of a dormant seed. The need for water by protoplasm is a basic reality of plant life.

Water has many uses in plant tissues besides making protoplasm active. No mineral nutrient can enter plant cells, from the soil or the air, unless dissolved in water; and no organic compound can move from one cell to another except in solution. The universal solvent, water is itself a plant nutrient, for it is one of the raw materials in the process of photosynthesis by which green cells capture light energy as manufactured sugars. It is in water as a

Fig. 10-4. Microsprinkler in operation.

solvent vehicle that mineral salts move from root tips up through trees to the leaves. Tender new shoots and young leaves are enabled to hold themselves erect or spread out horizontally without any rigid framework because their cells are distended or turgid with water. Only when plant cells are turgid can they grow larger or divide, and only when leaves are fully spread out can they make most effective use of light. In times of moisture shortage, this turgidity is lost and leaves collapse into a wilted condition.

The amount of water needed for all these uses is really very small, however. For land plants, the big problem is that they constantly lose water from their tissues in the process called transpiration. The amount of water required for all other purposes is infinitesimal compared with the amount transpired daily from leaves, stems, and fruits of citrus trees. So long as the atmosphere surrounding the plant is not saturated with water vapor, the plant must lose water, and the drier the air, the faster the rate of water loss. Unless this water can be replaced promptly, the plant suffers, and so the possibility of replacement is of vital con-

Fig. 10-5. Young flatwood citrus planting showing typical double-row bed planting scheme and microsprinkler irrigation system lines.

cern. Practically all the water the trees use is absorbed by their roots from the soil, so we must examine the ability of soils to supply water.

Soil-Water Relations

In the discussion of soil in chapter 4, it was pointed out that the amount of available water a soil can hold is determined by the difference between percentages present at field capacity and at the wilting point.

A typical Astatula fine sand at the permanent wilting point has about 1 percent of water, at field capacity about 5 percent; it is therefore able to hold (by difference) a maximum of about 4 percent of available water. A soil of the Arredondo series, a phosphatic soil with slightly more organic matter, holds about 2 percent at the wilting point, 8 percent at field capacity, and so has around 6 percent of available water at maximum capacity. Thus each soil has it own characteristic water-holding capacity.

It would appear at first that the soil with the highest percentage of available water would be the one that could supply the most water to a citrus tree. But the total amount of water available to the tree is dependent also upon the volume of soil permeated by its roots, and this means primarily the depth of the soil to either a water table or a hardpan. A deep, well-drained soil with an effective rooting depth of five feet and a maximum of 4 percent of available water can hold for use by trees nearly twice as much water as a soil with 7 percent of available water at field capacity but a depth of only 1.5 feet to a hardpan. That is why low, moist soils often have greater need of irrigation than deep, sandy soils. During a drought, the shallow soil must be irrigated more frequently and can absorb less water at each irrigation than is the case with a deep soil.

Absorption of water by plants is not the only way that available water is removed from the soil. Evaporation from the soil surface removes much water, especially from the top foot of soil (there is little loss by evaporation below this depth). Shallow soils, therefore, lose a larger percentage of their available water through evaporation than deep soils and consequently must be irrigated more frequently than deep soils during dry periods.

Plant-Water Relations

The leaves of a tree with adequate moisture are turgid, but as the water content of the tree is reduced to a condition of moisture deficiency, the leaves gradually lose turgidity and become wilted. The first indications of this condition, called "incipient wilting," are found in early afternoon when transpiration exceeds absorption of water. This incipient wilting is not visible but can be demonstrated by suitable methods. Such a slight moisture deficit in the leaves occurs almost daily, except in rainy weather, and seems to have no harmful effect at all.

As the moisture deficiency within the tree becomes greater, however, as the result of a succession of days when transpiration exceeds absorption, the leaves begin to show a visible temporary wilting for a short but increasing interval each afternoon. This wilting disappears later in the afternoon at first, as decreasing transpiration enables the roots to replenish the moisture shortage, and so long as the wilting lasts only an hour or so there is not great loss resulting from it. Temporary wilting is an important indication that the soil moisture is approaching the permanent wilting point and that irrigation may be needed soon. As the moisture shortage continues, the leaves wilt earlier and recover later, often not until after dark, until eventually they fail to recover turgidity at night. By this time, the soil has now reached the permanent wilting point and the leaves will remain wilted permanently unless water is added to the soil. If the soil water supply is not increased within a certain length of time, the twigs and limbs will dry out and the tree may die or at best will lose all its leaves. If water is added by rain or irrigation soon enough, the wilted leaves can recover and the tree will have suffered no great permanent injury, although more or less dropping of leaves and fruits may have occurred.

Irrigation is most beneficial if water is supplied as soon as temporary wilting is observed. Some growers also watch cover crops because these plants have a much shallower rooting zone than the trees and tend to show moisture shortage by wilting before the trees do. It might be even better to make physical measurements of the soil moisture and thereby to be aware at all times of any growing shortage of moisture instead of waiting to observe wilting in plants. Methods and instruments are available for directly measuring soil moisture content, but unfortunately the number of samples that must be taken in a citrus grove to obtain reliable values for soil moisture make direct measurement too expensive for even the large, commercial grower, let alone for the small grove owner. An accounting system that subtracts daily losses of water by evaporation and transpiration (together known as "evapotranspiration"), which account for the greatest losses of soil moisture, and adds water supplied by rainfall and irrigation is being used to determine effectively the grove's need for supplemental water. Such an accounting system must allow for the type and depth of the soil in the individual grove. It must be diligently maintained by management, but it does take much guesswork out of the irrigation program.

Drainage

It may seem paradoxical that drainage should be a factor in irrigation, but for the citrus grove on low ground this is often the case. More than 50 percent of the citrus groves in Florida are now planted on poorly drained soil. Early citrus growers often considered the high, well-drained locations satisfactory as to drainage but very subject to drought, while the low, poorly drained lands were recognized as presenting drainage problems but considered as having little need for irrigation. Today it is generally accepted that the deeper the soil, the larger the rooting system a tree can develop and the less the need for irrigation. The poorly drained soils present the biggest irrigation problems.

Need for Irrigation

About once in every ten years, Florida experiences a drought of serious economic consequences; about one year in three the spring rainfall pattern does not provide sufficient soil moisture to take care of the needs of citrus trees properly, even on the best sites. The critical period is usually during the season from February to April, when fruit is setting and starting to increase in size. Most growers who expect to irrigate keep close watch on trees and weather records during this period. As soon as the rainfall record shows that rainfall is below normal for the season, the grower should be alert to detect the first temporary wilting, indicating that irrigation should begin. Too often, however, the grower, hoping that rain will come and make irrigation unnecessary, waits until the leaves are already badly wilted before starting irrigation.

In most sections of Florida, water has been readily available from lakes or shallow wells, and distribution through permanent or portable mains has been easy. Power sources and labor supplies have made possible extensive irrigation. But analyses of the economic results from irrigating have not shown that it was always a profitable operation. Growers have applied water when it was not really necessary, or have applied it too late to obtain benefit. Often a heavy investment in irrigation equipment has been made without any clear ideas on what use was going to be made of it; such equipment was just something a grove should have. And even when the equipment is bought with clear understanding of what could be done with it, it is easy for the grower to spend more money irrigating than he can gain from the operation unless he analyzes carefully the factors involved.

Fall irrigation may be worthwhile occasionally if the trees show severely wilted foliage or fruit begins to wilt and become flaccid before it is ready to harvest, but such occasions will be very infrequent. As a rule, fall irrigation is undesirable because it may induce a flush of growth that will be more easily injured by winter cold and will leave fewer buds to produce blooms in spring.

Irrigation in the spring, when temporary wilting appears, in a season of less than normal rainfall will increase the yield of fruit and is usually an economically justified operation. Even then, irri-

gation should be as limited as seems compatible with tree health
and fruit retention, for unnecessary application of water not only
adds to the cost of production but also tends to cause development
of fruit with lower content of solids, especially when applied late
in the season.

This program should be developed with the proper understanding of the water availabilities; labor, power, and equipment; and
the basic operating conditions. An economic feasibility study
should be made. The early citrus grower employed various means
of water distribution requiring high labor inputs and often simply
used the furrows between rows of trees in bedded groves. The
gasketed, lockjoint, aluminum portable pipe system later came
into vogue and was highly satisfactory during the 1940s. Surface
and deep-well water sources were generally available; gasoline
and electricity were the power sources; centrifugal and turbine
pumps presented no problems. Currently, with large expanses of
groves, water availability has become more of a problem and labor
for the portable irrigation line almost nonexistent. Systems that
require higher capitalization but far less labor have had to be developed. Volume guns with underground feeder lines that water
areas as large as a half acre or more, self-propelled mobile guns
that travel down the middle and require manpower only when
being moved from one middle to another, and, later, the solid-set
system of permanent risers with impact sprinklers set along each
tree row to cover the entire ground area evolved out of necessity.
The latest interest is in the drip, or trickle, system of distributing
water through shallowly placed polyvinylchloride (PVC) lines and
discharge through emitters (drippers) under each tree. Also
finding widespread use are various types of microsprinklers. In
fact, as water supplies become more limited in the future, drip
and microsprinkler systems are probably the only types of systems
that will be allowed by regulation. Many advantages and disadvantages can be found for each method of distribution and should
be considered in the feasibility study.

Pruning

Pruning, the cutting off of plant parts in order to develop a desired
shape or to remove dead, diseased, or poorly placed branches, has
been practiced with many kinds of fruit trees for centuries. The
early leaders of the Florida citrus industry were mostly men with

previous experience in growing deciduous fruit trees in the North, and they tried at first to use the same types of pruning for orange trees that they had learned to use on apple trees. Gradually they realized that there is no need for training to a particular system since citrus trees have naturally strong crotches and limbs seldom split away and, while the trees grew well with different types of pruning, they were apparently about as thrifty and productive with a minimum of pruning as with a good deal. Since pruning adds to production costs, growers have come to abandon pruning for form and vigor, and bearing trees are pruned largely for reasons of health maintenance or size.

Pruning needed during the first four years has been discussed in chapter 6. In the early, bearing years, from the fifth to the tenth year, little pruning is required except removal of sprouts as explained below. For trees older than ten years, more pruning may be needed for various reasons. The following pruning practices are fairly standard in mature, bearing groves.

Sprouting

Once a year, preferably in the months of April or May or as time permits, sprouts should be removed from the rootstock, trunk, and scaffold branches of trees that tend to have many competing branches arise in the main framework area. Failure to remove such sprouts may result in trees with less than desirable shape and in the case of rootstock sprouts, other problems come to mind. If rootstock sprouts are allowed to develop, they often proliferate at the expense of the scion portion of the tree thereby allowing the undesirable rootstock to become dominant. Since the rootstock plant is not the desired variety and the fruit is usually inedible, judicious removal of rootstock sprouts is extremely important.

Scion shoots should be pruned if they cannot become desirable permanent branches. Fruiting twigs should not be removed from the interior of the tree since yield would be reduced. Any shoots that will fill in a vacant space in the periphery of the tree should be left to become part of the permanent framework. All these sprouts should be removed when they are still so small that they can easily be cut with hand clippers. If older sprouts are present, overlooked in past years, they may require use of long-handled pruning shears. The work can be done rapidly but calls for exercise of some judgment. While sprout removal is a horticulturally sound practice, in most operations it is rarely performed since it is labor intensive and expensive. Regular pruning of rootstock sprouts, however, must not be ignored and should be conducted regularly as a part of the total production program.

Deadwood Pruning

There are various reasons for the presence of dead twigs and branches in a citrus tree, among them cold damage, waterlogging of soil, infestations of insects and mites, and fungal infections. Simply removing such deadwood without determining and correcting the cause is poor grove management. Hurricanes, freezes, and droughts, which are largely beyond man's control, may cause dying of large limbs as well as small. Even without these external causes, some twigs regularly die because growth of other branches shuts them off from light until they can no longer make enough food to maintain themselves, and others may be so weakened by the flow of food from them to a developing crop of fruit that they die of starvation.

Twigs that die from being too shaded will self-prune themselves and might be left to do so, and much other deadwood might be left to erode away except for its unattractive appearance and its causing scars by rubbing against developing fruit. However, dead twigs are an important source of melanose infections on fruits, and while it is not feasible to do a sufficiently thorough job of pruning of fine twigs to control melanose by pruning alone, removal of these infected twigs is very helpful as a supplement to spraying. There is also the fact that as larger limbs die back following freezes or fungal infections of the roots, they may carry decay back into permanent trunk or main limbs. Every three to five years, therefore, a pruning crew should go through the grove with lopping shears and pruning saws to cut out the dead branches of a diameter of one-fourth inch or larger. It is not economically feasible in commercial practice to try to prune out all small dead twigs, however desirable this would be in theory. Usually from thirty minutes to an hour per tree will suffice for this pruning. Lopping shears will easily cut branches to three-fourths inch in diameter, but larger limbs should be cut with a saw. All cuts should be made flush with the larger branch from which the dead branch arises, or with a lateral branch in heading back limbs, so that no projecting stub remains; and the final cut should always be below any dead tissue. It has been customary to treat any cut surface over an inch in diameter with pruning paint although even larger cuts will heal well without such protection when made on limbs with many healthy leaves supplying food for healing. This pruning operation is best done during the summer months because labor is most available for such work then. Furthermore, by this time it is possible to tell just how much damage was done if there was a freeze during the winter, so that cold-injured wood can be pruned with assurance. It is always a mistake to try to prune shortly after a freeze. As with sprout removal, this hand pruning is a horticulturally sound practice, but is rarely performed today due to the costs involved. Another factor contributing to the reduction in hand pruning is the regular use of mechanical pruning equipment in most mature groves to shape the trees by hedging and topping (which will be discussed later).

Special Pruning

Several types of pruning are sometimes needed that can be done along with pruning of deadwood.

Long, thin branches that bear little or no fruit because they are not sufficiently exposed to light, and therefore will never be able to bear more fruit in the future, should be removed so that their supply of water and nutrients will be available to better placed branches.

Tangerine trees may profitably be opened up by pruning out portions of the dense centers to allow more sunlight to penetrate the interior (making fruit color better) and to reduce slightly the number of fruiting branches (giving better fruit size). This objective is better accomplished by bulk pruning of a few large limbs than by pruning out many small branches. If the latter is done, it will be only a short time before the interior of the tree is as dense as ever. The earlier in the season of fruit development that this can be done, the better.

Grapefruit trees, because of the great weight of their fruit, are especially likely to have some of the lower limbs bending down until they are nearly on the ground. The fruit on these low-hanging branches is often of poor quality and is likely to have cuts or other injuries made by cultivating or mowing equipment. These branches also complicate the problems of pest control.

Raising the bottom of the canopy of these trees, called "lifting" or "skirting," is accomplished by pruning the branches that are touching the ground or very close to it. It is usually best to remove an entire branch at its origin on the trunk. To avoid having it tear away some wood and bark from the trunk, the limb should first be

Fig. 10-6. Double-boom hedger in operation.

cut upward to at least one-third of its thickness. In the case of quite large limbs, this first cut is made several inches out from the trunk and the downward cut made half an inch farther out. After the bulk of the limb is gone, the stub can easily be cut next to the trunk. In either case the final cut should be flush with the trunk. If removal of a whole branch would leave quite a prominent gap in the canopy of the tree, then it may be better to prune only those subordinate branches that hang near the ground. The best "lifting" of the canopy has been accomplished if the remaining branches, when loaded with fruit, are pulled down until the fruit barely or not quite touches the ground and, when relieved of the weight of the crop, do not hang lower than a foot from the ground.

A method of "lifting" that is used in some groves employs a powered circular saw. This is passed under the tree at a height of a foot or so above the ground and cuts all branches that hang lower than this. The pruning is quickly done, but such a saw is dangerous to handle and should be operated only under careful supervision.

Hedging

Since 1950 the process of "hedging" citrus trees has been developed in the state. Primarily it was developed as a remedy for the situation created in many groves where trees had been planted in rows twenty to twenty-five feet apart and had grown so large that they were badly crowded. By means of a gang of circular saws, the rows are hedged, with the sides vertical or slanting toward the center of the tree at a small angle, so as to leave a clear middle seven to nine feet wide between tree rows. This shape admits light to the lower part of the canopy, increasing the bearing area and improving the color of fruit on the lower branches, as well as reducing costs of spraying and picking.

Any one of several systems of hedging can be used, depending on how many sides of each tree need trimming and the frequency of the operation. One of the most satisfactory systems is to start the hedging operation at the time when the trees first begin to meet in the operating middle. By opening every other middle to good operating width (i.e., to about eight feet) at this time, and after two years opening the alternate middles similarly and shifting operations to them, there is provision for continuous good operation. In the fourth year, the first set of middles can again be opened, and the rotation followed regularly. In this system, hedging is done in one direction only, which is the direction of most convenient operation. Another possible system would be to open the middles in one direction at first, and then a few years later to open the middles at right angles.

Many possibilities for different hedging programs exist. Frequency of pruning is related to tree vigor (a combination of many factors) and distance between trees. In general, frequent light pruning is best because the least leaves and wood are thus removed each time. This helps to keep yields at an optimum level and keeps costs relatively low.

Most hedging is done to open drive middles up to a width of at least eight feet. An angled cut is used that is five to fifteen degrees from vertical to maximize sunlight interception and facilitate grove operations. Timing of this operation often coincides with harvest completion, and many groves are hedged just after the crop is picked. Of course, if harvest is in winter and the grove is subject to possible cold damage, hedging may need to be delayed. Hedging should be completed, however, before bloom is possible, or at least very shortly after bloom set, to minimize fruit losses.

Fig. 10-7. Grove that has just been lightly hedged.

A special case exists for Valencia orange since there is always a crop on the tree at any time of the year. Growers seem to be equally divided on timing, some choosing to prune immediately after harvest and others electing to prune carefully in late winter prior to harvest. In either case, pruning will have to be light so as not to remove the crop on the tree. This points to the importance of frequent, light pruning, especially for the late-maturing varieties.

Topping

Removal of a portion of the tops of trees is often necessary in contemporary citriculture. If trees are allowed to grow unchecked, they will become quite tall, resulting in shading and subsequent loss of lower canopy; such trees will be difficult to spray and harvest.

Topping is now a regular part of most pruning programs and is performed at regular intervals of one to four years. While many configurations are possible, the most widely accepted shape is a "roof-top" with the peak at around fifteen to sixteen feet and shoulders at ten to twelve feet.

Pruning Very Weak Trees

Following severe attacks of soil fungi or injury by hurricanes or freezes, old trees may have a tremendous amount of deadwood in proportion to that which is still productive. Unless vigorous growth gives evidence of prompt recuperation, the grower may well consider whether the cost of heavy pruning might not better be diverted to removal and replacement with young trees. Tree surgery, including filling of cavities and "wiring" of vigorous shoots from severely headed scaffold limbs, is hardly profitable in commercial groves. Trees in need of extensive and time-consuming repairs are better replaced unless they are dooryard trees with sentimental value to the owner (see "Grove Rehabilitation" in chapter 7).

Special Pruning Considerations

If, for any reason, large areas of trunk or limbs are exposed to the sun as the result of heavy pruning or of defoliation by cold or storm, the exposed surfaces should be protected by a coat of whitewash to prevent sunscald. In spite of their thick bark, these surfaces have been shaded by foliage and cannot endure the sudden exposure to direct sun. Sunscald can occur in winter as well as summer, but whenever it takes place, the trunk may be injured so seriously that the tree must be removed. Severe heading back to the top so that all foliage is removed is best done in spring when new shoots can be expected to renew the shade most quickly, with temporary whitewash protection of the bark in the meantime.

To paint or not to paint pruning cuts is not nearly as important as whether to make clean cuts that heal readily with no projecting stubs. And speaking of projecting stubs, each hedging operation, especially when the operation has been overly delayed, should be followed by pruners who will cut off the stubs left by mechanical equipment. If not removed, these stubs will shortly be hidden by new growth and will present a danger to operators and equipment in future work in the grove. While this practice is horticulturally sound, it is rarely employed today due to the great costs involved.

Cold Protection

The point has frequently been made in earlier chapters that injury by low winter temperatures is the greatest factor limiting the area for production of citrus fruit in Florida. A full discussion of the nature of cold hazard in the various citrus-growing areas of the state will be found in chapter 4, and in chapter 5 there is a consideration of the selection of sites for groves with greatest natural freedom from cold injury and of stocks and scions with cold hardiness.

Fig. 10-8. Citrus tree with stack-type grove heaters nearby. Stack covers are removed when heaters are ignited.

Having made the best available selection of site and chosen a combination of stock and scion suited to the general area, the grower can further avoid injury from cold by certain cultural practices. Banking of young trees has been discussed in chapter 5. Trees that are free from nutritional deficiencies and from weakening by pests will endure cold better than trees that are weak for any reason. In the section on "Weed Control, Cultivation, and Cover Crop Management" in this chapter, the effect of a cover crop on cold injury and the importance of clean culture in winter are made clear. Finally, the grower can avoid practices that tend to maintain trees in active growth in the fall. Such trees are more easily injured by cold than trees that have become dormant.

Finally, when growers have done all they can by careful planning and good culture to help their trees escape injury from low temperature, active cold protection measures may need to be taken. These measures may take several forms. During days of plentiful labor and cheap fuel, most cold protection was accomplished by heating or firing the groves. Other methods employed included wind machines and, more recently, the use of water.

Firing

Until the "big freeze" of 1894–95, citrus growers in Florida relied on favorable location for protection from cold. The first grove heating was done during the freeze of 1899, although far more growers then were in favor of covering trees with tents or lath (perhaps with supplementary heat). The cumbersome nature of covers and the good effects obtained with wood fires led to extensive grove heating after 1900. Since pine wood was abundant, resinous heartwood of slash pine (called "lighter wood" or "fat pine") was commonly employed for many years.

The last pine wood supplies were used up many years ago and growers turned to diesel fuel as a source of heat. At one time, the black smoke produced by incomplete combustion was considered desirable and beneficial. It is now well recognized that it is heat, radiant and convective, not smoke, that protects trees from cold. Stack heaters of various designs and pressurized oil systems, assuring more complete combustion, have gradually replaced less efficient types. Central systems are popular because they are clean, more efficient, easy to ignite, and require no labor for refueling. Furthermore, the equipment that is allowed is increasingly regulated in the interest of pollution control.

Even these more efficient sources of heat do not always assure freedom from cold injury. Sometimes the grower waits too long, permitting some freezing to occur, before lighting the heaters, and then has no benefit from the money spent for heating. Sometimes cold winds lower the temperature so far, and carry away the heated air so rapidly, that it is impossible for the heating to give full protection. Sometimes the cold period continues for two or three days or possibly longer, until the supplies of fuel oil have been exhausted, and though growers kept their trees from freezing for two days, they were injured on the third. But when the conditions are not too unfavorable, heating is very effective in keeping grove temperatures above damaging levels.

Thermometers are necessary so that growers know how well they are controlling temperature. There should be at least one thermometer within the grove and another outside the grove but close by; the former enables the grower to keep track of the temperature around his trees, while the other indicates whether the surrounding air mass is getting colder or warmer. These thermometers must be sheltered and by standard usage are placed horizontally at a height of four-and-a-half feet about the ground. An error of 1°F in the reading of these thermometers can have serious consequences in fruit or twig injury, so they should be checked for accuracy in the critical range (20° to 35°F) each fall before the first need to use them.

The time to light fires depends upon the desired degree of protection needed and the philosophy of the grower. Where fruit protection of tender varieties is needed, lighting may commence when grove temperatures reach 30°F. In most cases, however, economics preclude this expense and heating is usually done only to protect the tree from substantial damage and protection of the crop (if one is on the tree) may be ignored. In such cases, the temperature is allowed to drop to 28°F, or even as low as 24°F before cold protection is commenced.

Heaters should be spaced more closely on the side or sides of the grove from which drift of cold air is expected so that the air is warmed as it enters the grove and maintains safe temperatures as it moves through the grove with much less assistance from other heaters. Otherwise, thirty-five heaters per acre are commonly used in the portions of the grove needing heating.

Growers tend to overestimate the amount of heat that is produced and are surprised to find later that there was some tree injury in spite of heating. On nights of only moderate cold, the grower might be well advised to estimate the damage likely to occur if he does not fire, and compare this value with the cost of heating, for heating is an expensive operation. At any rate, the grower should avoid making overly optimistic estimates.

Other Methods

Sprinklers are sometimes used, especially to protect nurseries or specimen trees. Even though ice may form on twigs, the internal temperature of the plant tissues cannot fall below 32°F so long as the continuous adequate volumes of water are applied. If the temperature falls far below freezing, there may be a thick coat of ice formed and its weight may cause much breakage of limbs. Nursery trees are so low that the ice usually forms a framework resting on the ground and does not put any load on the branches. Sprinkling is feasible only for groves so small that the sprinkler system will cover all the trees.

With the development of permanent irrigation systems with risers spaced regularly through groves, it seemed logical to adapt the systems for cold protection during the winter. This principle of water use was employed during the cold wave of December 1962, with disastrous results. Applying the water at the rate of 0.1 inch per hour allowed it to freeze immediately, subjecting the wood and foliage of the trees to lower temperatures than would have been experienced with no protection. Severe damage, with excessive cold cankers, occurred while adjacent trees, left unsprinkled, often showed no damage. Aside from the problems of keeping mud dauber wasps from building nests in the sprinkler mechanisms and the actual freezing up of the sprinklers, there is the necessity of applying sufficient water to maintain a slush ice on the trees at all times during the entire freezing periods. For lack of good information and fear of a repetition of the events of 1962, overhead sprinkling as a method of cold protection in bearing groves is today discouraged unless an uninterruptible source of water is ensured and sprinkler precipitation is well in excess of the previously mentioned 0.1 inch per hour rate.

Recent experience with microsprinkler irrigation systems has shown that they can provide some protection as well. In this situation, the water stream is usually directed on the tree trunk and not into the canopy. This procedure has worked well with young trees, especially when used in conjunction with insulating tree wraps. The combination of water and wraps has provided protection for young trees down to temperatures in the low teens. Of course, part of the top of the tree is lost in such scenarios, but the main portion of the trunk can be saved, and such trees usually regrow quite rapidly the following season.

Wind machines are also used in Florida groves for cold protection. Like oil heaters, they were used for some years in California before being tried here. The machine is essentially one or two large airplane propellers mounted on a tower that can be rotated in a circle. They are operated by electric, gasoline, or diesel motors. The principle on which they are based is that on still, clear nights there is a stratification of air, colder next to the ground and increasingly less cold up to a height of from forty to two hundred feet, above which temperature falls again with height. The height at which this change occurs is called the "inversion point," and the increase in temperature with height up to this point is called a "temperature inversion" since air temperatures are normally colder with altitude. If the inversion is large, that is, if the air temperature forty feet above the ground is several degrees warmer than the temperature near the ground, then a wind machine can blow this warmer air down and mix it with the cold air. If there is a breeze, or if the night is quite cloudy, there is likely to be little or no inversion. The use of these machines must be tailored to the particular grove, and no recommendations can be made without study of the individual grove.

Fig. 10-9. Double-bladed wind machine.

Cold Injury to Fruit

Citrus fruit is first damaged when the temperature has fallen to 28°F and remained there from two to four hours. The first evidence of injury is the presence of ice crystals in the fruit early in the morning following the low temperature. When the ice has melted, tiny white crystals of hesperidin are formed along the walls of the fruit segments, especially in sweet oranges. These crystals do not indicate that the fruit is harmful to eat but do indicate in most cases that the fruit has been frozen, although in rare cases they may be formed from other causes. If the freezing has ruptured the juice sacs near the stem end, fermentation is likely to start in a few days, and then several days later the tissues at the stem end begin to dry out, with twisted segment walls. While fermentation is going on, it is better not to eat much fruit, but either before or after this the frozen fruit is perfectly healthful, although containing less juice when some of the juice sacs are dry.

Fruit that has been damaged by freezing may show a water-soaked appearance or evidence of previous water-soaking, ruptured juice sacs, mushy condition of the pulp, or dryness, depending on the severity of freezing and the length of time since freezing occurred. These damages are almost always at the stem end of the fruit and only rarely found at the stylar end.

Two types of freezing damage to fruits are recognized by the citrus laws of the state of Florida: *damaged* and *seriously damaged.* Damaged fruits are those showing drying or other evidence of freezing at the stem end for over one-fourth-inch depth in oranges or grapefruit, or one-eighth-inch in mandarins, or an equivalent fruit volume, if occurring elsewhere than the stem end. If the extent of the freezing injury is more than twice the minimum for damaged fruit, it is considered seriously damaged.

Another slightly different form of cold injury is produced in small citrus fruits by freezing due to direct radiation of heat to the sky. When any fruit is fully exposed to the sky, it radiates heat from its upper surface out into space. If this loss of heat continues until the fruit temperature falls below the critical point, the cells in this area are killed. Decay organisms invade the injured rind, and rot develops where the cells are dead. This type of injury is rarely seen in oranges, grapefruit, and tangerines, probably because they have very thick rinds, but it is often found in the small-fruited citrus species such as calamondin, limequats, and kumquats, which are often grown in cold areas.

The Florida Department of Citrus, in cooperation with the Citrus and Vegetable Inspection Division of the State Department of Agriculture, maintains constant field service during and following any freeze to determine the extent of damages and to make sure that only fruit of sound condition is sent to market. Shipping holidays are also imposed following a severe freeze so that cold injury will have time to be manifest before fruit is shipped; when shipping is resumed, fruit inspectors examine carefully all fruit packed for shipment to eliminate any showing freeze damage.

Severe freezes kill many twigs or even large branches. Growers often hasten to prune out this deadwood, but experience has shown that such pruning should not be attempted until after the spring flush of growth has matured. Trees injured seriously by cold need to make unusually vigorous vegetative growth and so may need more fertilizer and water than trees of the same size that have not been subjected to cold damages.

Costs and Returns

Frosts and freezes decrease profits because groves that have been injured by them cannot be operated at greatest efficiency. In addition to immediate loss of fruit, there may be decreased crops the next year or next several years. If crop and trees are saved by some method of cold protection, there has been a great increase in cost of production of each box of fruit and thus a decrease in expected net returns, although sometimes the loss of a large portion of the crop raises the value of what is uninjured enough to compensate for the cost of protection. The prospective purchaser of a grove needs to be especially careful to inquire into the history of cold damage. On a warm summer day or during a mild winter, when there has not been a freeze for two or three years, it is easy to be overly optimistic regarding freezes. If one has not seen the grove following a period of freezing weather over the state, it would be well to seek advice from someone who knows well the freeze history of the area.

11 /
Crop Harvesting, Maturity, and Grade

The purpose of a citrus grove is, of course, to produce a crop of fruit; and, if sound practices have been faithfully carried out, there should be a good crop to harvest every year, barring climatic catastrophes. Two questions that arise are when to harvest this crop and how. The latter question is more easily answered and so will be taken up first.

If growers belong to a cooperative marketing organization or sells fruit on the tree, the fruit will likely be picked by crews supplied by a packinghouse or processor. If growers have their own pickers, they should be very aware that a well-grown crop of fruit can be greatly reduced in value by careless picking and handling. Fruit that is going to the processing plant is utilized so soon after harvesting that care in picking is not of great importance, but a crop destined for the fresh-fruit market has more of a chance to break down before it reaches the consumer if it is not harvested carefully. In spite of their leathery rinds, citrus fruits cannot be handled roughly and stay in good condition, and any cuts or punctures made in picking offer easy entrance for decay organisms.

Prior to 1900, most citrus fruits were pulled from the twigs, often carelessly, and sent to market after a few days of curing in the packinghouse. A great deal of the fruit was injured by "plugging" (the leaving of some rind tissue with the fruit stem attached to the twig when the fruit is pulled away), and such fruit spoiled rapidly on its way to market. Because of this problem, the industry turned almost entirely to clipping each fruit from its stem, a slower process but one that gave a much higher percentage of sound fruits. From 1900 to 1940, fruit clippers were used regularly, but a shortage of labor during World War II brought about a return to pulling of oranges and grapefruits for faster harvesting. It was found that with suitable care to leave only the "button" on the tree, pulling caused no more injury to the crop than usually occurred from clipper cuts or punctures.

Mandarin types "plug" easily when pulled because of their

Fig. 11-1. Citrus harvester.

fragile rinds, and they should be clipped instead. By the time oranges and grapefruits are well matured, the fruit should separate readily when pulled properly. This means turning the fruit at right angles to its stem and exerting a sideways stress, not pulling straight away from the twig, which technique may cause plugging even with fully mature fruit.

A labor force for harvesting the citrus crop has dwindled, and the costs of labor have increased rapidly for a good many years. This has led to considerable research by experiment stations, commercial companies, and grower organizations directed toward mechanized harvesting methods. Studies have been conducted along three lines: (1) development of best tree sizes, shapes, and spacings to facilitate effective equipment use; (2) discovery of abscission (growth regulator) compounds to reduce pull force necessary to sever the fruit from a fruiting branch; and (3) invention of equipment to actually accomplish the harvest. Progress has been made. New plantings are spaced to anticipate hedging (pruning) practices. Abscission chemicals have been cleared by the U.S. Environmental Protection Agency for use on an experimental basis. Harvesting equipment (tree and limb shakers, blowers, water guns, and augers) reflects the innovative thinking of engineers and horticulturists. The concerted effort of the entire citrus industry has shown results. Hand harvesting is still the method of choice; as long as it is affordable and suitable labor is available, it will likely continue to be.

Quality Standards (Maturity)

Knowing when to harvest citrus fruit involves the question of fruit maturity. Properly speaking, there is no ripening process in citrus fruit and no such thing as "tree-ripe" fruit or ripe fruit of any kind.

Fig. 11-2. Citrus harvester with picking tub.

In peaches and avocados, as in most other familiar fruits, there is a stage of maturity at which softening takes place rapidly, and in a few days a hard fruit passes through this ripening process and becomes overripe. Citrus fruits pass from immature to mature and finally to overmature condition while remaining on the tree, but the changes are slow and spread over several months. When picked at any stage of maturity, the fruit does not change after picking except as it may be infected by fungi and spoil or may slowly dry out. There is a considerable period of time during which the fruit has desirable quality, although some mandarins may have a short time between legal maturity and internal drying.

Citrus growers want not only a large crop but one that will bring a good market price, which is based on both the internal and external quality of the fruit. Internal quality is concerned with juice quantity and flavor components, while external quality reflects eye appeal. Although fruit for processing does not need to have such high external quality as that for the fresh-fruit market, the internal quality must be very good.

For persons who have only a few trees, it is easy to determine when any of the sweet citrus fruits have sufficiently matured to give the grower a high-quality product if harvested. They feel no pressure for getting the crop off the trees. They can sample fruits at intervals until satisfied that the crop has reached prime eating condition before picking it in quantity for family use. No chemical tests are needed to measure the fruit's maturity, and no regulations assuring that only fruit of acceptable quality is shipped need to be considered.

It would be equally possible for every grower, large or small, to use the same criteria for determining maturity, but only in a utopian society could this assure best quality for the consumer. Long ago, too many growers proved willing to ship immature fruit to distant markets, and as early as 1911 legislation was initiated to protect the reputation of Florida fruit. As the Florida citrus industry has increased in size and complexity, more and more laws and regulations have been necessary to control the operations of grower, packer, and shipper for the best interests of the whole industry and to assure the marketing only of a product that the consumer can buy with confidence. These regulations pertain to maturity, sizes, and grades of fruit that can be handled commercially, and they are rather extensive since it is necessary to set up different standards for each of the different kinds of citrus fruits. Each shipment of fresh fruit and each lot of fruit delivered to the cannery or concentrate plant is inspected to see that it meets the applicable legal and regulatory standards.

What constitutes maturity in citrus fruits is defined by state law in each citrus-growing state, with the further federal statute that applies whenever a state fails to enforce its laws properly. Florida citrus fruits cannot be shipped commercially until they are mature as defined by Florida laws. The Florida Citrus Commission of the Department of Citrus is authorized under these laws to issue regulations for determining maturity and for the limits of the various sizes and state grades. However, not all fruit that meets maturity requirements and is properly classified by size and grade can be shipped. To further ensure orderly marketing, the citrus industry operates under voluntary Federal Marketing Order 905. The Citrus Administrative Committee is authorized under the Federal Marketing Order 905 to issue regulations determining the limits of the various sizes and U.S. grades for interstate and export shipments (subject to the approval of the U.S. Secretary of Agriculture). These regulations are enforced by

Fig. 11-3. Dumping citrus tub into truck in field.

the Fruit and Vegetable Inspection Division of the Florida Department of Agriculture and Comsumer Services. All are somewhat flexible so that requirements may be made more stringent or be relaxed somewhat in accordance with the nature of the crop being marketed.

Table 11-1.
Factors used in minimum-quality requirements
for Florida fresh citrus fruits
(as of 1 August 1978)

Fruit	Color break	Juice content	Brix	Acid	Brix/acid ratio Required[a]	Minimum
Oranges[b]	Yes	Yes[c]	Yes	Yes	Yes	Yes
Grapefruit	Yes	Yes[d]	Yes[e]	No	Yes	Yes
Tangerines	Yes	No	Yes	No	Yes	Yes
"Temples"[b]	Yes	No	Yes	Yes	Yes	Yes
Tangelos	Yes	No	Yes	Yes	Yes	Yes
Lemons[f]	No	Yes[g]	No	No	No	No
Limes[h]	No	Yes[g]	No	No	No	No

SOURCE: From Table 5, *Florida Citrus Quality Tests*, Florida Cooperative Extension Service Bulletin no. 188 (June 1979), p. 19.

a. For appropriate soluble solids.

b. Separate standards for natural color and color-added fruit.

c. Gallons per one and three-fifths bushel box.

d. Cubic centimeters per fruit.

e. Separate standards for seedless, white seedless, and pink and red seedless varieties.

f. Volume basis.

g. Restrictions on size of fruit.

h. Honey tangerines maximum acid 1.0% or minimum ratio of 12 to 1.

Minimum Maturity Standards

The first attempts to frame a legal definition of a mature citrus fruit were made in 1912. A single fruit character was sought that could be readily measured by physical or chemical methods and used to assure average consumer acceptance. This proved impossible in the case of most kinds of citrus. Only acid fruits (lemons and limes) can be judged suitable for shipment on the basis of a single character, the percentage of juice by volume, and this is not related to degree of maturity. These fruits develop their maximum acidity early in the season while they are quite immature, and they are picked as soon as they meet minimum size requirements, which are dictated primarily by market demand.

Limes are wanted only in a biologically immature state, hence legal maturity is defined only in terms of minimum size and juice

Table 11-2.
Factors used in minimum-quality requirements
for Florida processing fruit
(as of 1 August 1978)[a]

Fruit	Color break	Juice content	Brix	Acid	Brix/acid ratio Required[b]	Minimum
Orange[c]	No	No	Yes	No	Yes	Yes
Grapefruit[c]	No	No	Yes	No	No	Yes
Tangerines[c]	No[d]	No	Yes	No	Yes	Yes
"Temples"[c]	No	No	Yes	No	Yes	Yes
Tangelos[c]	No	No	No	No	No	Yes
Lemons	No	No	No	No	No	No
Limes	No	No	No	No	No	No

SOURCE: From Table 6, *Florida Citrus Quality Tests,* Florida Cooperative Extension Service Bulletin no. 188 (June 1979), p. 19.

a. 1 December through 31 July, unless noted otherwise.

b. Required ratio applies until 1 January.

c. From 1 August through 30 November, fruit must meet fresh-fruit standards.

d. No color break after 15 November.

content. The size requirement is to assure freedom from "green" taste and may change at times, but usually no Tahiti limes less than one and three-fourths inches in diameter may be shipped at all. The general requirement is 42 percent juice by volume, with a size restriction at or slightly below one and three-fourths inches as set by marketing agreement regulations each season. There is no size requirement for Key limes, but they also must be 42 percent of juice by volume.

No single character has been found to measure consumer acceptance of the nonacid citrus fruits; a group of five interrelated characters is therefore employed. These are color break, juice content, soluble solids content, acid content, and ratio of solids to acid (see tables 11-1 and 11-2).

Color Break

Immature citrus fruits are green, like leaves, because their rinds contain large amounts of chlorophyll. If temperatures are not too high, chlorophylls begin to diminish in quantity as the citrus fruits begin to mature so that the yellow pigments, carotenoids, which are also present in green fruits (and leaves), become evident. Eventually the green color is likely to disappear entirely in fully matured fruits and is replaced by yellow in lemons and grapefruits, orange in oranges, and orange-red in some mandarins and tangelos. This breakdown of chlorophylls takes place only when the temperature is relatively low, as in fall and winter in Florida. In the tropics, oranges are still more or less green when fully mature; and Valencia oranges that have lost the green color in early spring may regreen if left on the trees into April or later in Florida.

Normally, citrus fruits exhibit a change of color with maturity; and the first indication of change from leaf-green to a yellowish green, if it is developed naturally, is termed "color break." Florida law requires that citrus fruits (other than limes and lemons) show a color break to some extent before they can be shipped as fresh fruit. Treatment with ethylene gas in the degreening room in packinghouses greatly accelerates the breakdown of chlorophylls if the process has already begun naturally and makes it possible to develop satisfactory color for the market. Oranges, grapefruits, tangerines, Temples, and tangelos have a minimum color break requirement all through the season for fresh fruit, but there is no such requirement after 1 December for cannery fruit.

Temperature is not the only factor involved in color break, for light plays a part too. Fruits in the outside canopy will show this change earlier than those in the more shaded parts of the tree; early in the season, it is therefore often necessary to spot-pick exposed fruit. Sometimes, especially in a warm fall, shaded fruit may remain quite green after it has become satisfactorily mature internally. Satsumas, some tangerines, and tangerine hybrids, which are most highly prized when they have developed a deep red or orange color, may pass the condition of prime eating quality and be somewhat overmature before shaded fruit shows much color in the rind. Parson Brown, Hamlin, and some navel oranges may also be fully mature when still exhibiting some green rind color. Warm, rainy weather in the fall causes slow development of color break and duller color when the fruit is fully matured. The grower may also influence the development of color break by cultural practices, some of which (e.g., oil sprays after mid-July or excessive nitrogen fertilization) may delay this process, while others (e.g., properly balanced nitrogen with potash fertilization) may hasten it slightly.

Brightest rind color of citrus fruits is developed under conditions of bright sunshine, low humidity, and relatively low temperature during the maturation period. Climatic conditions in Florida are not such as to cause high coloring of oranges, although internal fruit quality may be excellent. Therefore, after the degreening room treatment, some yellow oranges are dipped into a dye solution to enhance their eye appeal. Temples and tangelos may also be so treated. This process is rigidly supervised to prevent fruit of unsatisfactory eating quality from being made to appear properly mature. Later in the season, as natural color develops in the rind, these fruits are usually shipped without coloring.

Juice Content

The juice sacs in citrus fruits become engorged with juice as the fruit matures. Good palatability involves a sufficient amount of readily released juice of desirable taste, and the laws specify the minimum quantities that must be present. These are easily determined but are stated in different ways for different fruits. The required juice content of oranges is stated in terms of gallons of juice that can be squeezed from the fruit in a standard packed box, with the minimum requirement of four and one-half gallons per box. Juice content of grapefruits is stated as the cubic centimeters per fruit, with a minimum quantity for each standard size. No juice content is specified for mandarins, Temples, tangelos, or other hybrids. As mentioned previously, the juice requirement for limes and lemons is stated as a percentage of their volume.

The high juice content characteristic of Florida citrus fruits, especially of oranges, is an outstanding factor in their reputation. Early or late in the season, some fruits may have less than the minimum, but as a general rule Florida citrus fruits run far above the minimum requirement for juice. Sometimes the pink and red seedless grapefruit varieties have difficulty in meeting the requirement early in the season.

Soluble Solids Content

The earliest minimum maturity standards set up in Florida were based on percentage content of sugar, the direct measurement of which required considerable time and elaborate chemical laboratory equipment. Later it was found that sugars constituted quite

regularly over 75 percent of the total weight of the compounds
—organic and inorganic—dissolved in the juices, the so-called soluble solids. The percentage of soluble solids can be determined by
measuring the density of the solution, and thus the sugar content
is easily determined indirectly. There is a steady increase in
soluble solids, and proportionally of sugars, throughout the season
until the fruit is well past acceptable maturity. In addition to
sugars, the soluble solids include certain organic acids (largely
citric acid), vitamins, and very small amounts of inorganic salts
and organic compounds that are responsible for the flavors
characteristic of the various citrus fruits. The off-flavors that
sometimes develop in fruits because of improper handling or over-
maturity are usually due to changes in these flavor compounds unless micro-organisms have invaded the fruit.

Soluble solids begin to accumulate in early fall and reach
levels of desirable palatability in the fall, winter, or spring, depending on the variety involved. Density of the juice is measured
with a hydrometer floating in a cylinder of juice, and the reading
of this hydrometer in degrees Brix is converted by tables, after
correction for temperature, into percentage of soluble solids.
Although late in the season of any variety the values may be
higher, the following figures give the usual range of total soluble
solids during the normal harvesting season for the important citrus fruits: oranges, tangerines, Temples, and tangelos, 9 to 14 percent; Honey tangerines (Murcotts), 12 to 16 percent; grapefruits, 7
to 12 percent. Minimal values of solids are required for shipping
these fruits.

Acid Content

Citric acid is the organic acid chiefly found in citrus fruits, but
small amounts of malic, oxalic, and tartaric acid are also present.
Acid percentage is highest in immature fruit, decreasing steadily
as the fruit matures. There is a gradual change in taste from sour
to pleasantly tart to sweet without noticeable acidity; and then,
very late in the season, to an insipid sweetness (caused by an
acidity too low to make the taste pleasant).

There is no maximum permissible acidity specified for any citrus fruit, but the percentage must always be determined in order
to calculate the required ratios. Minimum acid content required
for oranges and tangelos is 0.4 percent, but not for other

citrus fruits. The acidity is determined by titration of the juice with a standard solution of a base; the equivalent acidity as anhydrous citric acid can be calculated easily from the quantity of base used. The amounts usually found in sweet citrus fruits during their normal harvesting season range from 1 percent early in the season to 0.5 percent late in the season. Limes and lemons, which are valued for their high acidity, have from 4 to 7 percent of acid according to variety.

Ratio of Total Soluble Solids to Total Acid

While the flavors of the different citrus fruits are chiefly due to small amounts of certain organic compounds, as explained previously, the taste (sweet or sour) is dependent on the relative amounts of sugar (determined as soluble solids) and acid in the juice. Extensive research into consumer preferences for several sweet citrus fruits, using the technique of "taste panels," has shown that no particular sugar content will alone assure acceptable taste. The average consumer wants a pleasantly tart or subacid fruit, and this requires certain proportions of sugar to acid. The percentage of total soluble solids (in degrees Brix) divided by the percentage of total acid gives the ratio of soluble solids to acid, always stated on the basis of acid as unity. Data from thousands of taste tests with fruits of all degrees of maturity made possible the charting of what constituted satisfactory ratios for a wide range of soluble solids and acids, and from these findings the present laws were drawn.

Early in the season of any fruit, the solids are low and acid high, giving a low ratio. As the season advances, the solids increase and the acid decreases, giving progressively higher ratios. The laws require that fruit early in the season have a certain minimum content of soluble solids and minimum ratios of percentage of solids to percentage of total acid. The minimums for oranges are listed in table 11-3. (Similar tables for grapefruit, tangerines, Temples, and tangelos have been developed by the Division of Fruit and Vegetable Inspection, Florida Department of Agriculture.) A higher ratio is necessary to give acceptable taste when the sugar content is low than when it is high. Therefore, if fruit exceeds the minimum percent soluble solids requirement, it is permitted to have a lower ratio. Because the percentage of sugar (and hence of soluble solids) increases as the fruit becomes more mature, the ratio required decreases as the season advances.

Table 11-3.
Oranges: soluble solids and soluble-solids-to-acid ratio

Minimum soluble solids (%)	Range of soluble solids (%)	Soluble solids/acid minimum ratio
Note 1	8.0–8.09	10.50 to 1
	8.1–8.19	10.45 to 1
	8.2–8.29	10.40 to 1
	8.3–8.39	10.35 to 1
	8.4–8.49	10.30 to 1
Note 2	8.5–8.59	10.25 to 1
	8.6–8.69	10.20 to 1
Note 3	8.7–8.79	10.15 to 1
	8.8–8.89	10.10 to 1
	8.9–8.99	10.05 to 1
Note 4	9.0–9.09	10.00 to 1
	9.1–9.19	9.95 to 1
Note 5	9.2–9.29	9.90 to 1
	9.3–9.39	9.85 to 1
	9.4–9.49	9.80 to 1
	9.5–9.59	9.75 to 1
	9.6–9.69	9.70 to 1
	9.7–9.79	9.65 to 1
	9.8–9.89	9.60 to 1
	9.9–9.99	9.55 to 1
	10.0–10.09	9.50 to 1
	10.1–10.19	9.45 to 1
	10.2–10.29	9.40 to 1
	10.3–10.39	9.35 to 1
	10.4–10.49	9.30 to 1
	10.5–10.59	9.25 to 1
	10.6–10.69	9.20 to 1
	10.7–10.79	9.15 to 1
	10.8–10.89	9.10 to 1
	10.9–10.99	9.05 to 1
	11.0–11.09	9.00 to 1

SOURCE: Taken from *Florida Citrus Quality Tests,* Florida Cooperative Extension Service Bulletin no. 188, Appendix I, "Minimum Quality (Maturity) Standards," pp. 2–3.

Note 1. Minimum soluble solids (in Brix %) for oranges for processing, 1 Dec. through 31 July.

Note 2. Minimum soluble solids (in Brix %) for natural color oranges, 16 Nov. through 31 July.

Note 3. Minimum soluble solids (in Brix %) for (a) color-added oranges, 16 Nov. through 31 July; and (b) natural color oranges, 1–15 Nov.

Note 4. Minimum soluble solids (in Brix %) for (a) color-added oranges, 1 Nov. through 15 Nov.; and (b) natural color oranges, 1 Aug. through 31 Oct.

Note 5. Minimum soluble solids (in Brix %) for color-added oranges, 1 Aug. through 31 Oct.

Oranges with 11 percent soluble solids, for example, need only have a ratio of 9.0 to 1. Percent acid decreases with increasing maturity so that the same ratio is attained with lower solids and the minimum solids requirement decreases as the season advances. Although naturally colored oranges must have 9.0 percent soluble solids until the end of October to be shipped, they need have only 8.5 percent soluble solids after 15 November.

Citrus fruits just approaching satisfactory maturity often have an unpleasant, raw taste that disappears as they become fully matured. This unpleasant taste cannot be measured by simple chemical tests. Higher ratios early in the season act to decrease the possibility that "green"-tasting fruits will reach the market. On the other hand, fruits with very high sugar content at the end of the season may be insipid. The minimum ratio specified (9.0 to 1 for oranges with 11 percent soluble solids) assures that no such fruit will be marketed.

A certain ratio is not in itself a guarantee of quality unless it is tied to a percentage of total soluble solids. Oranges with 6 percent soluble solids, a very low value for oranges, but only 0.5 percent acid would have a 12 to 1 ratio but very poor quality.

Testing for Maturity

A test for maturity is no more accurate than the sample that is taken from a group of trees or lot of fruit. To be useful, a sample must be representative, that is, it must reflect as nearly as possible actual conditions on the trees or among the lot brought to the packinghouse or cannery.

Some years ago, all of the fruits on a large, heavily laden Valencia orange tree at the Lake Alfred Citrus Research Center were picked and tested individually. This study showed that fruits on the south side of a tree were higher in soluble solids and had a higher soluble-solids-to-acid ratio than those on the north side of the tree. There was an increase in soluble solids and soluble-solids-to-acid ratio as fruits were picked from successively greater heights. Fruits on the outside portion of the tree were brighter in color and higher in soluble solids and soluble-solids-to-acid ratio than those partially shaded in the canopy or fully shaded near the trunk. Fruits in the top of the tree, whether in full sunshine or partially shaded, were more brightly colored and higher in soluble solids and soluble-solids-to-acid ratio than either outside or canopy fruits. Total acid tended to be lowest in fruits from the northeast side of the tree and to increase in inside fruits picked from successively greater heights. A systematic pattern of juice content was not encountered, although large, coarse-textured, poorly colored inside fruits tended to have less juice. A sample taken from the outside on all sides at a height of three to six feet was representative of the entire tree. Citrus trees are harvested in two ways: spot-picking, when only certain fruits or portions of a tree are taken, and clean-picking, when all of the fruits except those that are obviously immature are picked. Early in the season, some varieties may be spot-picked for size, color, or maturity to obtain higher prices for the fruits. Specialty fruits, such as tangerines, Temples, and varieties for the gift trade, are best spot-picked if suitable labor is available. Oranges, grapefruit, and other varieties going to a cannery or when fully mature are, as a rule, clean-picked.

Spot-Picking—Spot-picking involves selection of certain fruits from the trees; hence, samples should be harvested with the knowledge that fruits from the top outside and outside portions, especially on the south and southwest sides, will be the most brightly colored and have the highest soluble solids and soluble-solids-to-acid ratios. Fruits from the canopy or inside portions will be less well colored and lower in soluble solids and soluble-solids-to-acid ratio than the average for the entire tree. Enough samples should be taken to ensure that variations within a grove are included. Twenty to fifty fruits properly chosen will be more representative than several times that number casually picked from the trees.

Systematic sampling will help to answer the question whether the fruits should be harvested at any particular moment. Where clean-picking is contemplated, or where checking the progress of internal quality is the object of testing, samples of outside fruits taken from all sides of the trees at a height of three to six feet from the ground should be representative of the entire crop. When maturity is marginal and any error may mean that the picked fruit must be destroyed, it is wise to "weight" the sample by deliberately picking low and reaching into the leafy canopy. A number of boxes representative of the block should be sampled from the trees, taking into consideration variety, rootstock, soil, draining, cultural factors, and size of fruits.

In summary, legal maturity for Florida citrus fruits is defined by laws and regulations that require a color break, minimum juice content, minimum percentages of total soluble solids and acid, and required solids-to-acid ratios. A lot of fruit must meet all of the applicable requirements, as shown in tests by federal-state inspectors, before it is certified for handling or shipping. Minimum requirements for legal maturity of Florida citrus fruits have become higher and more complex through the years, and it can be said with pride that the interests of the consumer have been a concern of the people who lead the industry that produces and markets these delectable fruits. These marketing restrictions are now understood and accepted as "minimum quality standards" rather than purely technical legal requirements.

Fruit Sizes and Containers

The market sizes of citrus fruits correspond to the number of fruits of uniform size that can be packed by set patterns in a standard shipping box of four-fifths bushel capacity. Each size is defined by the maximum and minimum diameters of the fruit in it, since there is a small range of diameters for each size. On entering a packinghouse for sweet citrus fruits, which are more or less spherical, it is easy to recognize the "sizers." On these machines the fruits move along slightly tapered rollers until they reach an opening equal to their diameter and drop between the rollers into a bin with others of the same size. Limes are longer than they are wide and are not so easily sized in this way; more often they are sized by weight as they move over a series of counterbalanced trapdoors, the heaviest fruit dropping out first.

In citrus fruits, there is no relation between size and grade as there is in apples. Certain sizes are more popular with consumers than others, however, particularly those in the middle of the range of sizes for any kind of citrus fruit. Extra large sizes may be less juicy than average, are more difficult to squeeze juice from, and cost more per fruit; fruits in the small sizes are usually higher in juice and sugar than the average, but more of them must be squeezed to get the same volume of juice. The preference for fruits of medium size is well known to all fruit handlers and is recognized by the marketing agreement committees, which may restrict the sizes as well as the grades of any citrus fruit that may be marketed. When the crop is running heavily to small sizes, smaller sizes will be permitted to go to market than when the bulk of the crop is of medium or large sizes.

Legal market sizes vary for the different kinds of citrus fruits and are defined in United States standards as regulated and amended by the Florida Department of Citrus. The standard nailed one and three-fifths bushel box for which sizes were originally established was formerly used almost exclusively for shipping citrus fruits but is no longer in use. Commercial shipping sizes are 48, 64, 80, 100, 125, and 163 for oranges, Temples, and tangelos, and 18, 23, 32, 40, 48, and 56 for grapefruits in regular four-fifths bushel cartons. Sizes for tangerines in the four-fifths bushel carton or wirebound box are 100, 120, 150, 176, 210, 246, and 294. Cartons of two-fifths bushel size and five- and eight-pound polyethylene and plastic mesh bags are also used for shipping. Fruit in bags is sold by weight; hence bags may include more than one size of fruit. Limes are not packed by standard sizes, although fruits in any one container must be uniform in size within a range of one-fourth inch in diameter.

Grades

U.S. standards for grades of Florida citrus fruits are defined by the Consumer and Marketing Service of the United States Department of Agriculture. Florida standards for grades, which apply to citrus fruits shipped within the state only, are similar in most respects to the federal standards. They are established under regulations of the Florida Citrus Commission. Regulations of the several federal marketing agreements issued by the U.S. Secretary of Agriculture upon the recommendation of the Growers Administrative Committee specify what grades and sizes of citrus fruits may be shipped outside of the production area (south of Georgia and east of the Suwannee River). These regulations are established at the beginning of each shipping season and are revised or amended as crop and market conditions warrant during the season.

The grade for citrus fruit is based mostly on external appearance and represents the degree of satisfactory appeal to the eye of the consumer. However, no fruit may be placed in a grade unless it meets minimum requirements for maturity.

Four grades are commonly recognized: U.S. Fancy, U.S. No. 1, U.S. No. 2, and U.S. No. 3. Fruit that has not yet been graded is tabulated on packinghouse records as Unclassified. The U.S. Fancy grade is seldom packed since it represents fruit of external perfection very difficult to produce. Most citrus fruit moves as U.S. No. 1, and growers attempt to practice grove care that will enable most of their crop to be packed in this grade. Occasionally they can also ship some which grades U.S. No. 2. Fruit of U.S. No. 3 grade is rarely shipped to fresh-fruit markets but is sent instead to the processing plants.

To be classed in any grade, citrus fruits must be mature, similar in varietal characteristics, and free from unhealed cuts and bruises. The Fancy grade requires that fruit be well colored, well shaped, firm, fairly smooth in texture of rind, and free from blemishes on the rind due to pests or mechanical causes (except that up to an average of 10 percent of the surface of any lot of fruit may be discolored by rust mites). These represent the external characters that the purchaser considers to indicate highest quality. The various lower grades specify the extent to which fruit may progressively vary from these ideals.

The U.S. No. 1 and U.S. No. 2 grades are further divided into subclasses based on discoloration due to rust mites. Some people suppose that russetted fruit is a different variety from bright fruit, and others believe it to be sweeter than bright fruit. As mentioned in chapter 9, rust mites affect only the appearance of the rind and do not have any effect on the internal quality of fruits on which they feed. Russetted fruit is just as good to eat as bright fruit, and some markets even pay a premium for it, although it is usually discounted somewhat for poor external appearance and may not keep as long.

The subclasses are separated on the basis of the proportion of the rind that is discolored and the percentage of fruit showing russetting. U.S. No. 1 grade has five subclasses: U.S. No. 1 Bright, U.S. No. 1 (no subclass name), U.S. No. 1 Golden, U.S. No. 1 Bronze, and U.S. No. 1 Russet; while U.S. No. 2 has Bright and Russet subclasses. All these subclasses have the same grade characters except for rind color and represent progressively greater amounts and intensity of discoloration. U.S. No. 1 Bright may contain no fruit with more than one-fifth of the whole area of its surface discolored, while U.S. No. 1 Russet must have at least a third of the fruits (by count) with more than one-third of the surface discolored. The discoloration becomes darker as the affected portion of the rind becomes larger. Sometimes the discolored area is dull and will not take a shine (early season damage), which is undesirable; in other cases, this area is glossy, although discolored, and will take a shine from the polishing brushes, which is desirable from the marketing standpoint.

U.S. grades for Tahiti limes are U.S. No. 1, U.S. No. 2, and U.S. Combination, which contains at least 60 percent of U.S. No. 1 grade. Each grade requires fruit to be mostly green in color, but has sub-classes, Turning and Mixed Color, for fruit that is becoming yellow. The minimum grade that may usually be shipped is U.S. Combination Mixed Color, although this requirement is subject to change upon the recommendation of the Lime Administrative Committee in accordance with the needs of the industry as indicated by the current crop condition. Key limes must meet standards for U.S. No. 2 Tahiti limes except for no color specification.

In summary, maturity denotes a certain minimum of acceptable edibility, size is defined by the number of fruits that can be packed in standard boxes, and grade indicates a certain degree of acceptability of external appearance.

Fruit for Processing

The discussion thus far has been centered on fruit that is to be shipped to market as fresh fruit since sizes and grades are primarily applied only to such fruit. The requirements of the citrus processor must also be considered, however, since over 80 percent of the total crop now goes to processing plants. This is not equal for all types of citrus fruits. In the 1987–88 season, over 93 percent of sweet oranges were processed (mostly to frozen concentrate); 57 percent of the grapefruits went to processing plants; and 34 percent of the tangerine crop was processed. Temples, Murcotts, and tangelos were also processed in relatively small amounts (see table 11-4).

Internal quality is of greater importance to the processor than external appearance. When fruit is in short supply, the processor is glad to overlook external appearance unless there are rind blemishes that will flake off into the juice or the fruit is so abnormal in size or shape that it cannot be handled by the processing machinery. As fruit begins to dry out, either through natural processes as it becomes overmature or because of freeze injury, the value to the processor decreases sharply. Any fruit with less than average juice content is penalized.

Fruit is sold to canneries on the basis of pounds-solids (pounds of juice times percentage of total soluble solids) or pounds-juice per box or load, the latter for single-strength (canned) juices.

Table 11-4.
Utilization of Florida citrus fruits
(quantities in thousands of 90-pound boxes)

Fruit	1976–77			1988–89		
	Fresh	Pro-cessed	Percent pro-cessed	Fresh	Pro-cessed	Percent pro-cessed
Oranges						
Earlies and mids	6,325	84,675	93.0	5,436	79,864	93.6
Orange, late	5,376	67,624	92.6	3,020	58,280	95.1
Grapefruits						
Seedy	71	7,229	99.0	a	3,350	100.0
White seedless	10,179	19,221	65.4	8,030	19,670	71.0
Colored seedless	9,540	3,760	28.3	15,859	7,841	33.1
Temples	2,135	2,565	54.6	868	2,882	76.9
Tangelos	1,721	2,479	59.0	1,348	2,452	64.5
Tangerines[b]	1,891	1,609	46.0	1,638	1,262	43.5
Limes	481	239	33.2	950	300	24.0
Totals	37,719	189,401	83.4	37,149	175,901	82.6

SOURCE: Florida Agricultural Statistics Service, *Citrus Summary, 1988–89.*
   a. Fresh sales insignificant; included in processed.
   b. Honey tangerines ("murcotts") not included prior to 1981–82.

Random samples are taken for fruit quality (maturity) tests from each load upon arrival at the cannery. Information furnished the processor not only includes the usual figures on Brix (total soluble solids), acids, and Brix-acid ratio obtained from a regular maturity test to assure compliance with legal requirements, but also the number of box equivalents or weight of fruit in the load and the weight of the juice per box equivalent. These data enable the processor to make necessary calculations as to probable yield of final product and how the load should be blended with others for efficient plant operation.

   Citrus canneries in Florida process a multitude of products in six principal forms—frozen, chilled, and canned juices and frozen, chilled, and canned sections and salads—plus numerous valuable by-products, including peel oils, molasses, dried pulp, etc. About

80 percent of all of the fruit delivered to processors goes into two products, frozen concentrated orange juice and chilled juice including orange-grapefruit blends. Fresh orange juice must have a minimum Brix-acid ratio of 10 to 1 and reconstituted juice a minimum ratio ranging from 13 to 1 to 19.5 to 1 under U.S. and Florida standards for frozen concentrated orange juice. The product is manufactured principally as either a 3-plus-1 or 4-plus-1 concentrate. A can of the former has a Brix of from 45° to 47° as purchased in the grocery store. Fresh juice is concentrated in a multistage high-vacuum process to about 55° Brix, after which fresh juice is added back to reduce the Brix to the proper range. Addition of fresh juice (and oil flashed off during concentration) is essential to produce a high-quality product. Other frozen concentrated juices include grapefruit, tangerine, lemon, and lime.

An increasing proportion of the oranges and grapefruits sent to canneries is being processed as chilled juice. Juice from fruit of concentrate quality is extracted, flash pasteurized, chilled to near freezing, and put into containers ranging from tank cars or ships to four-ounce cartons for shipment to market, where it is sold in grocery stores or delivered to individual homes. Widespread acceptance of frozen concentrated and chilled juices has led to an increasing number of various types of sections and salads being made available in either frozen or chilled form. A diminishing proportion of fruit is being processed into canned products, with consequent lower returns to the grower whose fruit will not meet concentrate standards and must be diverted to single-strength juice.

Today, it is recognized by knowledgeable growers that virtually every phase of the cultural program from the initial choices of a rootstock and site to the fertilizer, spray, and other components of the program has an influence upon fruit qualities and yield. Growers of fruit for processing have, moreover, a convenient yardstick in pounds-solids per acre against which they may measure the overall efficiency of their operations. Most growers realize, however, much as they would wish to sell all of their produce to a single outlet, that a healthy, viable fresh-fruit market is also essential to their success in supplying fruit profitably to processors. Their well-being is assured as long as the purchaser continues to identify the juice reconstituted from a small can or poured from a carton with freshly squeezed juice or cut-up fresh fruit. There are many synthetic citrus or citrus-like products around ready to become substitutes should this image ever be lost.

Determining the Value of Fruit

Citrus crops may be sold in a variety of ways. Some are sold in bulk, and the grower is paid for the crop based upon an agreed-upon estimate of its value. For example, a buyer may agree to purchase a grower's crop of Valencia oranges in a certain five-acre block for $10,000. The grower would then be paid the $10,000 as a flat sum.

Frequently the crop is sold on some sort of unit basis such as a certain price per standard box (a box of oranges being 90 pounds, grapefruit 85 pounds, and tangerines 95 pounds). For example, a grower may sell a crop for $5.00 per box. The fruit is harvested, weighed, the weight converted to box equivalents, and the grower paid at the $5.00 per box rate. Fruit destined for the fresh-fruit market is usually sold this way, and the price is usually strongly related to the external quality of the fruit. Fruit of superior quality will bring a greater price since more of the fruit can be packed as a higher grade and less will have to be sent to the cannery due to rind blemish problems.

Fruit sold for processing is usually priced in one of two ways, either on the basis of pounds-solids per box or pounds of juice per box. Fruit going to fresh or chilled juice is usually priced on the basis of pounds of juice per box. For example, if the fruit harvested averaged 45 pounds of juice per box and the price per pound of juice was 10 cents, the fruit price would be $4.50 per box.

Fruit for concentrate is usually priced on the basis of pounds-solids per box. To arrive at the box value, one needs to determine the percent solids (degrees Brix), multiply by the pounds of juice per box, then multiply that figure by the price per pound of solids. For example, assume 12 percent solids and 45 pounds of juice per box with a pounds-solids price of $1.00 per pound. Multiply .12 times 45 to determine pounds-solids per box, yielding 5.4 pounds. Multiply 5.4 times the pounds-solids price ($1.00) to yield the per-box price of $5.40.

Some prices are understood to be delivered-in prices. In those cases, the grower must pay the picking and hauling costs out of the proceeds. Other prices are quoted as on-tree prices, in which cases the buyer pays for picking and handling. A careful analysis of the various selling options will usually result in a best method for selling the crop.

12 /
Citrus Fruits for the Home

A persistent promotional ploy used during the Florida land boom of the 1920s exhorted the prospective purchaser to buy a home and "pick oranges from your piazza." While this is a little too much to expect, certainly one of the satisfactions that nearly all homeowners in Florida can have is to be able to pick some kind of citrus fruits from their own trees. The number of different kinds that may be grown will vary with size of the home grounds and with the climatic conditions of their location.

Many types of citrus can readily be grown by the dooryard grower in central and south Florida. Some varieties, such as the satsuma mandarin and kumquat, may be grown in warm locations of north and west Florida. Table 12-1 classifies some of the most popular varieties in order of season of ripening to enable the dooryard grower to select varieties that will produce fruit over the longest possible period.

Considering the various types of citrus fruits in turn, the citrus industry lists them as staples (sweet oranges and grapefruits), which are accepted as a regular part of the diet and eaten in some form practically every day by many people; specialty fruits (tangerines and tangerine hybrids), which are excellent for holiday or dessert uses; and acid fruits (lemons, limes, and others with high citric acid content), which find use as thirst-quenching drinks, garnishes on the dinner table, and ingredients for refreshing pies and delicious cakes. For landscaping the homesite, fruit trees that have additional ornamental value enhance the beauty of the surroundings, and a specimen tree of some exotic type adds interest as a "conversation piece." If the homesite is large enough, several cultivars of each type may be selected.

Sweet orange is the first choice, and if only a single citrus tree is to be grown, it may well be an early variety such as Hamlin or one of the navel oranges, except where the danger of cold makes it necessary to substitute Owari satsuma. If there is room for more than one or two sweet orange trees, a midseason variety such as Pineapple could be considered, and the late Valencia would be

246

Table 12-1.
Dooryard citrus varieties

Fruit	Season	Seeds	Relative size
Oranges			
Navel[a]	Very early	Very few	Large
Hamlin	Early	Few	Small
Parson Brown	Early midseason	Many	Medium
Pineapple	Midseason	Many	Medium
Queen	Midseason	Many	Medium
Valencia	Late	Few	Medium
Grapefruits			
Marsh	Midseason	Few	Large
Duncan	Midseason	Many	Large
Red blush	Midseason	Few	Large
Thompson (Pink Marsh)	Midseason	Few	Large
Specialty			
Satsuma	Very early	Very few	Medium
Robinson	Very early	Varies[b]	Varies
Sunburst	Early	Varies[b]	Medium-large
Orlando	Midseason	Varies[b]	Varies
Minneola[a]	Midseason	Varies[b]	Large
Temple	Late midseason	Few to many	Medium
Dancy	Midseason	Few to many	Small
Murcott	Late midseason	Few to many	Medium
Kumquat	Early midseason	Few	Very small
Acid			
Calamondin	Year-round[c]	Few	Very small
Persian lime	Year-round[c]	None	Medium
Key lime	Year-round[c]	Few	Small
Lemon[d]	Year-round[c]	Few	Varies
Limequat	Year-round[c]	Few	Small

a. Shy bearer.

b. These varieties vary in yield, size, and number of seeds depending on pollination. For best results, a pollinator tree should be nearby.

c. Acid citrus bears largest crop in late summer but some fruit ripen all year.

d. Many varieties can be grown such as: Lisbon, Bearss, Villafranca, Meyer, Ponderosa, etc.

another choice. In the area north of Ocala, however, Valencia is not recommended because the fruit is too often injured by cold. Where Valencia can be grown successfully, these three varieties will supply fresh fruit continuously from early November to August.

Grapefruit is usually second choice in citrus fruits. The Duncan variety is one of the best for home use, its quality compensating for its seediness. Many people will prefer a red-fleshed variety like Redblush because of the combination of flesh color and seedlessness. Usually a single grapefruit tree will suffice whereas several sweet orange trees are wanted.

Among the mandarins, satsumas (usually a substitute for sweet oranges) mature during late November but hold quality on the tree for only about four to six weeks. The mandarin hybrids (Lee, Osceola, Robinson, Page, and Sunburst) should have much interest as early-maturing tangerine substitutes. Robinson and Sunburst are now favored. Dancy tangerines may reach fair eating quality by Thanksgiving, but Dancy is usually better later. The homeowner may well decide to substitute a tangor or tangelo for a tangerine when choice must be limited. Temple tangor is superb in quality as well as appearance, and so is Minneola tangelo; and many people would choose one of these in preference to grapefruit if a choice were necessary. Some of the cultivars (especially the hybrids) may be difficult to locate at local nurseries. This is certainly true of the newer varieties and some of the older ones that may have fallen out of favor with commercial producers.

Acid fruits include lemons and limes, but even where cold permits them to be grown the true lemon is not recommended for a home fruit because of its susceptibility to scab. For southern Florida, the Tahiti lime makes a satisfactory acid fruit for the home since fruit can be picked any time of the year. The Meyer lemon and Eustis or Lakeland limequat can be grown wherever sweet oranges can be, and the calamondin is a good acid fruit for home use anywhere in the state.

Dual-purpose fruits are those which combine ornamental value with useful fruit. The kumquats, calamondin, and Meyer lemon are notable examples. Conversational fruits might cover such items as Ponderosa lemon, Ruby blood orange, or shaddock. These fruits always excite the horticultural interests of guests.

Rootstocks should be chosen for hardiness, long life, and fruit quality rather than primarily for yield. Wherever satsumas are grown for hardiness to cold, they should be on trifoliate-orange stock. In northern Florida, other citrus fruits may be grown on either trifoliate-orange or sour orange stock. In central Florida, sour orange and Cleopatra mandarin will probably give the best fruit quality. Any citrus trees bought for the home planting should be certified free of the common virus diseases as well as free from nematode infestation. As pointed out in chapter 7, the homeowner who wants citrus trees should also be very careful not to plant ornamentals that may be infested with nematodes; doing so will render futile the caution used in choosing nematode-free citrus trees.

Any well-drained site that is suitable for building a home and having a garden is likely to be satisfactory for citrus trees if temperatures are not limiting. These trees will tolerate light shade but will be more productive if they are not shaded by other trees. They should also not be planted so close together that they cut off light to the lower branches of neighboring trees. For home plantings, the spacings recommended for commercial plantings should be enlarged.

Vigorous one-year-old nursery trees should be planted; these should preferably have been container grown. They will cost more than the bare-rooted trees used in grove planting, but they will be more likely to live and thrive with minimum attention. For the person planting only a few trees, this assurance and relief from care is usually worth the difference in cost. These trees may be set out at any time when they do not have tender new growth, but it is unwise to plant before 15 February in southern Florida or 1 March in the northern part of the state. They should be set slightly higher than they grew in the nursery row or container, and be provided with a basin to hold water around each tree. This basin should hold about five to ten gallons of water and is periodically filled to soak the root area of the young tree. Some of the soil should be removed from the root mass when the tree is planted. This will expose many of the outer roots and allow them to grow quickly into the new planting area provided. This soil removal is also important since the difference in soil between the potting mix and the planting site can make a drastic soil interface difference. This can result in difficulty in watering and subsequent root growth. If subfreezing temperatures are forecast after trees are planted, they should be protected as described in chapter 5.

Water is the first requirement of the young tree, and it will be used up rapidly by trees with a good head of foliage, which container-grown trees should have. If a garden hose reaches the trees easily, let it run in each basin for ten or fifteen minutes each week, long enough to fill the basin, for the first month. Thereafter, whenever new growth is seen to wilt in midafternoon, fill the basins again. If a hose cannot be used, supply about eight to ten gallons at each watering. Need for irrigation will be less as the trees increase their root systems each year, but some occasions for watering may be expected through the fourth year.

Fertilization should start when swelling buds indicate that growth is beginning. The first year it is well to apply fertilizer about every six weeks from early April until September. A 6-6-6 analysis is a good general one for garden use, including citrus trees, and may be used at rates from a half cupful for the first application to one-and-a-half pints in September, increasing the quantity steadily all season. For the second, third, and fourth years, the fertilizing schedule given in chapter 6 can be followed. Fertilizer should cover the basin area the first year. In succeeding years, a good rule of thumb is to spread the fertilizer as many feet beyond the drip of the canopy as the age of the tree in years (up to ten). For the home garden, it is convenient to remember that one pint of mixed fertilizer weighs about one pound. (*Caution*—Do not use a one-pound coffee can or similar container since such a can may actually hold nearly three pounds of mixed fertilizer.)

Citrus trees in home gardens are much less likely to suffer from deficiency of mineral elements than in commercial groves because of the greater amount of organic matter usually present in garden soils. As a precaution against the possible development of deficiencies, however, it is wise to use during the first few years fertilizer mixtures containing microelements. These are readily available at fertilizer stores. If zinc deficiency symptoms appear, it will be necessary to apply a spray as described in chapter 9, but this need is rather rare in gardens on sandy soils. On alkaline soils, however, zinc and manganese deficiencies may be expected to appear unless annual nutritional sprays are applied. Iron deficiency may also occur and should be corrected with soil applications of chelated iron materials.

Many home gardeners have grown citrus trees successfully without any attention to soil reaction. If the garden is on sandy soil and sulfur is not used in a regular program of pest control, the gardener is justified in not worrying about this matter. If the trees do not have healthy foliage, however, and the cause is not obviously an insect infestation, it would be well to take a sample of soil to the

County Extension Office or local garden center for checking the acidity. If the soil is not in the pH range of 5.5 to 6.5, the situation should be corrected as recommended or as explained in chapter 8. If the soil is naturally basic, it will be next to impossible to change the reaction.

Fertilization of bearing citrus trees in the home grounds is best based on age rather than yield because of the difficulty of keeping yield records. The recommended fertilizer applications given in table 6-1 will be quite satisfactory for the home gardener to follow. However, these amounts are for trees growing without competition of lawn grass. Citrus trees in the home garden will grow best if they are cleanly cultivated or else kept heavily mulched with grass, leaves, or pine straw, but sometimes they are planted in the midst of an expanse of green lawn. In such cases, the turf should be kept from growing closer than three feet from the trunk of the tree, and in the first ten years the amount of fertilizer should be increased about 25 percent at each application to provide enough for grass as well as tree. If grass clippings are not carried away but are left to decay in place, there will be a return to the soil of the elements needed by the grass thereafter, and the trees will no longer have competition. Fertilizer applied for tree use will injure the grass if it is not promptly washed down into the soil with water. Under a mulch system, weeds should be suppressed by the mulch, and there is no occasion to cultivate then. The mulch should be kept at least six inches away from the trunk to avoid foot rot.

Pest control should be undertaken only as need for it becomes evident. Citrus trees in the home garden may thrive for years with little trouble from pests. When they do appear in sufficient intensity to require action, the homeowner will usually find it more satisfactory to have the spraying done by a pest control operator or a neighboring commercial grower rather than to spray the trees himself. This latter may be perfectly feasible with trees up to bearing size, but larger trees require spraying equipment of larger capacity and power than is likely to be profitable for the grower of a few trees to own. The discussion of pests and their control in chapter 9 is just as valid for the home garden citrus grower as for the commercial operator. However, the dangerous qualities of some insecticides are more important to the home gardener, since he is less likely to have adequate protective equipment to use in applying them and his house and family are more likely to be affected, than they are to the commercial operator.

Appendixes

Appendix 1
Citrus Grove Records

Citrus growing is a business, and every good business needs excellent records for evaluation of performance. In fact, good grove records are in many ways just as important as good cultural practice. Valuable in many ways, records are indispensable at tax time. Other uses include comparative studies over several years to evaluate performance over time and to compare one grove with others in the state. Such comparisons are relatively easy to make since annual studies are conducted by the University of Florida IFAS Cooperative Extension Service (examples are included elsewhere in this text). If the grower uses record-keeping forms similar to those used by the Cooperative Extension Service in compiling data, the IFAS studies, comparisons should be rather straightforward.

Keeping good grove records should not be looked upon as a bothersome chore but rather as an opportunity to improve grove and management performance. Suggested guidelines and forms to facilitate record keeping are contained in IFAS Extension Circular 428 by R. P. Muraro and L. K. Jackson. Most of the text that follows here is excerpted from that publication for the reader's reference and convenience. Copies of Circular 428 should be available from most local IFAS Cooperative Extension Offices.

Records should be kept each season on every grove and should include the following:

1. Inventory of equipment owned.
2. Grove chart and inventory of trees by age, variety, and rootstock.
3. Dates and description of all operations.
4. Costs of operations.
5. Rate, analysis, and composition of fertilizers applied.
6. Sprays and dusts applied, with dates, materials, and rates.
7. Amount and date of irrigation applications.
8. Rainfall record for the year.
9. Temperature record for the year, emphasizing low temperatures.

10. Number of boxes harvested (by variety), disposition, and financial returns.
11. Number and variety of resets planted, with locations (a reset map may be helpful).

Fiscal Year

The most common fiscal period for citrus grove records is September through August. However, any fiscal period is satisfactory as long as monthly records are kept. Results measured in fruit yields should be from the bloom that occurred in the spring of the fiscal period evaluated. For example: a grove record for September 1989 through August 1990 would produce fruit harvested in the period of September 1990 through August 1991 and would be chiefly the result of grove practices and treatments during the 1989–90 period.

Record Forms

Forms best suited to supply the desired information should be used. Large columnar sheets are often used to good advantage, as are monthly data sheets with seasonal summaries. The number of groves involved should also be considered before deciding on forms.

Outlines of a few forms that might be used in keeping a grove record are shown in the tables in this appendix. Information which is received from these forms over a period of years will be helpful in finding more profitable methods of organization, operation, and management of the grove. Such information is also valuable in obtaining credit when needed and in preparing tax returns.

Grove Inventory

Table A1-1 is a form for recording tree numbers by variety, rootstock, age, and planting distance. This inventory is made at the beginning of each season. The first inventory may necessitate an actual tree count or can be made up from a grove chart or plat (see table A1-7). Each succeeding tree inventory may be readily made from the previous one by adding one year to all ages, adjusting tree counts for trees removed, and adding resets.

Equipment Inventory

Table A1-2 is an inventory sheet for equipment owned by the grove operator. The first item on this inventory sheet is an es-

Table A1-1.
Citrus Grove Record

Grove: _____   Business Year: _____ to _____
       (name, number, etc.)

Acres: _____   Condition: _____

Legal description: _____   Sec._____ Twp._____ Range_____
                                          If irrigated
Soil type: _____   source of water: _____

Kind of cover crop: _____   Light:_____ Medium:_____ Heavy:_____

TREE RECORD

Class	Variety	Rootstock	Age	Planting distance	Number of trees	Acres
Early Oranges						
Midseason Oranges						
Late Oranges						
Seedy Grapefruit						
Seedless Grapefruit						
Tangerines						
Temples						
Other: _____						
Totals						

Table A1-2.
Grove and Equipment Inventory

Grove: _____ Business Year: _____ to _____
(name, number, etc.)

		Make these entries beginning of business year		Make these entries end of business year				
Property and description	Quantity	Value as of ___		Additions and repairs	Machinery sold	Value as of ___	Appre- ciation/ deprec.	% for other accounts
Real estate: Land		$		$	$	$	$	
Trees								
Buildings:								
Irrigation: Wells or lake								
Pumps								
Motors								
Mains: surface								
underground								
Volume or traveling gun								
Permanent sprinklers								
Equipment: Tractor								
Disc								
Chopper								
Mower								
Fert. spreader								
Sprayer								
Duster								
Water & supply truck or tank								
Trailer								
Truck								
Auto								
Miscell. tools								
Grove supplies								
Totals		$		$	$	$	$	

timate of the value of the land and trees in the grove. This figure should be the amount the grove is considered to be worth for long-time fruit-producing purposes.

This figure also is useful for determining an interest charge on investment in land and trees. An interest charge on the investment should be considered in all business operations. The inventory may be summarized and prorated to the various grove records included on an acreage or use basis if this equipment is used on more groves than those included in the particular account. There is no equipment inventory to be recorded where grove work is done by a caretaker, since these costs are included in caretaking charges.

Grove Receipts

Table A1-3 is designed to show on-tree receipts and boxes of fruit handled or picked by methods of sale. The data desired are the number of boxes of fruit by variety and the amount of money the fruit brought on the tree.

Grove Expenses

Table A1-4 is an example of a monthly expense sheet. A large, multiple-column sheet could be used with a column for the date of grove operation. However, such a method does not provide for as much detailed information as table A1-4. Table A1-4 is divided into three sections:

The first section is designated as General Expenses. This section is for recording labor, gasoline, oil, repairs, insurance, irrigation, and all other expenses where equipment is owned by the operator. Purchases of equipment may be itemized and entered in the miscellaneous column if such is to be written off as current expenses. Equipment that is to be charged to more years of operation than the current one, should be entered on the equipment inventory sheet (table A1-2) in the "additions and repairs" column.

The second section is for fertilizer analysis and tonnage schedule. This division is used only in those months when fertilizer is applied. Attempts at a grove analysis from the standpoint of fertilizer added will be of little value unless complete information is recorded. Therefore, it is important that the fertilizer tonnage and complete fertilizer analysis be recorded. The columns at the right of the sheet allow for recording the total cost of each fertilizer application as well as the cost per acre.

Table A1-3.
Grove Receipts

Grove: _____   **Business Year:** _____ to _____
          (name, number, etc.)

Date	Variety of fruit & number of boxes	Method of sale[1]	Value received ($/box, p.s.)	Marketing expenses		Net return		
				Pick & haul	Pack & selling	Per box	Total	
			$	$	$	$	$	
Total			$	$	$	$	$	

Miscellaneous Receipts

Date	Item and description	Value
	Crop insurance payment	$
Total		$

[1]Cash sale (CS), Participation (P), Consignment (C), Fresh (F), Bulk (B), Cannery or Eliminations (CE), etc.

Table A1-4.
Grove Expenses

Grove: _____ (name, number, etc.)

Business Year: _____ to _____

General Expenses

Date	Item description	Quantity	Labor	Truck & tractor repairs	Gas and oil	Other grove equip	Irrigation repairs	Irrigation gas and oil	Miscellaneous grove work	Total
			$	$	$	$	$	$	$	$
Total			$	$	$	$	$	$	$	$

Fertilizer Schedule

Variety	Quantity per acre	Analysis											Cost			
		N	P₂O₅	K₂O	MgO	MnO	CuO	ZnO	Fe₂O₃	B₂O₃	Lime or Dolm	Application	Material	Total	Cost per acre
												$	$	$	$
Total												$	$	$	$

Spray And Dust Schedule

Variety	Spray program (P. bloom, S. oil, etc.)	Quantity/cost per 500 gallon tank												Concentration per tank (dilute, 2X, 5X, 10X, etc.)	Cost per tank	Total tanks	Cost		
		Copper	Zinc	Manganese	Chloro-benzilate	Ethion	Tri-thion	Kel-thane	Oil	Beniate	Other	Sulphur dust	Other				Appl	Material	Total
															$		$	$	$
Total																	$	$	$

The third section is for the spray and dust analysis and schedule. Columns are provided to record the type of spray program being applied as well as the materials used in each spray program along with the cost of those materials. Columns at the right of the sheet allow for recording the cost per tank and the total cost for each spray program.

Accumulative Grove Expenses

Often a grower will want to determine expenditures as of a particular date. Table A1-5 enables the grower to keep an accumulated cost by date and by grove practice. This sheet will be useful when summarizing the grove records at the end of the fiscal year as well as aiding in developing a cash flow chart for financial planning.

Summary Statement

A summary sheet for combining costs and returns for a season is shown in table A1-6. This is a summary statement for the grove for one year, and it renders an easy comparison with other groves in other seasons. There are several points that should be taken into consideration in making such comparisons. The most important of these are the average age of trees and varieties of fruit in each grove. Also, the summary statement shown on table A1-6 will allow direct comparison of citrus grove care costs, which are now being made available by the Cooperative Extension Service. (Copies of some of these reports may be found in Appendix 2 of this text. Contact your local IFAS Extension Office for current reports.)

Tree Chart

Growing orchard crops such as citrus is a long-term investment, unlike many other agricultural endeavors. Therefore, every effort should be made to maintain each tree at top efficiency. There is nothing the grower can do to assist in this effort that will be more valuable than a grove tree chart or plat. One method of making such a chart is shown on table A1-7. This chart will assist in checking questionable trees to determine whether their production is profitable or whether they should be replaced.

A grove history showing the source and variety of rootstock and scion should be included with the grove chart. Knowledge of the parent trees will assist growers and technical workers should grove problems develop.

Table A1-5.
Accumulative Grove Expenses

Grove: _____ (name. number. etc.)

Business Year: _____ to _____

Date	Description	Disc	Chop	Mow	Labor. general grove wk.	Herb-icide	Ferti-lize	Spray/dust	Hedging	Topping	Tree removal	Irrigation	Young tree care	Miscel-laneous	Grove taxes	Total costs	Accumul. total costs
		$	$	$	$	$	$	$	$	$	$	$	$	$	$	$	$
Total		$	$	$	$	$	$	$	$	$	$	$	$	$	$	$	$

Table A1-6.
Summary of Grove Record

Grove:_____ Business Year: _____ to _____
              (name, number, etc.)

Acres in Grove:_____   Total Boxes of Fruit:_____   Boxes Per Acre:_____

Item	Grove total for year	Per acre	Per box
Total Revenue	$	$	$
Grove Expenses: Disc	$	$	$
Chop			
Mow			
Labor, General Grove Work, Pull Vines			
Herbicide			
Spray			
Dust			
Fertilizer			
Hedging and Topping			
Brush Removal			
Tree Removal			
Young Tree Care			
Irrigation			
Miscellaneous			
Grove Taxes			
Interest Expense			
Depreciation on Buildings & Equipment			
Total Grove Expenses	$	$	$
Net Returns	$	$	$

*Include costs of labor, power and material for operations when applicable.

Table A1-7.
Tree Chart of Citrus Grove (Example)

	1	2	3	4	5	6	7	8	9	10	11
1	R	M	M	M	V	M	M	M	M	M	M
2	R	M	M	M	M	M	M	M	M	V	M
3	R	M	G	V	M	M	V	M	M	M	M
4	R	G	G	V	M	M	G	M	M	M	M
5	R	G	G	V	M	M	M	M	M	M	M
6	M	V	M	V	M	M	M	M	M	M	M
7	M	G	M	V	M	G	M	M	M	V	M
8	M	M	V	V	M	V	M	V	M	M	V
9	G	V	M	V	G	G	G	M	M	V	M
10	G	G	V	M	M	M	M	V	M	V	M
11	M	M	V	V	M	M	M	M	M	V	M
12	G	G	G	M	M	M	M	M	R	M	M
13	M	M	M	M	M	M	M	M	M	V	V
14	G	M	G	M	M	M	M	V	V	V	V
15	G	V	V	M	M	M	V	V	V	V	V
16	G	M	G	M	M	M	M	M	M	M	V
17	M	M	M	M	V	R	M	V	P	V	V
18	M	M	M	M	V	V	M	M	V	V	V
19	M	G	G	M	V	M	M	M	V	V	V
20	M	M	G	M	M	M	M	M	V	M	V
21	M	G	V	M	M	G	G	M	M	V	M
22	V	V	V	V	V	V	V	M	V	V	V
23	V	V	V	V	V	V	V	V	V	V	V
24	V	V	V	V	V	V	V	V	V	V	V
25	V	V	V	V	V	V	V	V	V	V	T
26	V	V	V	V	V	V	V	V	V	V	V
27	V	V	V	V	V	V	V	V	V	V	V
28	V	V	V	V	V	V	V	V	V	V	R
29	V	V	V	V	V	V	V	V	V	V	V
30	V	V	V	V	V	V	V	V	V	V	V
31	V	V	V	V	V	V	V	V	V	V	V
32	V	V	V	V	V	V	V	V	V	V	V

Legend, Year Set, Number of Trees, and Acreages

	Year Set	Trees	Acres
P = Pineapple oranges	1952	1	.01
V = Valencia oranges	1952	173	2.43
G = Seedy grapefruit	1952	28	.40
M = Marsh seedless grapefruit	1952	140	2.01
T = Tangerines	1952	2	.03
R = Resets	1971	8	.11
Totals		352	5.02

Planting distances = 25 ft. × 25 ft.

In charting a grove, use paper having parallel lines drawn horizontally and vertically with the resulting squares of sufficient size for writing in symbol for each tree. In most cases, the chart should be oriented on the charting paper with the top of the sheet representing north, or as near north as possible. For purposes of locating individual trees on the chart, the lines and columns should be numbered. One good method of numbering is shown on this chart. Begin at the upper left, or northwest, corner and number downward for lines. Begin at the same position and number to the right for columns. Then two numbers will represent the position of any tree on the chart. For example, the designated position of the Pineapple orange tree would be 17-9 (line 17, column 9).

A tree chart like the one pictured is somewhat unusual because a mixed planting is represented. Frequently a chart will show only a single variety in a block, and in that case symbols could be used to represent tree condition or yield. An integral part of any chart would be a listing of scion variety, rootstock, source of trees, and tree age plus any permanent features such as buildings, wells, roads, or the like.

Concluding Statement

Keeping and using records analytically contributes to the efficiency of any citrus enterprise. It is important to maintain data regularly on grove conditions and production costs. Grove practices and elements of management become more meaningful when responses are available on paper for study and comparison. Keeping good grove records is merely an exercise unless they are used regularly. These records are important management tools and should be consulted before making changes in programs that may affect returns.

Appendix 2
Estimated Comparative Indian River Citrus Production Costs, 1988–1989

Types of production expenses[a]	Total cost per acre			
	1988		1989	
Irrigated processed fruit production				
Mechanical mow middles		25.07		26.94
Chemical mow (2 times)		21.64		23.60
General grove work (2 labor hrs/acre)		15.68		16.86
Herbicide (1/2 tree acre treated)[b]				
Application	33.30		30.99	
Material	82.99		86.11	
Total herbicide cost		116.29		117.10
Spray 2X (one 500-gal tank/acre)				
Post bloom				
Application	32.36		34.04	
Material	40.20		48.66	
Total post bloom cost		72.56		82.70
Summer oil				
Application	32.36		34.04	
Material	39.61		39.06	
Total summer oil cost		71.97		73.10
Dust (sulphur)				
Application (aerial)	5.18		6.00	
Material	10.34		11.02	
Total dusting cost		15.52		17.02
Fertilizer (bulk)				
3 applications	17.85		17.40	
Material (12-2-15-2.4 MgO, 1,500 lbs)	115.50		131.49	
Total fertilizer cost		133.35		148.89
Topping		31.98		33.58
Remove brush from trees		12.12		13.03
Hedging		19.19		20.15
Chop brush		11.87		12.98

Remove trees: pull, stack, and burn trees using front-end loader	13.55	14.43
Young trees (1–3 yrs old; 3 trees/acre)		
Water (avg. 5 waterings)	10.07	10.83
Fertilizer (application and material)	23.76	24.88
Sprout, Ridomil/Aliette, etc.	3.35	3.40
Prepare site and plant resets	32.89	33.76
Total young trees	70.07	72.87
Irrigation[c]		
Microsprinkler system	59.02	63.45
Clean ditches (weed control)	7.57	8.14
Checking irrigation system	10.13	10.64
Fixed/variable expense	25.99	28.19
Total irrigation costs	102.71	110.42
Total production costs, processed fruit	733.57	783.67

Irrigated fresh fruit production

Supplemental post bloom spray		
Application	32.36	34.04
Material	38.24	38.30
Total supplemental spray cost	70.60	72.34
Fall miticide spray		
Application (aerial)	6.84	6.00
Material	22.75	22.69
Total fall miticide spray cost	29.59	28.69
Total production costs, irrigated fresh fruit	833.76	884.70

SOURCE: Ronald P. Muraro (extension farm management economist, CREC, Lake Alfred, Florida), April 1989.

NOTE: The listed estimated comparative costs are for the example grove situation described in the Economic Information Report Series entitled "Budgeting Costs and Returns: Indian River Citrus Production" and may not represent your particular grove situation in the Indian River production area, i.e., the citrus producing counties on Florida's east coast

a. The budget cost items have been revised to reflect current grove practices being used by growers—e.g., chemical mowing, different spray materials, higher rates of fertilization, microsprinkler irrigation, more reset trees, etc. Therefore, the revised costs shown may be higher than previously reported.

The budget cost items in this report represent a custom managed operation. Therefore, all equipment costs are based upon the average custom rate costs, and a 10 percent handling and supervision charge is added to the material cost.

Although the estimated annual per acre grove costs listed are representative for a mature Indian River white seedless grapefruit grove, the grove care costs for a specific grove site may differ depending upon the tree age, tree density, and the grove practices performed. For example, a Temik application would add $133.24 per acre; water control and maintenance of ditches and canals could average $58.14 per acre; extensive tree loss due to blight or tristeza could at least double, if not increase more, the tree replacement and care costs; travel and set-up costs may vary due to size of citrus grove and distance from grove equipment barn, and so forth.

b. Where *equipment use* or *application* is listed (mowing, hedging, spray application, etc.), an average custom charge (cost) is used, which includes a charge for equipment repairs, maintenance, labor, and overhead. A *management charge* for equipment supervision and fruit marketing is not included.

Other cost items that are not included in the budget are ad valorem taxes and interest on grove investment. In addition to these cost items, overhead and administrative costs, such as water drainage/district taxes, crop insurance, and other grower assessments, can add up to 12 percent to the total grove care costs. These costs vary from grove to grove depending on age, location, and time of purchase or establishment.

Also, a supervision (or handling) charge of 10 percent of cost is included in the materials expense.

c. Irrigation expenses for 1989 include the following:

	Flood	Volume gun	Micro-sprinkler	Drip
Variable operating expense	82.64	189.98	63.45	50.75
Checking irrigation system	—	—	10.64	8.95
Fixed-variable expense (annual maintenance repairs to system; cleaning ditches/weed control)*	5.91	16.11	28.19	23.70
Total cash expense	88.55	206.09	102.28	83.40
Fixed-depreciation expense	8.66	50.03	56.56	45.25
Total cash and fixed expenses	97.21	256.12	158.84	128.65

* Where applied, there may be an additional cost of $32.93 per acre for water control in/out of ditches and canals plus $25.21 per acre for ditch and canal maintenance.

Appendix 3
Estimated Comparative Southwest Florida Citrus Production Costs, 1988–1989

Types of production expenses[a]	Total cost per acre			
	1988		1989	
Irrigated processed fruit production				
Mow middles (6 times per year)		50.16		53.88
General grove work (2 labor hrs/acre)		15.68		16.86
Herbicide (1/2 tree acre treated)[b]				
Winter/spring application				
Application and material	34.50		30.99	
Fall cleanup application				
Application and material	88.48		89.14	
Total herbicide cost		122.98		120.13
Post bloom				
Application (250 gal/acre)	18.86		20.28	
Material	26.50		32.86	
Total post bloom cost		45.36		53.14
Summer oil				
Application (250 gal/acre)	18.86		20.28	
Material	32.60		32.03	
Total summer oil cost		51.46		52.31
Fall miticide				
Application (aerial)	6.84		5.75	
Material	28.08		30.55	
		34.92		36.30
Fertilizer (bulk)				
3 applications	17.85		17.40	
Material (12-2-15-2.4 MgO, 1,500 lbs)	120.00		120.97	
Total fertilizer cost		137.85		138.37
Topping		31.98		33.58
Remove brush from trees		12.12		13.03

269

Hedging		19.19	20.63
Chop brush		12.07	12.98
Remove trees: pull, stack, and burn		18.01	19.24
trees using front-end loader (4 trees)			
Young trees (1–3 yrs old; 4 trees/acre)			
Water (avg. 5 waterings)	13.43		14.44
Fertilizer (application and material)	32.37		33.17
Sprout, Ridomil/Aliette, etc.	2.45		2.63
Prepare site and plant resets	28.92		29.69
Total young trees		77.17	79.93
Irrigation[c]			
Drip system	77.58		83.40
Clean ditches (weed control)	7.57		8.14
Ditch and canal maintenance	23.45		25.21
Water control (in/out of ditches	30.63		32.63
and canals			
Total irrigation costs		139.23	149.38
Total production costs, irrigated		768.18	799.76
processed fruit			

Irrigated fresh fruit production

Supplemental post bloom spray			
Application (aerial)	6.84		5.75
Material	21.88		22.74
Total supplemental spray cost		28.72	28.49
Fall miticide spray			
Application (aerial)	6.84		5.75
Material	20.68		20.63
Total fall miticide spray cost		27.52	26.38
Total production costs, irrigated		824.42	854.63
fresh fruit			

SOURCE: Ronald P. Muraro (extension farm management economist, CREC, Lake Alfred, Florida), April 1989.

NOTE: The listed estimated comparative costs are for the example grove situation described in the Economic Information Report Series entitled "Budgeting Costs and Returns for Southwest Florida Production" and may not represent your particular grove situation in Southwest Florida.

The term "Southwest Florida" refers to the counties listed in the Florida Agricultural Statistics Service "Southern Production Area." However, the costs shown are applicable to other South Central Florida counties such as Desoto and Sarasota counties.

a. The budget cost items have been revised to reflect current grove practices being used by growers—e.g., chemical mowing, different spray materials, higher rates of fertilization, microsprinkler irrigation, more reset trees, etc. Therefore, the revised costs shown may be higher than previously reported.

Although the estimated annual per acre grove costs listed are representative for a mature Southwest Florida Hamlin orange and red seedless grapefruit grove, respectively, the grove care costs for a specific grove site may differ depending upon the tree age, tree density, and the grove practices performed. For example, a Temik application would add $122.22 per acre; extensive tree loss due to blight or tristeza could at least double, if not increase more, the tree replacement and care costs, and so forth.

   b. Except for ground spray application costs, where *equipment use* or *application* is listed (mowing, hedging, fertilizer application, etc.), an average custom charge (cost) is used. A *management charge* for equipment supervision and fruit marketing is not included.

   Other cost items that are not included in the budget are ad valorem taxes and interest on grove investment. In addition to these cost items, overhead and administrative costs, such as water drainage/district taxes, crop insurance, and other grower assessments, can add up to 12 percent to the total grove care costs. These costs vary from grove to grove depending on age, location, and time of purchase or establishment.

   Also, a supervision (or handling) charge of 10 percent of cost is *not* included in the materials expense. This charge is normally added when the grove maintenance is handled by a custom operator.

   c. Irrigation expenses for 1989 include the following:

	Flood	Volume gun	Micro-sprinkler	Drip
Variable operating expense	82.64	189.98	63.45	50.75
Checking irrigation system	—	—	10.64	8.95
Fixed-variable expense (annual maintenance repairs to system; cleaning ditches/weed control)*	5.91	16.11	28.19	23.70
Total cash expense	88.55	206.09	102.28	83.40
Fixed-depreciation expense	8.66	50.03	56.56	45.25
Total cash and fixed expenses	97.21	256.12	158.84	128.65

* Where applied, there may be an additional cost of $32.93 per acre for water control in/out of ditches and canals plus $25.21 per acre for ditch and canal maintenance.

Appendix 4
Estimated Comparative Interior Citrus Production Costs, 1988–1989

Types of production expenses[a]	Total cost per acre			
	1988		1989	
Nonirrigated processed fruit production				
Disking (2 times)		17.62		16.40
Mowing (3 times)		29.28		31.68
General grove work (2 labor hrs/acre)		15.06		15.40
Herbicide (1/2 tree acre treated)[b]				
Application (2 times)	19.88		20.34	
Material	64.61		64.59	
Total herbicide cost		84.49		84.93
Spray (2 times)				
Post bloom				
Application (April)	32.38		29.26	
Material	33.66		41.74	
Total post bloom cost		66.04		71.00
Summer oil				
Application	32.38		29.26	
Material	43.74		50.00	
Total summer oil cost		76.12		79.26
Fall miticide				
Application	22.74		24.23	
Material	24.07		25.01	
Total fall miticide cost		46.81		49.24
Fertilizer (bulk)				
3 applications	26.31		20.61	
Material (16-0-16, 1,325 lbs)	106.00		120.49	
Total fertilizer cost		132.31		141.10
Topping (cost year of topping)		30.83		32.37
Remove brush from trees		11.58		12.16
Hedging (cost year of hedging)		22.52		23.65
Chop brush/mow brush		9.48		10.19
Remove trees: pull, stack, and burn		14.20		15.12

trees using front-end loader (3 trees)
Young trees (1–3 yrs old; 3 trees/acre)

Water resets (avg. 5 times/yr)	10.26		11.03	
Fertilizer (application and material)	10.63		11.25	
Tree wraps, sprout, Ridomill/Aliette, etc.	15.43		15.80	
Prepare site and plant resets	23.20		23.80	
Total young trees		59.52		61.88
Total production costs, nonirrigated processed fruit		615.86		644.38

Irrigated processed fruit production
Irrigation[c]

Permanent overhead system	102.00		109.65	
Operating variable costs	20.91		22.48	
Check irrigation system and maintenance	2.42		2.60	
Total irrigation costs		125.33		134.73
Total production costs, irrigated processed fruit		741.19		779.11

Irrigated fresh fruit production
Supplemental fall miticide spray

Application	32.38		29.26	
Material	25.97		24.23	
Total supplemental fall miticide		58.35		53.49
Total production costs, irrigated fresh fruit	799.54		832.60	

SOURCE: Ronald P. Muraro (extension farm management economist, CREC, Lake Alfred, Florida), April 1989.

NOTE: The listed estimated comparative costs are for the example grove situation described in the Economic Information Report Series entitled "Budgeting Costs and Returns: Central Florida Citrus Production" and may not represent your particular grove situation in the Central Florida production area, i.e., Polk and Highlands counties. The costs presented in this table are also generally applicable to other counties such as Hardee, Hillsborough, Lake, and Orange.

a. The budget cost items have been revised to reflect current grove practices being used by growers—e.g., chemical mowing, different spray materials, higher rates of fertilization, microsprinkler irrigation, more reset trees, etc. Therefore, the revised costs shown may be higher than previously reported.

The budget costs in this report represent a custom managed

operation. Therefore, all equipment costs are based upon the average custom rate cost and a 10 percent handling and supervision charge is added to the material cost.

Although the estimated annual per acre grove costs listed are representative for a mature Central Florida Valencia orange grove, the grove care costs for a specific grove site may differ depending upon the tree age, tree density, and the grove practices performed. For example, a Temik application would add $133.24 per acre; extensive tree loss due to blight or tristeza could at least double, if not increase more, the tree replacement and care costs; travel and set-up costs may vary due to size of citrus grove and distance from grove equipment barn, and so forth.

b. Where *equipment use* or *application* is listed (disking, hedging, spray application, etc.) an average custom charge (cost) is used, which includes a charge for equipment repairs, maintenance, labor, and overhead. A *management charge* for equipment supervision and fruit marketing is not included.

Other cost items that are not included in the budget are ad valorem taxes and interest on grove investment. In addition to these cost items, overhead and administrative costs, such as water drainage/district taxes, crop insurance, and other grower assessments, can add up to 12 percent to the total grove care costs. These costs vary from grove to grove depending on age, location, and time of purchase or establishment.

A supervision (or handling) charge of 10 percent of cost is also included in the materials expense.

c. Irrigation expenses include the following:

	Micro-sprinkler	Permanent overhead	Traveling volume gun
Variable operating expense	63.45	109.65	189.98
Checking irrigation system	10.64	2.60	—
Fixed-variable expense (annual maintenance repairs to system)	28.19	22.48	16.11
Total cash expense	102.28	134.73	206.09
Fixed-depreciation expense	56.56	59.54	50.03
Total cash and fixed expenses	158.84	194.27	256.12

Appendix 5
Costs for Establishing, Planting, and Maintaining a Citrus Grove through Four Years of Age, South Florida Flatwoods Area

	Costs per acre	
	Range	Average
Land costs[a]		
Improved pasture land	$1,500– $2,500	$1,740
Raw land and semi-improved pasture	1,000– 2,000	1400
Land preparation—clearing		
Pasture and light palmettos	80– 225	160
Raw land (heavy pines, palmettos)	200– 400	310
Land preparation—leveling		
With laser	200– 350	275
Without laser	100– 250	160
Land preparation—bedding		
2 rows (short rows: 1,350+ ft.)	125– 325	200
Soil amendments		
Dolomite, 2 tons	– –	65
Superphosphate, 500 lb.	– –	45
Canals, ditches, dikes, reservoirs, roads	250– 400	315
Throw-out pumps for water movement	– –	40
Culverts and pipes	85– 125	105
Drainage tile	140– 160	150
Irrigation systems		
Microsprinkler, with well[b]	1,000– 2,000	1,360
Microsprinkler, without well	375– 1,000	705
Drip, with well[b]	800– 1,300	1,015
Drip, without well	240– 800	540
Water permits and environmental studies		
Cost	10– 35	30
Time in months	3– 6	5

(*continued*)

| | Percent land utilization | |
	Range	Average
Planted to citrus	50– 89	73
Ditches and canals	5– 10	8
Water retention	3– 25	13
Roads and service areas	3– 15	6

| | Year | Costs per tree, South Florida | | | |
		1	2	3	4
Solidset planted trees					
Drip irrigation		.50	.50	.50	.50
Fertilize tree		.30	.45	.50	.55
Supplemental fertilization through irrigation		.25	.30	.35	.40
Spray		.40	.45	.55	.60
Uninsulated tree wrap		.50	.15	.15	.15
Sprouting (labor)		.20	.20	.20	.20
Herbicide		.40	.40	.40	.40
Ridomil/Aliette		.45	.45	.45	.00
Cultivation/mowing		.30	.30	.30	.30
Miscellaneous		.15	.15	.15	.15
Total cost per year		3.45	3.35	3.55	3.25
Reset trees (year 4 = cost of trees 1 through 4 years old)		3.45	6.80	10.35	13.60
Cost of planting trees[c]		5.85			

SOURCE: Ronald P. Muraro (farm management economist, CREC, Lake Alfred, Florida), November 1985.

a. Land cost will vary from one county to another as well as from one parcel to another.

b. Irrigation costs include distribution system, power unit, and well (where indicated). The higher cost ranges reported also included a cost for fertigation equipment.

c. Tree cost (bare root) = $4.20; stake, plant, and water tree = $1.65.

Index

Miami, Florida, 60
Microcitrus, 11
Microelements, 250; deficiencies of, 254
Micronutrient, 163, 164; toxicity of, 165
Midsweet (orange cultivar), 30
Milam (citrus hybrid cultivar), 71, 154, 160
Mineral nutrients, 138, 204
Mineral salts, 4, 209, 254
Minneola (tangelo cultivar), 56, 57; crossed with Clementine to Page hybrid, 62; as scion susceptible to xyloporosis, 159; and nonpest sprays, 202
Mites: and the nursery row, 80; and spraying, 142; and citrus decline, 150; control of, 187; and pest management, 192, 193; and predatory insects, 201; and Fancy Grade fruits, 241
Moisture deficiency, 207
Molasses, 21, 243
Molybdenum: in grapefruit, 70; as nutrient element, 164, 173; and soil reaction, 165; and yellow spot, 181
Moragne, Dr. N. H., 40
Morton citrange, 71
Mowing, 200
Muck soils, 92
Mudding-in, 134
Murcotts (tangelo cultivar): compared to Oneco, 44; as citrus hybrid, 53; and xyloporosis virus, 159; and application of nutrient elements, 177; and scab, 186, 195
Mutation, genetic, 32, 33
Myakka soil, 107, 109
Mycoplasma, 71

Nagami (kumquat cultivar), 17, 41
Naples, Florida, 114
Natural nutrient, 124
Navel oranges, 29, 232, 246
Nematicides, 135
Nematodes: and stocks, 71; and the nursery row, 79; and grove management, 114; affecting production cost, 124; and grove rehabilitation, 150; as disease organisms, 153, 159; infestation in home gardens, 249
Nicholson, D. J., 30
Nitrogen: and fertilization, 140; as nutrient elements in fertilizers, 166–68, 177, 178; in relation to potassium, 169; in relation to magnesium, 170; and soil reaction, 174; and cover crops, 201, 202
Nonpest sprays, 198
Northwesterly winds, 103
Nova (tangelo cultivar), 58, 62, 159
Nucellar embryony, 14, 64, 65
Nucellus, 14
Nursery adaptability, 66
Nursery canker, 61
Nursery row, 79; water basin, 249–50
Nursery trees: bare root, 249; container grown, 249–50
Nutrient elements, 162, 173, 177
Nutrients, 139, 143, 166–73
Nutrient supply, 110
Nutritional sprays, 198
Nutritional stress, 60

Obeni-mikan (tangerine cultivar of Japan), 43
Ocala, Florida, 26, 43
Off-flavors, 234
Oil (in fruit): bitterness of, 15
Oil sprays (in pest control), 236
Okeechobee County, 115, 116

Peel oils, 243
Perrin, 28
Perrine, Dr. Henry, 49
Persian (lime cultivar), 50
Pests: control of, 183, 185, 251
Pests, insects, 202
Pesticides, 183, 187
pH: and the water table, 106; as
    expressed on a scale, 111; and
    soil reaction, 165–66; and soil
    amendments, 174–75
Philippe, Dr. Odette, 31
Phosphates, 166
Phosphoric acid, 177
Phosphorus, 163, 167, 172,
Photosynthesis, 103, 162, 204
Physiological sprays, 198
Pickers, 225
Picking costs, 245
Pineapple (orange cultivar):
    commercial importance of, 24;
    as sweet orange cultivar, 26;
    compared to Pope Summer, 28;
    and citrus for the home, 246
Pineda soil (type), 109
Pinellas County, 106, 112, 113, 115,
    116
Plant bugs, 192
Plant foods, 163
Planting, 132
Plant tissue, 92
Plugging (of fruit), 225
Polk County, 30, 95, 112, 113, 114,
    115, 116, 117, 160
Pollination, 14
Pollution control, 219
Polyethylene bags, 75
Pomelo, 31
Pomological Committee of the Flor-
    ida Fruit Growers Association,
    25, 40, 43
Poncirus trifoliata, 12, 61, 70
Ponderosa (lemon cultivar), 48

Ponkan (tangerine cultivar), 41, 43,
    44
Poorly drained soils of the coastal
    areas, 107
Pope, F. W., 28
Pope's Summer (orange cultivar), 28
Potash, 169, 177
Potassium, 108; as primary nutrient
    element, 163, 164, 165, 166; and
    soil reaction, 166; with respect to
    excessive nitrogen, 167; as ele-
    ment in fertilizer, 169
Pratylenchus coffeae, 161
Predacious mite, 198
Preserves, 18, 21
Pricing of fruit, 245; per box, 24
Processing, 242
Protein, 163
Protoplasm, 204
Protoplasmic fusion, 54
Pruning, 210–21; and Murcott culti-
    var, 60; and mechanized grove
    operations, 125; and production,
    143; and grove maintenance,
    199, 210, 211, 212–13; types of,
    211–17; of grapefruit trees, 213;
    of tangerine trees, 213; equip-
    ment of, 213–18; protecting sur-
    faces, 217; and cold injury to
    fruit, 224
Pruning paint, 217
Psorosis virus, 72, 131; strains A and
    B, 156; concave gum, 156
Puffiness (of fruit), 102
Pulling, 225
Pulp, 21; dried, 243
Purple scale, 189, 190, 197
Putnam County, 112, 115, 117

Quality: external, 227; internal, 227
Queen (orange cultivar), 28

Radiation of heat, 92

Radopholus citrophilus, 160
Rafinesque, 14
Rainfall: as climatic consideration, 91, 100, 101; and fertilizing bearing citrus trees, 166; and soil reaction and nutrient availability, 170; and citrus pest management, 186; and irrigation, 213
Rangpur (lime cultivar): as citrus fruit, 51–52; and other stocks, 71; and exocortis virus, 158; and xyloporosis virus, 159
Ray Ruby (grapefruit cultivar), 38
Read grove, 40
Reasoner, P. W., 41, 44, 68
Reasoner Brothers, 52
Rectangular system (of planting), 126
Red albedo, 37
Red-alga spot, 196
Redblush (grapefruit cultivar), 32, 36
Red Dancy (tangerine cultivar), 40
Red grapefruit, 33
Redheaded scale fungi, 198
Red Marsh (grapefruit cultivar), 36
Red rust, 171
Regreening, 25
Regulations: maturity, 228
Regulatory bodies, 8
Relative humidity, 91, 102
Replanting, 152
Rhode Red (orange cultivar), 25–26
Ridge Pineapple (orange cultivar), 71, 160
Rind, leathery: in hesperidium subfamily, 11; and by product usage, 21; and other desired characteristics for commercial trade, 25; and crop harvesting,

226; in Fancy Grade and fruit processing, 241, 242
Ripening process, 226
Rivers Nursery, 25, 65
Riviera soil, 107
Robinson, 57, 63, 159, 198
Rockdale, 109
Roe, W. G., 30
Rollerston Nursery, 43
Root rot, 153, 154, 155, 196
Roots, 90, 133
Rootstocks: rough lemon, 6, 28, 67, 70, 71, 98; eremocitrus lime, 11; trifoliate orange, 15, 17; for citranges, 16, 61; and propagation of citrus trees, 67; as consideration for maturity, 35, 238; and citrus fruits for the home, 248, 249; sour orange stock, 249
Root systems, 250
Root weevils, 193
Royal (grapefruit cultivar), 34, 37
Royal Palm Nurseries (Oneco, Florida), 17, 36, 37, 44
Ruby (blood orange cultivar), 28, 33, 36, 248
Rue family (Rutaceae), 11
Rusk citrange, 16, 66, 71
Rust mites, 175, 188, 193

Safety Harbor, 31, 35
St. Augustine, Florida, 5, 45, 53, 112
St. Johns River, 5, 29, 114
St. Lucie County, 112, 113, 114, 115, 116, 117
Salt concentration, in soil, 150
Sampling (maturity testing), 238
Sampson (tangelo cultivar), 57, 58
Sand hill decline, 68, 153
Sandy soils, 92, 127, 134
Sanford, Gen. H. S., 28, 47, 65
Sarasota County, 115, 116
Satsuma: xyloporosis virus on, 8;